FLAWED PERFECTION

What It Means to Be Human
&
Why It Matters for Culture, Politics, and Law

FLAWED PERFECTION

What It Means to Be Human
&
Why It Matters for Culture, Politics, and Law

JEFFREY A. BRAUCH

LEXHAM PRESS

Flawed Perfection: What It Means to Be Human and Why It Matters for Culture, Politics, and Law
Copyright 2017 Jeffrey A. Brauch

Lexham Press, 1313 Commercial St., Bellingham, WA 98225
LexhamPress.com

You may use brief quotations from this resource in presentations, articles, and books. For all other uses, please write Lexham Press for permission. Email us at permissions@lexhampress.com.

Unless otherwise noted, Scripture quotations are from *ESV® Bible* (*The Holy Bible, English Standard Version®*), copyright © 2001 by Crossway Bibles, a publishing ministry of Good News Publishers. Used by permission. All rights reserved.

Scripture quotations marked (NIV) are taken from the Holy Bible, New International Version®, NIV®. Copyright © 1973, 1978, 1984, 2011 by Biblica, Inc.™ Used by permission of Zondervan. All rights reserved worldwide. www.zondervan.com The "NIV" and "New International Version" are trademarks registered in the United States Patent and Trademark Office by Biblica, Inc.™

Print ISBN 9781683590248
Digital ISBN 9781683590255

Lexham Editorial: Abigail Stocker, Elliot Ritzema, Elizabeth Vince
Cover Design: Jim LePage
Typesetting: ProjectLuz.com

24 xii / US

To Cynthia, Melissa, Christina, and Jeffrey.
I could not be more thankful or proud to be your dad.

CONTENTS

PART 1
HUMAN NATURE

CHAPTER 1:
WHY HUMAN NATURE MATTERS

How does our understanding of human nature affect how we address the pressing questions of our day?

The average person in Rwanda, they would no sooner kill their neighbor than you or I. But when the killing began by those who were ready to do it, the fear just took a hold of people, and it went like wildfire.

—CARL WILKENS,
Adventist Development and Relief Agency[1]

O ver the course of one hundred days in 1994, Rwandan Hutus slaughtered more than 800,000 of their countrymen. Men, women, children. Over three hundred per hour. Over five per minute.

The trigger was the April 6, 1996, explosion of a plane carrying the Hutu president of Rwanda, Juvénal Habyarimana, along with the president of Burundi. Hutus, blaming the explosion on Tutsi rebels, immediately launched attacks on Tutsis and other Hutus perceived to be Tutsi sympathizers. While organized by leaders of militia groups and the armed forces, the genocide involved the whole population. Leaders turned citizens into killers of neighbors and even their own family members. Between 100,000 and 200,000 Hutus participated in the genocide. While some killers had guns and grenades, most wielded low-tech weapons such as nail-studded clubs and—especially—machetes. They used rape, too, as a means of genocide; the United Nations estimates that between 250,000 and 500,000 women were raped during the genocide.

Journalist Philip Gourevitch traveled around Rwanda afterward, interviewing survivors and gathering information. In his book *We Wish to Inform You That Tomorrow We Will Be Killed with Our Families*, he relates a particularly chilling account of a massacre that took place in Nyarubuye. When Tutsis asked the local Hutu mayor how they might be spared, he told them to seek sanctuary in a church. They did, and Gourevitch writes that a few days later the mayor himself "came at the head of a pack of soldiers, policemen, militiamen, and villagers; he gave out arms and orders to complete the job well. No more was required of the mayor, but he also was said to have killed a few Tutsis himself."[2]

After many hours, the killers still had not finished massacring the refuge-seekers. So they cut the Achilles tendons of the survivors, feasted on cattle taken from the victims, drank beer, and rested. The next day, "The killers at Nyarubuye went back and killed again. Day after day, minute to minute, Tutsi by Tutsi: all across Rwanda, they worked like that."[3]

A radio station, Radio Télévision Libre des Mille Collines (RTLM), fueled the killing frenzy. After the president's plane exploded, the station called for a "final war" to "exterminate the cockroaches."[4] It broadcast names of people to be killed along with instructions on where to find them.[5] The radio station and genocide leaders consistently downplayed the victims' humanity; in speeches and "consciousness raising meetings" held in advance of the genocide, leaders referred to Tutsis as "scum" and "devils" ("horns, hoofs, tails, and all").[6] RTLM urged listeners to "leave no grave half full"[7] and to "take no pity on women and children."[8] Other nations stood by and refused to intervene. In part, their attention was on other crises, such as a war in Bosnia that was itself turning into a genocide. But nations like the United States were also influenced by the failed intervention in Somalia that occurred just months before in 1993 (captured in the book and movie *Black Hawk Down*).

While the United Nations had deployed a peacekeeping force of about 2,500 to Rwanda in November 1993 in response to a civil war, it refused to allow its soldiers to use force. On April 21, two weeks into the genocide, Lieutenant-General Roméo Dallaire, Canadian commander of the UN troops, requested additional troops. He insisted that with 5,000 soldiers he could bring an end to the genocide.[9] The Security Council refused. It instead adopted—with strong support from the United States—a resolution reducing UN forces by nearly 90 percent to 270 troops.[10] Western nations evacuated their own citizens but did nothing to stop the killing until it was too late. President Bill Clinton later called the failure to intervene in Rwanda one of the greatest regrets of his presidency. In 2013 he told CNBC: "If we'd gone in sooner, I believe we could have saved at least a third of the lives that were lost ... it had an enduring impact on me."[11]

Carl Wilkens was the lone American to remain in Rwanda, and he stood as witness to the genocide that shocked the world and still haunts us today. Looking back, he summarized his emotions: "By the time the genocide was over, I was so angry at America— America the beautiful, America the brave."[12]

These appalling events bring our attention to a set of larger questions about human nature:

1. **What is the value of human life?** For three months in 1994, the lives of Tutsis were worth very little. They were considered scum. Devils. Cockroaches. Tutsi pastors, fearing for their lives and those of their congregations, wrote Hutu Pastor Elizaphan Ntakirutimana, Adventist Church President of Kibuye, seeking help and protection. He reportedly told them, "God no longer wants you."[13] While Western nations evacuated

and saved their own citizens, they did little to protect the lives of Africans. The Africans were on their own.

2. **How are humans capable of such evil?** In 1945, after the Holocaust, the world collectively declared, "Never again." We created the UN and ratified the Convention on the Prevention and Punishment of the Crime of Genocide. How could this have happened at the end of the twentieth century—less than fifty years later? How did so many ordinary citizens pick up machetes and strike down neighbors and friends?

3. **To what extent should humans be held responsible for such evil actions?** The events of 1994 raise difficult questions regarding human accountability. Leaders and planners are unquestionably to blame for the genocide, but what about ordinary citizens? As Wilkens noted, "The fear just took a hold of people." How do we decide whether—or to what extent—to blame the tens of thousands of individuals who killed while caught up in hysteria, fear, or ethnic and social pressure to participate? And what is the appropriate punishment for genocide?

We need to address these fundamental questions—and, thus, to properly understand human nature—if we want to address the pressing issues of our day in an informed way.

A HOUSE DIVIDED

Our fundamental beliefs about human nature don't just influence our perceptions of and reactions to events that are widely regarded as atrocities, like genocide. They also matter in the domestic legal and policy issues confronting Americans every day. Our core beliefs about human nature are the building blocks with which we craft specific public policies and legislative agendas—and yet, it's easy when confronting legal and policy challenges to focus on a plethora of cosmetic changes rather than the foundational issues. Take as an example what may be the defining characteristic of American public life today: the significant—and increasing—polarization between political parties. Red states and blue states. The inability of Congress to reach a consensus on any significant piece of legislation (including something as basic as an annual budget).[14] Nominations to the Supreme Court—and at times to lower courts—have given rise to pitched partisan battles.

As a result, the American public is skeptical and at times even pessimistic. We don't feel we can trust our political leaders. According to Gallup, out of fifteen key institutions in society (including the military, police, business, and the criminal justice system), Americans have the least confidence in Congress.[15] In 2016, only 9 percent of Americans expressed "a great deal" or "quite a bit" of confidence in Congress. The next lowest group on the confidence scale was big business, at 18 percent.[16]

And our growing polarization is not just a matter of perception. In June 2012, the Pew Research Center released findings of a 25-year study, which stated that Americans' "values and basic beliefs are more polarized along partisan lines than at any point in the past 25 years."[17] It reported that the divide between Democrats and Republicans on core values and beliefs was greater than divisions over race, class, age, or gender.[18] Key issues experiencing increasing divides include:

- **The role and scope of government**: In 1987, there was only a 6-point gap between the 65 percent of Republicans and 59 percent of Democrats who agreed that "when something is run by the government, it is usually inefficient and wasteful."[19] In 2012, there was a 36-point gap; 77 percent of Republicans versus only 41 percent of Democrats agreed.[20] More recent Gallup polling verifies that this division over the role of government remains. Today, 57 percent of Democrats prefer a more active government while only 15 percent of Republicans do.[21]

- **Immigration:** For over twenty years, Pew has tracked survey responses to the following proposition: "Immigrants today strengthen the country because of their hard work and talents." In 1994, there was barely a gap between Republicans and Democrats; 30 percent of Republicans and 32 percent of Democrats agreed with the proposition. In 2016, 34 percent of Republications agreed, compared with 78 percent of Democrats—a difference of 43 points.[22]

2016 PRESIDENTIAL ELECTION

The deep political divisions in the United States were on full display in the 2016 presidential election between Republican Donald Trump and Democrat Hillary Clinton. Two weeks before the election, *US News & World Report* declared: "The nation is sharply divided on nearly every topic, from race relations to what problems the next president should fix first, and a record percentage of people believe the country is on the wrong track."[23]

The nation's divisions were evident on election night. Donald Trump won the presidency with a victory in the electoral college of 304 to 227; Hillary Clinton won the popular vote by nearly three million votes. Seven electors voted for someone other than their party's nominee.

In the weeks following the election, thousands filled the streets in cities across America protesting Trump's election. Hundreds of thousands of women marched on Washington on January 21, the day after Trump's inauguration. By some estimates the number of marchers significantly exceeded the number of inauguration attendees from the day before.[24]

So now we live in a world where there is more profound disagreement over high-profile social issues than ever before. A 2016
Gallup survey found significant differences between Republicans
and Democrats on the following propositions:[25]

	Republicans agreeing	Democrats agreeing	Gap
Doctor-assisted suicide is morally acceptable	44 percent	64 percent	20 points
Medical research using stem cells obtained from human embryos is morally acceptable	44 percent	73 percent	29 points
Gay or lesbian relations are acceptable	44 percent	75 percent	31 points

These are all important issues that go to the core of who we
are as a society. Effectively addressing these issues will be necessary for us to function as a society and thrive. However, there is
no clear path to consensus on these and other issues that confront
us. It seems clear that it will not come from being more educated
or obtaining more data. We have plenty of data—more than at any
time in history. No, our disagreements are not over data collection
or interpretation. They go much deeper than that.

IN SEARCH OF FOUNDATIONS

In 1981, in considering the hot-button issues of his day, theologian
Francis Schaeffer wrote:

> The basic problem of the Christians in this country in the
> last eighty years or so, in regard to society and in regard
> to government, is that they have seen things in bits and
> pieces instead of totals.

They have very gradually become disturbed over permissiveness, pornography, the public schools, the breakdown of the family, and finally abortion. But they have not seen this as a totality—each thing as being a part, a symptom, of a much larger problem. They have failed to see that all of this has come about due to a shift in worldview—that is, through a fundamental change in the overall way people think and view the world and life as a whole.[26]

Schaeffer's diagnosis is still true in the twenty-first century. The disagreements in our society are not just over particular policies. They are disagreements over presuppositions—over foundational principles that undergird these policies.

My own search for foundational principles brought me to teach at Regent University School of Law in 1994. I was drawn by the school's mission: "To provide an excellent legal education from a Christian perspective, to nurture and encourage our students toward spiritual maturity, and to engage the world through Christian legal thought and practice." In each course I've taught at Regent, I've explored with students what biblical principles exist that might provide answers to the legal and policy challenges facing us.

But over the years, I've become convinced that legal and policy answers aren't generally found in individual passages from Leviticus or Deuteronomy. It's too easy to take such passages out of context or use them as proof texts. I'm much more confident approaching legal and policy questions using foundational principles demonstrated through the whole of redemptive history—the overarching biblical story of creation, fall, and redemption.

One of the most foundational—and most helpful—principles is the nature of human beings. With an accurate understanding of human nature, we can more thoughtfully and faithfully engage pressing legal and political questions. Getting human nature right will help us understand, prevent, and respond to human-rights abuses like human trafficking and genocide. It also helps us address the seemingly intractable divide over the proper role of government. That is the premise of this book: Getting human nature right is key to confronting the most pressing issues facing our nation and world. I will begin in chapter 2 by laying out what Scripture has to say about the nature of humans. I will look at three critical concepts: First, we are made in the image of God. Each of us has dignity and worth that do not depend on race, gender, income, power, or influence. Second, we are fallen. While we are made in God's image, that image is obscured and flawed in a profound way; humans are capable of both great good and great evil. Third, we are accountable moral agents. While we are influenced by our genes, upbringing, and culture, we are responsible for the moral choices we make—and for the consequences of moral failure.

The remainder of the book explores the implications of the biblical understanding of human nature for a wide variety of legal and policy issues, both global and domestic. The next four chapters explore global issues. Chapter 3 describes the fastest-growing criminal enterprise in the world: trafficking in human beings. In all the different forms this trafficking takes, it ultimately stems from both human fallenness and failure to see other human beings as made in God's image, with dignity and worth. I will then consider steps lawyers, legislators, and others can take to uphold moral accountability and combat human trafficking. Chapters 4 through 6 explore the implications of a biblical understanding of human nature on such global issues as the use of biotechnology, genocide, and the international human rights movement.

The book also explores how getting human nature right matters for addressing pressing domestic issues. Chapter 7 looks at the role of government and the importance of the rule of law. When structuring and carrying out governmental functions, it is essential for societies to acknowledge human dignity and worth, but we must also acknowledge human sinfulness and moral accountability. Sin affects leaders and institutions as well as ordinary citizens. By reviewing examples, both good and bad, the chapter explores how a nation can seek to create an effective government and legal system that promotes freedom, equality, and dignity.

Chapters 8 and 9 explore implications of a biblical understanding of human nature for challenging, important questions confronting the criminal justice system. Are individuals responsible for a crime if they are genetically or culturally predisposed to engage in certain acts? What if they were influenced by a particularly traumatic or difficult event or upbringing? How and why should we punish? Are longer prison sentences the answer? Should we focus on rehabilitating offenders?

In chapter 10, I urge Christians to carefully and humbly pursue legislative reform efforts, but with a cautionary note. It is not the case that if we just have the right laws—or the right party in power—we can make our communities everything they should be. I detail the church's failed attempts to micromanage moral behavior and explain that while these efforts were well-intentioned, they did not work because they did not properly account for human sinfulness—of both lawmakers and citizens. Changing the law, while both necessary and useful, cannot become our primary means for seeking social change.

Since I am a lawyer and law professor, I will often be examining the various issues in this book from a legal perspective. But each chapter will also address grassroots steps that can be taken—by lawyers and non-lawyers alike—to address issues in a productive and biblical way. God's call to "do justice" (Isa 1:17) is a call to his people as a whole, not just to those who have a legal background. In the same way, this book is written for anyone wishing to explore how they might faithfully and biblically engage the challenges confronting their world, nation, churches, and families.

HUMAN NATURE AND LAW

While this book examines the implications of a Christian view of human nature for a wide range of issues, it does not address these issues exhaustively. It is intentionally broad in scope. This reflects in part my teaching experience at Regent. Since 1994, I have taught Christian Foundations of Law, International Human Rights, Criminal Law, International Criminal Law, Civil Procedure, Torts, and Origins of the Western Legal Tradition. These courses cover a broad spectrum of issues. In every course, however, I have observed that human nature is key to understanding these issues.

NUREMBERG TRIALS

World War II produced a devastating loss of life. It is estimated that as many as 50 million people died as a result of the war, including many civilians. In the Holocaust, Germans murdered six million European Jews as well as nearly that many non-Jews.

When the war ended, the Allies determined that one of the important steps to promote justice and prevent a recurrence of these events was to criminally punish those responsible. From 1945 to 1949, the Allies held a series of thirteen trials in Nuremberg, Germany, to try individuals for crimes against peace, war crimes, and crimes against humanity. The most famous trial was the Major War Criminals Trial, held between November 1945 and October 1946. The twenty-two defendants included Hermann Göring, creator of the Gestapo.

The Nuremberg trials were an important statement by the world community that justice and reason should triumph over vengeance and power.

Indeed, human nature is key to law itself. Despite all of its failures and shortcomings, law continues to be a means for the image of God in us to be displayed. Human reason, inclinations, and will have been damaged by the human race's fall into sin. But we still have a certain capacity to know right from wrong; our consciences can still be pricked. The Holocaust, supported by an entire structure of Nazi law, showed humans' incredible capacity for evil. But it was followed by the Nuremberg trials and the world's declaration that genocide is fundamentally wrong and must be punished.

While it goes by different names, there remains a higher law of right and wrong that is known to some degree by all people. J. Budziszewski, in his book *What We Can't Not Know,* writes: "There is a common moral ground. Certain moral truths really are common to all human beings. Because our shoes are wet with evasions the common ground may seem slippery to us, but it is real; we do all know that we shouldn't murder, shouldn't steal, should honor our parents, should honor God, and so on."[27]

Anyone who has traveled extensively has observed how much food and attire differ among nations and cultures. However, among these nations and cultures there is a remarkable similarity in certain fundamental legal provisions. In *The Abolition of Man,* C. S. Lewis demonstrates the similarity of core legal provisions from ancient Mesopotamia to medieval Nordic nations to modern industrial democracies.[28] This is not by accident. There are core moral principles that are known to all, as noted earlier by John Calvin:

> While men dispute among themselves about individual sections of the law, they agree on the general conception of equity. In this respect the frailty of the human mind is surely proved: even when it seems to follow the way, it limps and staggers. Yet the fact remains that some seed of political order has been implanted in all men.[29]

While our work is filled with difficulty and pain, we still have the ability to create and produce. While human relationships are damaged and at times even dysfunctional, our ability to engage in those relationships still reflects the image of God. And while law and legal systems can be corrupted, there is a core knowledge of moral right and wrong that makes the discussion and application of law and policy meaningful.

Whether the issues of law and policy are international or domestic, criminal or civil, the only way we can understand and address them properly is if we get human nature right. Getting human nature right is vital, and it begins by seeing what Scripture says about who we really are.

CHAPTER 2:
CHRISTIANITY ON HUMAN NATURE

Are humans anything more than the product of time, matter, and chance?

Our plight is not that the image of God has been abolished. It is far worse, namely that while its structures of relationship remain, they are distorted at every point.

—CHARLES SHERLOCK,
The Doctrine of Humanity[1]

It was October 21, 1861, in Loudoun County, Virginia. Twenty-year-old Lieutenant Oliver Wendell Holmes Jr. lay bleeding on the ground. He had been shot in the chest during the Battle of Ball's Bluff. Bleeding from the mouth, Holmes expected to die.

Like many young men of his time, Holmes was filled with idealism when he had enlisted in the Union army as soon as the Civil War began in April of that year. As he described many years later, he had been "deeply moved by the Abolition cause."[2] He donated money to the cause and even served as a bodyguard to an abolitionist during the 1861 meeting of the Massachusetts Anti-Slavery Society. Holmes enlisted though he was just two months away from graduating from Harvard College. He was permitted to graduate when the Harvard faculty allowed him and fellow enlisters to return to take final exams during the summer.

Holmes's idealism quickly clashed with the cold reality of war. After being wounded at Ball's Bluff, he briefly considered taking an overdose of the laudanum he carried in case the pain "became unbearable."[3] Holmes recovered, however, and returned to the fight. Less than a year later he was wounded again, this time shot through the neck at Antietam Creek. Within another year he was shot a third time—in the foot at Chancellorsville. Holmes was disappointed that the wound was not more serious. Had his foot been amputated, he could have returned home.

Holmes's wartime experience left him disillusioned. He wrote his mother: "It's odd how indifferent one gets to the sight of death—perhaps, because one gets aristocratic and don't value much a common life—Then they are apt to be so dirty it seems natural—'Dust to dust'— I would do anything that lay in my power but it doesn't much affect my feelings."[4] He wrote his sister:

> I've pretty much made up my mind that the South have achieved their independence & I am almost ready to hope spring will see an end ... Believe me, we never shall lick 'em—The Army is tired with its hard, & its terrible experience & still more with its mismanagement & I think before long the majority will say that we are vainly working to effect what never happens—the subjugation (for that is it) of a great civilized nation. We shan't do it—at least the Army can't.[5]

Returning home after his three-year enlistment, Holmes chose not to reenlist, telling his parents, "I am not the same man."[6]

The war didn't just affect his decision about reenlistment; it affected his view of human beings and of truth itself. His idealism had turned to skepticism. Despite having enlisted to fight for the rights of slaves, the postwar Holmes was skeptical about the very idea of rights. Years later he wrote, "You respect the rights of man—I don't, except those things a given crowd will fight for."[7] He even noted, "All my life I have sneered at the natural rights of man."[8]

Holmes was also skeptical about truth. Despite identifying himself as a Christian while in college, Holmes now doubted the very existence of a truth beyond people's opinions. "Do you like sugar in your coffee or don't you? ... So as to truth."[9]

> As I probably have said many times before, all I mean by truth is what I can't help believing—I don't know why I should assume except for practical purposes of conduct that [my] *can't help* has more cosmic worth than any other—I can't help preferring port to ditch-water, but I see no ground for supposing that the cosmos shares my weakness.[10]

Holmes was also skeptical about the value of human life. Chief Judge Richard Posner of the United States Court of Appeals for the Seventh Circuit notes that Holmes was a "social and biological Darwinian."[11] Holmes's own words bear this out: "My bet is that we have not the kind of cosmic importance that the parsons and philosophers teach. I doubt if a shudder would go through the spheres if the whole ant heap were kerosened."[12] Similarly: "I see no reason for attributing to a man a significance different in kind from that which belongs to a baboon or to a grain of sand."[13]

Holmes was no longer committed to the abolition movement. Indeed, he was skeptical of almost all social welfare causes. What he did embrace was eugenics, the theory that selective breeding could improve the human species and its survival. Holmes's skepticism about the value of human life and of social movements to improve it is summarized well in a letter he wrote in 1915 to Dean John Wigmore of the Northwestern University Law School: "Doesn't this squashy sentimentality of a big minority of our people about human life make you puke?" Holmes was speaking "of pacifists—of people who believe there is an upward and onward—who talk of uplift—who think that something particular has happened and that the universe is no longer predatory. Oh bring in a basin."[14]

The story of Oliver Wendell Holmes isn't just a tale of a battle-scarred and disillusioned veteran. It is also a story about worldview and its impact on the legal system. Holmes went on to study and teach law at Harvard Law School. In 1882 he was appointed a justice of the Massachusetts Supreme Court. In 1902 President Theodore Roosevelt appointed Holmes a justice of the United States Supreme Court, where he served until 1932.[15] As a teacher, writer, and judge, Holmes had a profound and lasting impact on the development of American law. For example, Holmes's writings on freedom of speech continue to inform the courts' understanding of the First Amendment.

OLIVER WENDELL HOLMES AND THE FIRST AMENDMENT

Justice Holmes often wrote in colorful and memorable language. One of his most famous opinions was in the World War I case of *Schenck v. United States* (1919),[16] in which a unanimous Supreme Court upheld a conviction under the Espionage Act. Holmes wrote: "The most stringent protection of free speech would not protect a man in falsely shouting fire in a theatre and causing a panic. ... The question in every case is whether the words used are used in such circumstances and are of such a nature as to create a clear and present danger that they will bring about the substantive evils that Congress has a right to prevent." Both the "fire in a theatre" metaphor and the "clear and present danger" test have strongly shaped our understanding of the First Amendment's protection of free speech.

Sadly, Holmes's philosophical outlook also continues to influence the law. Holmes was essentially a materialist—he believed that everything can be understood in relation to matter. Geneticist Richard Lewontin explains the materialist view well: "We exist as material beings in a material world, all of whose phenomena are the consequences of material relations among material entities."[17] Under a materialist view, there is no reality aside from matter. As Holmes put it, humans have "no cosmic importance"; they are nothing more than physical products of an evolutionary process.

How does this materialist view of human nature relate to Christian teaching on human nature? To answer that question, we must look at three biblically rooted principles that are central to understanding a Christian view of human nature that spans theological traditions.

CREATED IN THE IMAGE OF GOD

According to the Christian view of humans, we are not simply the product of time, matter, and chance. Instead, we were created by God and in his image. Genesis records the following about the sixth day of creation:

> Then God said, "Let us make man in our image, after our likeness. And let them have dominion over the fish of the sea and over the birds of the heavens and over the livestock and over all the earth and over every creeping thing that creeps on the earth." So God created man in his own image, in the image of God he created him; male and female he created them. And God blessed them. And God said to them, "Be fruitful and multiply and fill the earth and subdue it, and have dominion over the fish of the sea and over the birds of the heavens and over every living thing that moves on the earth." (Gen 1:26–28)

This passage makes clear that God is our creator, and we are the product of his sovereign choice and will. We hold a different status from animals; we are much more than Holmes's ant heap. That we have great worth is evident in the striking statement that God created us "in his image." God gave us the important role to take charge of creation and of the animals around us. He gave us dominion.

Psalm 8 speaks very similarly about the place and role of humans. In it, David asks God: "What is man that you are mindful of him, and the son of man that you care for him? Yet you have made him a little lower than the heavenly beings and crowned him with glory and honor. You have given him dominion over the works of your hands; you have put all things under his feet, all sheep and oxen, and also the beasts of the field, the birds of the heavens, and the fish of the sea, whatever passes along the paths of the seas" (Pss 8:4–8). This passage affirms the same prominence, worth, and dominion found in Genesis.

But what does it mean to be created in the image of God? Scholars have wrestled with this question for thousands of years. Most agree, though, that being God's image-bearers means at least these things:

- **Humans can reason and plan**. We have the capacity for self-reflection and can ask why we should or should not take certain actions. The creation narrative makes clear that this reflects God himself. God displays rational self-reflection when he says, "Let us make man in our image."[18]

- **Humans are creative.** Just as God creates man, he tells Adam to create things and impart value to them.[19] As humans, we have the ability to know and appreciate beauty and to create beautiful things.

- **Humans have dominion over their environment, including animals.** This is related to our creative ability. We can express God's lordship over our environment; we have "mastery over created things."[20] While we are accountable to God, as his "vice-regents" we are "to manage and utilize together the created world."[21] Anglican theologian J. I. Packer puts it this way: God is glorified "when the possibilities of his creation are realized and developed by human enterprise, provided that this is done responsibly, in a way that benefits others."[22]

- **Humans also share in God's moral image.** Adam is created as a righteous man. He is instructed to live righteously and has the power to do so. He is also endowed with free will and can choose to disobey, as he did.[23] All humans are created with a conscience and with a moral law written on our hearts (Rom 2:14–15).

- **Humans were made for relationship—with God and others.** The Catechism of the Catholic Church notes that man is the only creature (of the "visible creatures") "able to know and love his Creator."[24] We are naturally inclined to seek meaning and the good, and our fulfillment can only be found in God. Before sin, we were naturally inclined to seek him. Indeed, "only in God will he find the truth and happiness he never stops searching for."[25] We were built to relate to others as well. In Genesis 2, God gives Adam a companion, noting that "it is not good that the man should be alone" (v. 18). He creates woman to be "a helper fit for [Adam]." Philosophers through the ages have agreed that humans are social beings.[26]

Humans have tremendous value in God's eyes. This is seen not only in creation but especially in redemption. God's own son Jesus Christ sacrifices his life so that human beings can have eternal life—and he becomes human to do so. Paul in Philippians 2 urges us to have the same mind that Christ did, "who, though he was in the form of God, did not count equality with God a thing to be grasped, but emptied himself, by taking the form of a servant, being born in the likeness of men. And being found in human form, he humbled himself by becoming obedient to the point of death, even death on a cross" (Phil 2:6–8). That God himself would take on human form and die for humans is a powerful testimony to the value God places on those who bear his image.

One of the most common ways of expressing what it means to be God's image-bearers is that we possess dignity. For example, the Catholic Catechism's summary states well the consensus of various Christian traditions: "Being in the image of God the human individual possesses the dignity of a person, who is not just something, but someone."[27] This is especially true because we, uniquely among all creatures, can be in relationship with God. "The dignity of man rests above all on the fact that he is called to communion with God."[28]

The concept of human dignity is one that resonates even with those who do not profess to be Christians. For instance, the Charter of the United Nations declares its purpose "to reaffirm faith in fundamental human rights, in the dignity and worth of the human person."[29] Similarly, the Universal Declaration of Human Rights affirms that "all human beings are born free and equal in dignity and rights."[30] Such language gives Christians common ground for discussion and understanding with those who embrace very different views of the world.

We must be careful here, however. Christian and secular views of human dignity are not the same. They perhaps differ most in their account of the source of human dignity. For many, human dignity is rooted in our autonomy—our ability to will and to make choices. In his excellent book *God, Freedom and Human Dignity*, Ron Highfield points out that the biblical concept of humans possessing inherent dignity changed significantly during the Renaissance and especially the Enlightenment. The revised view of dignity tells us, "The more self-sufficient and self-defining we are, the more dignity we have."[31] This view can be found in the writings of thinkers like Immanuel Kant and Friedrich Nietzsche. "Kant rooted human dignity in the independent, inherent and universal power of autonomy and asserted that even God had to respect it."[32] Similarly, Nietzsche insisted, "Dignity must be earned and can be acquired only by people who make themselves worthy by their own bold action."[33]

THE ENLIGHTENMENT

The Enlightenment, or "Age of Reason," was a period in the eighteenth century in which leading thinkers in many fields sought to improve humanity's welfare by rigorously applying reason and logic. Important Enlightenment figures include Thomas Hobbes, René Descartes, Galileo, Isaac Newton, John Locke, Thomas Jefferson, Voltaire, Jean-Jacques Rousseau, and Montesquieu. Many early Enlightenment thinkers sought to apply reason to understand God's world better, but others turned away from religion and the movement became focused on seeking progress purely through human reason and effort.

Enlightenment thinking heavily influenced eighteenth-century philosophy, science, literature, and politics, and it contributed to many advances in these fields. It also played a leading role in shaping the French Revolution.

This Enlightenment view of human dignity is very much evident in current law and policy. For example, the United States Supreme Court in *Planned Parenthood v. Casey* (1992) affirmed abortion (before a fetus reaches the point of viability outside the womb) to be a fundamental right under the Fourteenth Amendment of the Constitution.[34] The Court argued that essential to being human is the ability to have autonomy over key areas of life such as marriage, procreation, and child rearing. "These matters, involving the most intimate and personal choices a person may make in a lifetime, choices central to personal dignity and autonomy, are central to the liberty protected by the Fourteenth Amendment. At the heart of liberty is the right to define one's own concept of existence, of meaning, of the universe, and of the mystery of human life."[35]

The Supreme Court applied the same view of human dignity when requiring states to permit same-sex couples to marry in *Obergefell v. Hodges* (2015).[36] The majority declared that fundamental liberties "extend to certain personal choices central to individual dignity and autonomy, including intimate choices that define personal dignity and beliefs."[37] Later, the Court further emphasized the tie between dignity and personal choice: "There is dignity in the bond between two men or two women who seek to marry and in their autonomy to make such profound choices."[38]

Highfield writes that this view of dignity as hinging on autonomy is a "counterfeit dignity" in which the "greater our power or wealth the more independence we boast, and hence the more dignity we think we possess."[39] This contradicts the Christian view of dignity. Biblically, our dignity is not found in our autonomy or self-sufficiency—it is found in our *dependence* on God. We have dignity not because we have willed or earned it; we have dignity because God has graciously chosen to confer dignity upon us. "God's love for us is the fundamental ground of our worth."[40]

Our creation in God's image with authentic dignity and worth has always had significant implications for ethics, law, and policy. For example, after the flood, God gave Noah this instruction about what to do if a human being took another's life: "And for your lifeblood I will require a reckoning: from every beast I will require it and from man. From his fellow man I will require a reckoning for the life of man. Whoever sheds the blood of man, by man shall his blood be shed, for God made man in his own image" (Gen 9:5–6). The murder of a human being required a severe punishment—the death penalty. Why? Because killing a human being is killing an image-bearer of God.

The biblical concept of humans as made in God's image also prompted an important principle of due process in Israel's justice system. Deuteronomy 1:17 instructed judges: "You shall not be partial in judgment. You shall hear the small and the great alike." Regardless of their power, influence, or wealth, all individuals had the right to be heard in Israel because all were made in the image of God.

Similarly, Israel's criminal justice system had an important limitation on criminal punishment that was rooted in the fact that humans are made in God's image. Deuteronomy 25 records that a guilty person was to be beaten with the number of lashes his crime deserved, but there was an outer limit: "Forty stripes may be given him, but not more, lest, if one should go on to beat him with more stripes than these, your brother will be degraded in your sight" (Deut 25:3). Why did God insist that punishment not degrade the convicted criminal? Because even the criminal bears God's image.

The New Testament carries this principle into the ethical standards of how men and women are to speak to one another. James strongly urges believers to control their words. He says that the tongue "is a restless evil, full of deadly poison. With it we bless our Lord and Father, and with it we curse people who are made in the likeness of God" (Jas 3:8–9). Why should we exercise care in what we say? Because we have a duty to care for those who have dignity and worth as image-bearers of God.

FALLEN

The joyous story of human dignity, worth, righteousness, and communion with God does not last long in the biblical narrative. Almost immediately after creation, Genesis records the story of the fall. Adam and Eve were created in righteousness, but they were also given free will. And they used that free will to disobey God's command to not eat fruit from the tree of the knowledge of good and evil.

The impact of Adam and Eve's disobedience was tremendous. They were driven from the garden of Eden. They were told that they would experience pain and difficulty in childbirth, work, and in relationships with each other and their environment. Most significantly, decay and death were introduced into the world.

We cannot truly understand the nature of human beings only by considering human dignity. The fall profoundly affected human nature. A complete understanding of humans requires acknowledging that sin is now a part of our very nature. The apostle Paul paints a bleak picture in Ephesians 2:

> And you were dead in the trespasses and sins in which you
> once walked, following the course of this world, following
> the prince of the power of the air, the spirit that is now at
> work in the sons of disobedience—among whom we all
> once lived in the passions of our flesh, carrying out the
> desires of the body and the mind, and were by nature chil-
> dren of wrath, like the rest of mankind. (Eph 2:1–3)

Similarly, the prophet Jeremiah explains that "the heart is deceit-
ful above all things, and desperately sick; who can understand it?"
(Jer 17:9).

All humans are burdened with a sinful nature, and this sinful
nature does not affect us in a small way. Theologians use the term
"total depravity" when referring to the effect of the fall on human
nature. Total depravity does not mean that we are as bad as we can
be; it means that sin has affected every part of our being. Louis
Berkhof writes that "sin has corrupted every part of [each person's] nature and rendered him unable to do any spiritual good. ...
Even his best works are *radically defective*."[41]

Scripture agrees. It teaches that even our "righteous deeds" are
tainted by sin: "We have all become like one who is unclean, and
our righteous deeds are like a polluted garment. We all fade like a
leaf, and our iniquities, like the wind, take us away" (Isaiah 64:6).

Sin affects all of us, and it affects all parts of us. It affects
our wills, as Paul saw in his own life: "I know that nothing good
dwells in me, that is, in my flesh. For I have the desire to do what
is right, but not the ability to carry it out. For I do not do the
good I want, but the evil I do not want is what I keep on doing"
(Rom 7:18–19).

Sin also affects our minds. Paul in Romans describes the impact
of sin on our thinking. In chapter 1, Paul notes that God has made
himself known to all people and that all are accountable based on
that knowledge. He then describes why humans often fail to respond
properly to that knowledge: our minds, too, are damaged by the

fall: "For although they knew God, they do not honor him as God or give thanks to him, but they became futile in their thinking, and their foolish hearts were darkened" (Rom 1:21). Paul explains this further in chapter 8: "For those who live according to the flesh set their minds on the things of the flesh, but those who live according to the Spirit set their minds on the things of the Spirit" (Rom 8:5).

A Christian view of human nature recognizes that all parts of us have been affected by the fall. Sin affects the will, mind, inclinations, and emotions. John Calvin puts it well: "The whole man is overwhelmed—as by a deluge—from head to foot, so that no part is immune from sin and all that proceeds from him is to be imputed to sin."[42] He continues: "Whoever is utterly cast down and overwhelmed by the awareness of his calamity, poverty, nakedness, and disgrace has thus advanced farthest in knowledge of himself."[43]

JOHN CALVIN

John Calvin was a sixteenth-century French theologian. He was originally trained in the law, but after his conversion to Protestantism he turned to theology. Calvin was a well-known lecturer and preacher and an avid writer. He wrote many commentaries and treatises, including his most famous work, the *Institutes of the Christian Religion*. In his teaching and writing Calvin emphasized the depth of both human sin and the grace of God. He spent the last twenty-plus years of his life in Geneva, Switzerland, where he sought to shape a community based on biblical principles.

The picture is bleak. We are not sinful because we sin. We sin because we are sinful, and this sinful nature renders humans capable of great destruction and evil.

Does this mean the image of God in humans is destroyed? No. But it is flawed. We still bear God's reflection, but it is obscured. In his book *Doctrine of Humanity,* Charles Sherlock writes: "The structures which show the (ontological) reality of being made in God's image remain, but are corrupted, inverted. They work against their intended nature and purpose, dividing where they should unite, cursing where they should bless."[44]

The flawing of God's image in us is seen in several ways. First, it affects our ability to exert dominion over creation. While Adam continues to be tasked with cultivating the land, he will do so with pain and difficulty: "Cursed is the ground because of you; in pain you shall eat of it all the days of your life; thorns and thistles it shall bring forth for you; and you shall eat the plants of the field" (Gen 3:17–18).

Second, the flawed image is evident in our relationships. The ability and inclination to be in relationship with God and others is one of the most significant aspects of being made in God's image. Despite the fall, we are still drawn to and are capable of having meaningful relationships, but those relationships are damaged. The first sin was Adam's and Eve's rejection of God's instruction because of their desire to "be like God, knowing good and evil" (Gen 3:5). Our quest to be like God continues today. We still want autonomy and freedom from him. In human relationships, we can see the effects of the fall especially in the relationship between husband and wife. God created marriage to be a relationship of partnership and oneness, but after the fall, this relationship is infected with rivalry: "Your desire shall be for your husband, and he shall rule over you" (Gen 3:16). A World Council of Churches publication, *Christian Perspectives on Theological Anthropology,* summarizes well the impact of the fall on all of our relationships:

> Just as the reflection of Christ and of God's being in our humanity is bound up with our relatedness to God and to one another, so it is with our sin. Relationships which in Christ are characterised by love, truthfulness and reverence are replaced by aggression, exploitation, deceit, brokenness and violence.[45]

A third way in which we continue to see the image of God displayed but in a flawed way is in the creation and implementation of law—which, as noted in chapter 1, is a feature common to all societies and cultures. The ability to establish and maintain standards of right and wrong and order is an essential feature of exercising dominion, particularly in a fallen world. But we do not have to work hard to think of examples of laws that are painfully complex (e.g., the Internal Revenue Code, immigration law), subject to inconsistent or corrupt enforcement (e.g., Prohibition, some drug or gambling laws today), or even fundamentally unjust (e.g., Jim Crow laws, laws prohibiting individuals from converting to Christianity in some Middle Eastern countries). Throughout human history, law has provided a means for rulers to govern ineffectively or even corruptly. Law, too, clearly bears the effects of the fall's marring of the image of God in us.

ACCOUNTABLE

The fall leaves humans in a devastating position. We are sinners by nature, unable to come to God without his grace. While we are not as bad as we possibly could be, all aspects of human personality are impacted: our will, minds, inclinations, emotions—everything. As Ephesians 2:5 notes, we are "dead in our sins." We are hopeless apart from God's intervention. This conclusion might lead us to ask: "If our actions stem from our nature, is it just to hold individuals responsible for those actions?" Perhaps sin is akin to a disease, leaving humans as victims in need of treatment and cure rather than judgment.

Scripture rejects this view. Just as Scripture affirms the total depravity and helplessness of human beings, it also affirms that God holds humans morally accountable for their sinful choices that are consistent with that nature.

The biblical narrative directly following the fall reflects God's determination to hold humans morally accountable for their actions. Genesis 4 tells the story of brothers Cain and Abel. Both men brought an offering to God, but God was pleased with Abel's offering and not Cain's. Cain was jealous of his brother and became angry. God responded, "Why are you angry, and why has your face fallen? If you do well will you not be accepted? And if you do not do well, sin is crouching at the door. Its desire is for you but you must rule over it" (Gen 4:6–7). God understood the tremendous temptation Cain faced. Cain, like all of us, had a sinful nature and was confronted by circumstances that tempted him. Sin is pictured as crouching like a wild beast at Cain's door, ready to strike. But God insisted that Cain was responsible to rule over his passions. And God held Cain accountable when he failed to do so.

In the New Testament, we find that humans are held responsible for trusting in or rejecting Jesus and his saving work. Consider Jesus' blunt words to Nicodemus in John 3: "Whoever believes in [the Son of God] is not condemned, but whoever does not believe is condemned already, because he has not believed in the name of the only Son of God" (John 3:18). Nicodemus was morally accountable for his faith or lack of faith in Jesus Christ as Savior.

Further, the many biblical passages that discuss the last judgment show that God will hold individuals accountable for their acts in this life—despite their sinful nature and many strong internal and external temptations to sin. For example, Paul warns in 2 Thessalonians:

> God considers it just to repay with affliction those who afflict you, and to grant relief to you who are afflicted as well as to us, when the Lord Jesus is revealed from heaven with his mighty angels in flaming fire, inflicting vengeance on those who do not know God and on those who do not obey the gospel of our Lord Jesus. They will suffer the punishment of eternal destruction, away from the presence of the Lord and from the glory of his might, when he comes on

that day to be glorified with his saints, and to be marveled
at among all who have believed, because our testimony to
you was believed. (2 Thess 1:6–10)

The entire Bible shows us that sin is not just weakness or a
disease. It is not "merely a developmental flaw, a psychological
weakness, a mistake, or the necessary consequence of an inadequate social structure, etc."; instead, it is "an abuse of the freedom that God gives to created persons so that they are capable of
loving him and loving one another."[46] In *The Christian Nature of
Man*, J. Gresham Machen insisted: "An evil man inevitably performs evil actions; the thing is as certain as that a corrupt tree
will bring forth corrupt fruit: but the evil man performs those evil
actions because he wants to perform them; they are his own free
personal acts and he is responsible for them in the sight of God."[47]

In *Evangelism and the Sovereignty of God*, J. I. Packer discusses
the tension between the propositions that human beings are sinful
and without hope and that God holds humans responsible for their
sinful actions. Packer writes that we must hold to both of these
propositions firmly, just as God does:

Human responsibility is a fact, and a very solemn fact.
Man's responsibility to his Maker is, indeed, the fundamental fact of his life, and it can never be taken too seriously. God made us responsible moral agents, and He will
not treat us as anything less. His Word addresses each of
us individually, and each of us is responsible for the way
in which he responds—for his attention or inattention,
his belief or unbelief, his obedience or disobedience. We
cannot evade responsibility for our reaction to God's rev-
elation. We live under His Law. We must answer to Him
for our lives.[48]

CONCLUSION

The apathy and hopelessness of Oliver Wendell Holmes Jr. make sense if he was correct in his materialist view of the world. Human life lacks any lasting significance, and so the loss of life is meaningless.

From a Christian view of the world, by contrast, the life of every human is precious. We are not Holmes's ant heap; we have dignity and tremendous value in the eyes of God. Indeed, we are so valuable that God himself sent his son to live in human form and die to bring us eternal life.

A Christian view of human nature also provides hope. Because each human life has meaning, there is both a motivation and a basis to preserve, protect, and allow it to flourish. We are spurred on to pursue policies and laws that protect human dignity and respect moral accountability while recognizing we live in a fallen world that produced something as devastating as the Civil War or the Rwandan genocide. Exploring such policies and laws is the subject of this book. The following chapters explore how a Christian view of human nature provides guidance for how to approach key issues of our time. I will begin in the next chapter with one of the most challenging: human trafficking.

PART 2
GLOBAL ISSUES

CHAPTER 3:

HUMAN TRAFFICKING

What happens when we treat people as objects?

People were created to be loved. Things were created to be used. The reason why the world is in chaos is because things are being loved and people are being used.

–UNKNOWN[1]

Sixteen-year-old Asia Graves stood alone in a snowstorm—homeless, hungry, and desperate. She had had a troubled childhood in Boston's inner city. Her father was an alcoholic and her mother was addicted to drugs. A drug dealer molested Asia as a young girl. She was frequently shuttled from house to house until, at sixteen, she was living on the streets. A man approached her on this snowy night and told her she was too pretty to stay outside. He offered shelter and clothing, and Asia hoped that she had finally found a home, stability, and hope. She went home with him.

He soon made clear that strings were attached to his offer of shelter. He told Asia she would need to "earn her keep" and "showed [her] the ropes" of prostitution.[2] Under his control, Asia sold herself for two years to men all along the East Coast from Boston to Miami. She worked six nights a week, collecting up to $2,500 per night.

Sometimes Asia tried to leave, but the man turned violent. He stripped her naked and beat her. "If we didn't call him daddy,

37

he would slap us, beat us, choke us. … I couldn't leave because I thought he would kill me."[3] Columnist Yamiche Alcindor described the violence this way: "In one incident, her captor took a potato peeler to her face then raped her as she bled. Years later, the light scar remains just below her left eye. Other violent episodes left her with eight broken teeth, two broken ankles and a V-shaped stab wound just below her belly button."[4]

Asia stayed, even recruiting other young women to work as prostitutes. "We'd go to malls, schools, group homes, stations and look for girls who were by themselves or looked very vulnerable."[5]

Asia's nightmare ended after she suffered a miscarriage from a beating and finally went to the police. In the prosecution that ensued, six men pleaded guilty or were convicted of conspiracy or sex trafficking. Two were sentenced to twenty-five years in prison.[6]

FOUR TYPES OF HUMAN TRAFFICKING

Many believe that slavery died in the West in the 1800s, following a decades-long policy battle in Britain and a civil war in the United States. While legalized slavery did end, forms of slavery still exist today. Indeed, girls like Asia are victims of a form of modern-day slavery called human trafficking. The US State Department defines human trafficking as "the act of recruiting, harboring, transporting, providing, or obtaining a person for compelled labor or commercial sex acts through the use of force, fraud, or coercion."[7]

Asia's story is shocking, but it is by no means isolated. Consider the following numbers:

- **45.8 million**—the estimated number of slaves in the world at the time of this book's writing.[8] This is more than the number of slaves during the time William Wilberforce led the effort to abolish the British slave trade or before the US Civil War.[9]

- **800,000**—the number of people trafficked across international borders each year.[10]

- **5.5 million**—the number of children trafficked globally.[11]

- **1 million**—the number of children exploited by the global commercial sex trade each year.[12]

- **12–14**—the average age range of entry into prostitution for girls who were sexually exploited.[13]

- **11–13**—the average age range of entry into prostitution for boys who were sexually exploited.[14]

- **$150.2 billion**—the amount of illegal profits earned from human trafficking worldwide. Of this, $99 billion comes from sex trafficking; the remaining $51.2 billion comes from labor trafficking.[15] Human trafficking is the world's third-largest and fastest-growing criminal enterprise.[16]

Human trafficking takes place all over the world. The Global Slavery Index of 2016 estimates that India has more slaves—over 18 million—than any other nation.[17] China is second with 3.4 million, and Pakistan is third with 2.1 million. Measured as a percentage of the total population, the highest incidence of slavery is found in these five nations:[18]

- North Korea (4.4 percent of the population)

- Uzbekistan (3.97 percent)

- Cambodia (1.65 percent)

- India (1.4 percent)

- Qatar (1.36 percent)

As the story of Asia Graves makes clear, though, human trafficking is not just an "over there" problem. It takes place in the United States, too. The Global Slavery Index estimates that over

57,000 slaves live in the United States.[19] By one estimate, 14,500 to 17,500 foreign nationals are trafficked into the United States each year.[20] At least 100,000 children are trafficked within the United States each year.[21]

THE GLOBAL SLAVERY INDEX

The Global Slavery Index is compiled annually by the anti-slavery Walk Free Foundation. The index estimates the number of people held worldwide in any form of slavery, such as forced labor, sexual exploitation, and forced marriage. The foundation obtains data by conducting research in 167 nations and working with the Gallup Organization to survey 42,000 individuals in twenty-five countries.

Modern slavery looks different than it typically did historically. It occurs in a number of forms, from compelling people to work, fight, or provide sexual services to forcibly or fraudulently taking human organs.

FORCED LABOR

The State Department's 2014 Trafficking in Persons Report tells the story of Shyima Hall, an Egyptian girl who at age eight was sold by her parents to a wealthy couple. The couple immigrated to the United States, illegally bringing Shyima with them. Once in the United States, they put Shyima to work for up to twenty hours per day. They verbally and physically abused her. They also confiscated her passport and kept her from interacting with anyone around her. Shyima was rescued only after neighbors filed a report with child welfare authorities. Shyima described her experience this way:

> On the day I was rescued, I knew three words in English: "hi," "dolphin," and "stepsister." I now believe my captors

intentionally kept anything from me that might teach me the language, because knowledge of English could have given me more power. Something captors do well is keep their slaves powerless.[22]

Shyima was a victim of forced labor, in which individuals use threats, force, coercion, or deception to compel someone to work. This takes place in many ways. Some employers withhold payment to workers. Others refuse to allow workers to leave their employment. A common way employers do this with foreign nationals is to withhold passports and threaten to contact immigration authorities if workers do not do what they want.[23]

ORGAN TRAFFICKING

Mohammed Salim Khan, a thirty-three-year-old Indian man, was offered a construction job in a small town several hours away from where he lived. Khan was offered the equivalent of $4 per day, and he expected to work there for three months. When he arrived, a man locked him in a room and compelled him at gunpoint to give a blood sample and to take drugs that rendered him unconscious. Khan awoke to the sight of a man in a surgical mask standing over him. The man said, "We have taken your kidney. If you tell anyone, we'll shoot you."[24] Khan was never paid for his kidney; his recovery took months. Khan was the victim of a form of human trafficking called organ trafficking.

It is hard to know exactly how often organ trafficking takes place. At least 114,000 organ transplants take place every year, but this satisfies less than 10 percent of the global need.[25] Most transplants are done through legitimate means. Indeed, the purchase of transplanted organs alone is not considered trafficking. The transfer of an organ is viewed as human trafficking when victims, like Khan, are deceived or forced into giving up an organ, are not paid for the organ, are paid less than the promised price, or where organs are taken (often while the victim is being treated for an ailment that may or may not exist) without the victim's knowledge.[26]

There are special concerns when organs cross national borders. Most often, organ trafficking occurs when the recipient travels overseas to receive a transplanted organ, sometimes called "transplant tourism."[27] Approximately 5 percent of all organ transplants take place in this way.[28] In other cases, live donors are brought to another country to have an organ removed. The World Health Organization reports:

> In some cases, live donors have reportedly been brought from the Republic of Moldova to the United States of America, or from Nepal to India. In other cases both recipients and donors from different countries travel to a third country. More than 100 illegal kidney transplants were performed at St. Augustine hospital in South Africa in 2001 and 2002; most of the recipients came from Israel, while the donors were from Eastern Europe and Brazil. The police investigation in Brazil and South Africa revealed the existence of an international organ trafficking syndicate.[29]

CHILD SOLDIERS

Norman Okello lived with his family in northern Uganda during a period of warfare between the Ugandan army and the Lord's Resistance Army (LRA), led by the notorious warlord Joseph Kony. On January 1, 1994, when he was twelve years old, Norman and his father were quietly sneaking to their village from the family's rice field when they were surrounded by LRA soldiers. The soldiers took Norman from his father to a LRA camp, where four teenagers beat Norman with large sticks until he passed out.[30]

For the next two months, LRA leaders pushed Norman and other abducted boys until they were near the physical and psychological breaking point through beatings and forced marches. After two months were up, they ordered Norman and others to choose a weapon and to kill a fellow boy who had tried to escape. Norman selected a bayonet and thrust it into the boy's chest. Of the killing, Norman said, "When you kill for the first time, you change. Out of being innocent, you now become guilty. You feel like you're becoming part of the rebels."[31]

Norman became an "excellent soldier," killing many on behalf of the LRA. Eventually, Norman escaped and returned to his family. After years of therapy, he is married and a father himself.[32]

Norman was a victim of a form of human trafficking in which children are forced to become combatants in war or to serve as slaves to support combatants. Most often, boys are recruited and forced to fight. But both boys and girls are also pressed into service as messengers, porters, cooks, and as sexual partners for soldiers.[33]

The use of child soldiers has been a particularly large problem in war-torn nations in Africa. On March 14, 2012, a man from the Democratic Republic of the Congo named Thomas Lubanga became the first person ever convicted by the International Criminal Court (ICC) in The Hague. He was found guilty of "enlisting and conscripting of children under the age of 15 years and using them to participate actively in hostilities."[34] He was sentenced to fourteen years in prison.

Child soldiers gained worldwide attention through the work of Invisible Children, a nonprofit organization that used film to make known the atrocities committed by Joseph Kony and the LRA. Kony is believed to have kidnapped and deployed as many as 38,000 boys and girls as child soldiers in Uganda and the Central African Republic.[35] He, too, is under indictment by the ICC, though he remains at large.[36]

UNICEF estimated that, as of 2015, as many as 300,000 children were involved in more than thirty conflicts worldwide.[37]

INTERNATIONAL CRIMINAL COURT

The International Criminal Court (ICC) is the world's first permanent court established to try individuals for such international crimes as geno-cide, war crimes, and crimes against humanity. The ICC sits in The Hague, the Netherlands, and came into force in 2002 when sixty nations ratified the Rome Statute (the treaty that created the court). While the ICC has had some significant successes, including the conviction of Thomas Lubanga, it also faces challenges. African nations are concerned that the ICC has focused its attention almost exclusively on criminal law violations in Africa. In 2016, South Africa, Burundi, and The Gambia announced that they were withdrawing from the ICC. Further, the four most populous nations in the world (China, India, the United States, and Indonesia) have not ratified the Rome Statute and do not participate in the ICC's work. In fact, only three of the world's ten most populous countries have ratified the treaty.

SEX TRAFFICKING

The story of Asia Graves told at the beginning of this chapter paral-lels those of millions of victims of sex trafficking all over the world. In their book *Half the Sky*, Nicholas Kristof and Sheryl WuDunn tell the story of Meena, who grew up in northern India, near Nepal.[38] When she was eight or nine, she was kidnapped and sold. Her cap-tors held her in a rural home until she turned twelve. They then brought her to a brothel, to a man who had paid to have sex with her. Meena fought him off so fiercely that her captors had to return the money that the buyer had paid. Her captors then beat her with a belt, sticks, and iron rods. Five more times she was presented to buyers, and each time she fought them off.[39]

Meena's captors kept beating her. Finally, they drugged her, got her drunk, and a brothel owner raped her. Meena woke up hungover and hurting and realized what had happened. She concluded, "Now I am wasted."[40] She stopped resisting and began giving in to her captors and their customers.

Meena was not allowed to leave the brothel. She was forced to have sex with ten or more customers per day, seven days a week.[41] If she was sick or fell asleep, she was beaten. If she resisted, she was beaten in front of all the other girls. Indeed, she was beaten an average of five days per week. Her captors masked Meena's screams by turning up the stereo so loud that no one could hear them.[42] Meena endured this life for twelve years before someone bought her freedom.

Sex trafficking has millions of victims—adults and children—all over the world. The US State Department defines sex trafficking differently depending on whether the victim is an adult or a child. "When an adult engages in a commercial sex act, such as prostitution, as a result of force, threats of force, fraud, coercion or any combination of such means, that person is a victim of trafficking."[43] A child, on the other hand, is trafficked when he or she is "recruited, enticed, harbored, transported, provided, obtained, or maintained to perform a commercial sex act." In other words, proof of force, fraud, or coercion is not needed to constitute sex trafficking where a child is concerned.[44]

HUMAN TRAFFICKING AND HUMAN NATURE

Why does human trafficking exist? From a Christian perspective, human trafficking can only thrive because of our fallen human nature and because we fail to value human beings as made in the image of God.

HUMAN FALLENNESS

Human trafficking involves a most egregious display of the depravity of the human heart. President Barack Obama stated it well:

"When a little girl is sold by her impoverished family, or girls my daughters' ages run away from home and are lured—that's slavery. It's barbaric, it's evil, and it has no place in a civilized world."[45]

But human trafficking does exist in what to all appearances is a most civilized world. In 2012, news broke of a gang-controlled sex trafficking ring operating in wealthy Fairfax County, Virginia. The Underground Gangster Crips (UGC) enticed both teenage girls and adult women to join a prostitution ring using media sites and in-person recruitment at Metro stations and even local high schools.[46] They told recruits that "they looked pretty and could use their good looks to earn money."[47] The FBI tells how the gang was able to recruit and then maintain control over the girls: "Members of the enterprise invoked the gang to intimidate or coerce the victims into sexual activity, and they also regularly plied the victims with alcohol and drugs, including cocaine, PCP, ecstasy, and marijuana, in order to reward the victims and keep them sedated or compliant."[48] The gang's leader "personally enforced his will through a mix of manipulation, intimidation, and, where necessary, force—including chokings, beatings and rape."[49]

How was the gang able to do this? It targeted runaways and girls who were on the fringes of society. Gang members pretended to love the girls so that the girls—some for the first time—felt worth and acceptance. Only once they were fully drawn in did the girls experience the full measure of violence, abuse, and exploitation.[50] Thankfully, after relentless and effective investigation and prosecution, the UCG was broken. Gang members were sentenced to prison terms, some up to twenty-five years.[51]

This is not an isolated example. Accounts of human trafficking from all over the nation and world reveal the darkness of the human heart. Yamiche Alcindor tells of just three: "One girl was sold during a sleepover, handed over by her classmate's father. Another slept with clients during her school lunch breaks. A third was choked by her 'boyfriend,' then forced to have sex with 14 men in one night."[52] United States Attorney Neil MacBride, whose office prosecuted the UGC, gets to the heart of the matter: "They are as horrific and brutal and vile as any criminal cases we see."[53]

HUMANS AS CREATED IN THE IMAGE OF GOD

Human trafficking is only possible because all involved—the trafficker, the buyer, and sadly sometimes even the victim herself— see the victim as an object to be used or a commodity to be bought and sold. The American Psychological Association states that a person is sexually objectified when he or she is "made into a thing for others' sexual use, rather than seen as a person with the capacity for independent action and decision making."[54]

In 2003, professors Bridget Anderson and Julia O'Connell Davidson conducted a wide-ranging study on trafficking in persons for the International Organization for Migration. As part of the study they spoke with both sex workers and buyers around the world. They concluded that when buyers used prostitutes knowing they had been trafficked, they "did not perceive of sex workers as consenting subjects within the prostitution contract. Instead, they seem to think that in prostitution, women/girls actually became objects or commodities, and that clients could therefore acquire temporary powers of possession over them."[55]

The notion of possessing a person as an object or thing leads naturally to an environment where abuse, exploitation, and even violence are tolerated and encouraged. Consider these statements from Indian men who knowingly purchased the services of trafficked prostitutes:

> When there is violence ... it is mostly the prostitute's fault. See, I am going to buy something. If I am satisfied with what I am buying, then why should I be violent? I will be violent when I am cheated, when I am offered a substandard service, when I am abused or ill treated. ... Sometimes [violence] is because the prostitute wants the client to use condoms. They force it on the client. ... He will naturally

be disgruntled, and there will be altercations (Indian bank clerk, married, aged 54). ...

If [the prostitute] takes money and does not perform what she is expected to, then the customer will get angry. See, I understand that the prostitute is there in the first place because she has no choice or is forced there. I feel bad about this, especially if she is forced or sold. But the fact is that she is in the flesh market. The rules of the market apply to her as well as to one who is come out of her own choice. ... It may sound bad, but the fact is that she is a commodity offering a service and she should accept that. We should all (Indian civil servant, married, aged 39).[56]

It is not just traffickers and buyers who treat victims as objects; so do police in many nations. The World Health Organization (WHO) reports that police intervention to disrupt sex trafficking in some nations can result in the police abusing the women. "Research from Indonesia and India has indicated that sex workers who are rounded up during police raids are beaten, coerced into having sex by corrupt police officials in exchange for their release or placed in institutions where they are sexually exploited or physically abused."[57] Between 1999 and 2000, the WHO found that in Bangladesh, between 52 percent and 60 percent of sex workers reported being raped by men in uniform in the previous twelve months.[58] A survey in India revealed that 70 percent of sex workers reported having been beaten by the police.[59] These findings reveal that law enforcement officials, too, view victims as objects to be used and exploited rather than as human beings with worth and dignity. They also reveal why victims often fear police as much or more than their traffickers.

Objectification and depersonalization do not just occur in cases of sex trafficking. They are central to labor trafficking as well. In interviews with employers as well as trafficked domestic workers, professors Anderson and O'Connell Davidson found that some

employers view domestic workers as "objects of, rather than subjects to, a contract. This means that once a worker has entered
the home, voluntarily or through coercion by a third party, the
employer has certain rights over that person."[60]

Some employers admitted that they preferred trafficked/
unfree domestic workers to free domestic workers because the
former are easier to use and manipulate. Consider this statement
from a British employer:

> They're foreign and they're illegal and are scared and timid,
> and so they're not going to take up space. They're going to
> be very, very small, and that is generally easier to live with
> than someone who feels that this is their home. They're
> in really bad situations ... they're terrified (British female
> employer in London).[61]

None of this—from kidnapping and sale by traffickers to
purchase by buyers to abuse by police—would be possible if we
embraced the biblical view of human beings. All humans—regardless of sex, age, race, or national origin—have worth and value.
This is not because of their achievements, power, or influence. It is
because they are human beings created in God's image. Whatever
efforts we make to fight against human trafficking, they must
affirm the humanity of the victims who are trapped in the darkness of the trafficking world.

LEGAL AND POLICY IMPLICATIONS

Since 2000, much has been done in the legislative and policy
arenas to attack human trafficking. In 2000 the UN General
Assembly adopted and opened for ratification the "Protocol to
Prevent, Suppress and Punish Trafficking in Persons, especially
Women and Children." The protocol provides a clear, broad definition of human trafficking of various forms, including "sexual
exploitation, forced labour or services, slavery or practices similar
to slavery, servitude or the removal of organs."[62] Ratifying nations

agree both to make human trafficking a crime and to take steps to prevent it and protect victims. A total of 121 nations have ratified this protocol, and 80 have ratified one of its supplements.[63] It entered into force in 2003, and many nations have since enacted domestic laws seeking to comply with its terms.[64]

The United States has responded aggressively to human trafficking during the same time period. Congress passed the Trafficking Victims Protection Act of 2000 (TVPA). The act was the product of a widely embraced, bipartisan effort, passing the Senate 95–0 and the House 371–1 before being signed by President Clinton. The TVPA performs three major functions:

- **Protection.** The TVPA does several things to protect victims of human trafficking, including providing a special visa—the T visa—for foreign national victims who cooperate with the investigation and prosecution of traffickers.[65]

- **Prosecution.** The TVPA defines human trafficking broadly and enumerates a series of new crimes relating to sex and forced labor trafficking that can be punishable in a federal court. Sentences for violators range from 15 years to life in prison.[66]

- **Prevention.** The TVPA authorizes the United States to take comprehensive actions in researching and raising awareness about human trafficking as well as to work in conjunction with foreign governments in drafting laws and engaging in efforts to combat human trafficking generally. One of the concrete results of the act was the creation of the annual State Department Trafficking in Persons (TIP) Report, which has been a tremendous resource for monitoring trends and celebrating accomplishments in the fight against human trafficking.[67]

The TVPA has been reauthorized and revised several times since 2000. Two significant amendments include allowing victims to sue traffickers for civil damages in federal court (2003 reauthorization),[68] and prohibiting the United States from providing aid to countries using child soldiers (2013 reauthorization).[69]

In 2003 Congress also passed the PROTECT Act.[70] Among other things, this act established the national AMBER Alert program to issue notifications about abducted children, increased penalties for child abduction and child sex crimes, and prohibited sex tourism (travel by United States citizens to foreign countries for the purpose of "illicit sexual conduct," which includes commercial sex acts with a minor). Violators can be imprisoned for up to thirty years.[71]

PROTECT ACT

PROTECT is an acronym for the Prosecutorial Remedies and Other Tools to end the Exploitation of Children Today Act, which Congress enacted in 2003. One important aspect of this law is that it gives courts in the United States jurisdiction over acts that Americans commit overseas when engaged in what is known as sex tourism.

For example, it allowed a federal court to try American Michael Clark for molesting two young boys, ages ten and thirteen, in Phnom Penh, Cambodia. Evidence showed that Clark had moved to Cambodia in 1996 and had regularly paid young boys $2 to $5 in order to have sexual relations with them. His conviction under the PROTECT Act was upheld by the Ninth Circuit Court of Appeals in *United States v. Clark*.[72]

Beyond these legislative changes, law enforcement officials are taking much more aggressive action to enforce anti-trafficking laws. In the case of the sex-trafficking ring operating in Fairfax County, Virginia, mentioned above, the federal and state law enforcement officials worked side by side in a joint task force to combat trafficking together. Local communities, too, have established task forces or even special units to prosecute trafficking-related crimes.

INADEQUATE ENFORCEMENT

While much has been done on the legislative and law enforcement fronts to combat human trafficking, much more remains to be done. One of the great challenges confronting abolitionists today is that while nations have strong anti-human-trafficking laws, they often do not enforce them or do not enforce them effectively. This can be true for a variety of reasons. Law enforcement teams can be understaffed. Officials can be overwhelmed by the sheer number of other cases waiting for police, prosecutorial, or judicial action. More troubling, police, prosecutors, and judges can be bribed by traffickers and themselves become part of the trafficking apparatus.

Gary Haugen, president of International Justice Mission (IJM), one of the world's leading and most effective nonprofits fighting human trafficking around the world, describes this phenomenon as the "locust effect." In his book of the same name, Haugen points to a UN report that concluded, "Most poor people do not live under the shelter of the law, but far from the law's protections."[73] In light of UN estimates that there are at least 2.5 billion poor people in the world, Haugen asserts:

> If the condition affecting most of those 2.5 billion people is that they are outside the protection of law, then a lot of people are in big trouble—and a depth of trouble that the rest of us can scarcely imagine. To put it simply: They are not safe. They are—by the hundreds of millions—threatened every day with being enslaved, imprisoned, beaten, raped, and robbed.[74]

Haugen and IJM work around the world to support the creation of functioning justice systems in which police, prosecutors, and judges work transparently and without corruption to enforce the law. If the rule of law does not exist, the finest laws in the world will not protect victims or punish offenders. Desperately needed in the fight against human trafficking are men and women who are prepared to do the hard work of helping nations end violence and enforce the law.

Even in the United States, merely having laws against human trafficking does not solve the problem. Speaking of child sex trafficking, the Institute of Medicine and National Research Council of the National Academies has concluded: "Despite laws in every state that enable the prosecution of [child traffickers and those who purchase sex with minors] and despite the hard work of prosecutors and law enforcement in many jurisdictions, individuals who sexually exploit children and adolescents have largely escaped accountability."[75]

ADDRESSING PROSTITUTION

Law enforcement officials in the United States report that one of their great challenges in trying to stop sex trafficking is knowing how to address cases of prostitution. In many instances, prostitutes were or are victims of human trafficking. When arrested, however, many prostitutes fear the police and refuse to cooperate. There are several reasons for this. Sometimes, victims identify with their trafficker (often the result of drug or alcohol dependence or physical or mental abuse). Others, particularly foreign nationals, fear that the arrest will cause their legal status to be revoked. Police also report that it is sometimes difficult to know if prostitutes are underage and whether they are acting under force or coercion.

One of the most promising legislative models for dealing with these issues is the Swedish or Nordic model. The model bears its name because it was first adopted in Sweden in 1999 and has since been implemented in Norway, Iceland, and a few other nations.[76] The premise is that women and children involved in the commercial sex industry are victims. They are exploited and then bought and sold as commodities. The law therefore targets their exploiters—traffickers, pimps, and buyers.

The Nordic model's premise is to decriminalize the sale of sex and to criminalize the trafficking and buying of prostitutes. This means that Swedish prostitutes are not prosecuted; they are offered services to help them recover and transition to a life outside of the sex industry. However, a man buying sexual services in Sweden can be fined or sentenced to up to a year in jail.[77]

The proponents of this model argue that if one targets the demand for commercial sex services, the incidence of prostitution and trafficking associated with it will drop. Both Sweden and Norway have done comprehensive studies of prostitution in their nations and report significant success.

In 2008, the Swedish government appointed a special committee of inquiry to assess the first decade of its Ban Against the Purchase of Sexual Services.[78] Chancellor of Justice Anna Skarhed, formerly a justice in the Supreme Court of Sweden, chaired the committee.[79] The committee reported in 2010 that:

- The incidence of prostitution in Sweden was lower than it otherwise would have been had there been no ban on the purchase of sex. Street prostitution over the previous ten years was cut in half.[80] This contrasted with a substantial increase in street prostitution in neighboring Norway and Denmark during the same period.[81]

- Internet-facilitated prostitution had increased during this period but not at a level to replace the street prostitution that had declined:

The overall picture we have obtained is that, while there has been an increase in prostitution in our neighboring Nordic countries in the last decade, as far as we can see, prostitution has not increased in Sweden. There may be several explanations for this but, given the major similarities in all other respects among the Nordic countries, it is reasonable to assume that prostitution would also have increased in Sweden if we had not had a ban on the purchase of sexual services. Therefore, criminalization has helped to combat prostitution.[82]

- The ban on the purchase of sexual services also helped decrease human trafficking. The level of organized crime surrounding the sex industry in Sweden was "substantially smaller" in scale than in other comparable countries. According to the Swedish police, the ban on the purchase of sexual services acts as a barrier to human traffickers and procurers who are considering establishing themselves in Sweden.[83]

Seeing Sweden's success, other nations have followed its example. Norway, which had seen a significant increase in prostitution and trafficking during the first decade of the Swedish law, enacted its own ban on the purchase of sexual services in 2009.[84] A study of Norway's experience five years later found similar results to those in Sweden. As was hoped, demand for sexual services and the number of prostitutes in the country dropped. In Oslo, street prostitution dropped between 35 and 60 percent in that time. Even non-street prostitution dropped by 10–20 percent.[85]

This shrinking market for commercial sex services also cut down on the incidence of human trafficking. One of the findings of the two-hundred-page report was: "The enforcement of the law, in combination with the laws against trafficking in pimping, makes Norway a less attractive country for prostitution-based trafficking than what would have been the case if the law had not been adopted."[86]

The Nordic model is not without its critics. Some question the validity of the research touting the laws' success, claiming that the evaluations lack scientific rigor and demonstrate inconsistencies and flawed comparisons.[87] Others note that Sweden moved to this model from a system in which prostitution was legal.[88] They say that this makes it hard to project similar results in countries like the United States, where prostitution is illegal. Still others object to the laws' philosophical underpinning, which assumes that women in the commercial sex trade are victims.[89] They insist that some women make an independent choice to sell sexual services and should be empowered to do so. Indeed, one leading human rights organization, Amnesty International, has called for the complete decriminalization of prostitution, citing the "right" to engage in sex work.[90]

An additional criticism comes from police and prosecutors, who argue that decriminalizing the sale of sexual services actually can be counterproductive in the effort to combat prostitution and sex trafficking. For example, Scott Alleman, former assistant commonwealth attorney for Virginia Beach, claims that it is harder to obtain incriminating evidence against pimps and traffickers if law enforcement officials do not have the leverage of a possible criminal charge when questioning a prostitute.[91] He observes, too, that prostitutes frequently display some level of personal choice and responsibility in their actions so that it would be unjust to hold them completely blameless.[92] He advocates for laws that criminalize both demand and supply, while training law enforcement officials to carefully look for signs of force, fraud, or coercion that would indicate human trafficking.

What is the best approach? Prosecutions in the United States often punish prostitutes but do little or nothing to the buyers of sex.[93] This is misguided. It should never be viewed as acceptable to buy the use of another's body for self-gratification. Current law seems to reinforce the idea that prostitutes are objects and commodities, not individuals with value, worth, and dignity. A Christian view of human nature would demand that the law should criminalize the buying of a person for sex, and it should severely punish pimps and those who traffic women and children. This part of the Nordic model should be implemented.

United States law should also recognize that the vast majority of prostitutes did not become so voluntarily. Many began before age eighteen. Many others were drawn in by force, fraud, or coercion. The Bureau of Public Affairs reports: "The vast majority of women in prostitution don't want to be there. Few seek it out or choose it, and most are desperate to leave it. A 2003 study first published in the scientific *Journal of Trauma Practice* found that 89 percent of women in prostitution want to escape."[94]

The law, even if it criminalizes prostitution as Alleman suggests, should provide support and resources to allow victims of trafficking to escape that life. One example of how this is being done is an innovative program in Columbus, Ohio, called the CATCH (Changing Actions to Change Habits) Court.[95] It was begun by Paul Herbert, a judge who realized that many of the prostitutes being prosecuted in his court were victims of human trafficking and were trapped in a lifestyle from which they could not escape. Under this program, prostitutes who are arrested are given the opportunity to have criminal charges dropped if they agree to undergo a two-year program of drug and alcohol therapy and vocational training. This program affirms the humanity and worth of program participants and helps put them on a path to a productive life.[96]

In short, any steps to improve the law or the functioning of law enforcement must reflect an understanding of two things: First, prostitutes, who are often abused, addicted, or exploited, are persons with value, worth, and dignity. Second, many prostitutes—even those who are over eighteen—are or were victims.

They either started before age eighteen or were led to the life of prostitution by force, coercion, or fraud. Pimps often use deceptive practices, drugs, or physical abuse in recruiting women and girls to and keeping them in a life of prostitution. Few can truly be said to have voluntarily chosen the lifestyle.

IMPLICATIONS FOR THE CHURCH

There is a need for more than legislative change in the battle against human trafficking. The church as a whole has a crucial role to play.

In Isaiah 1 God addressed his chosen people in stark terms. He told them that he was tired of their sacrifices, prayers, and festivals—all things that he commanded them to do. Instead, he wanted this: "Stop doing wrong. Learn to do right; seek justice. Defend the oppressed. Take up the cause of the fatherless; plead the case of the widow" (Isa 1:16–17 NIV). Elsewhere in the Old Testament God insists: "Speak up for those who cannot speak for themselves, for the rights of all who are destitute. Speak up and judge fairly; defend the rights of the poor and needy" (Prov 31:8–9 NIV).

WILLIAM WILBERFORCE

William Wilberforce was the British Member of Parliament and social reformer who led the fight to abolish the slave trade in the British Empire. Wilberforce was first elected to Parliament when he was only 21 years old. Within a few years he became a Christian and seriously considered leaving public life, but as he thought and prayed he realized that God could use him to make a difference. He dedicated himself to what he called his two chief objects: "the suppression of the slave trade and the reformation of manners,"[97] or morality, in England.

Wilberforce repeatedly introduced legislation that would end the slave trade. For twenty years his efforts were rejected or ignored. Opponents argued that ending the slave trade would devastate the economy and diminish England's geopolitical influence. Despite facing death threats and severe health challenges, Wilberforce persevered. Finally, in 1807, Parliament voted to end the slave trade. When the vote was complete, his fellow members of Parliament stood to cheer Wilberforce. In 1833, on the day Wilberforce died, Parliament voted to ban slavery itself.

This appeal is still God's call for justice today. God is calling for modern-day activists to arise and, like William Wilberforce, lead the modern abolition movement. Wilberforces are needed in multiple roles and on multiple fronts. My colleague and former student Ashleigh Chapman, who now serves as the executive director of the Alliance for Freedom, Restoration, and Justice, describes the needed multipronged approach to combating human trafficking as the "Freedom Strategy." It involves five elements:

- **Prevention.** Awareness and prevention efforts can take place in schools and churches and through the media, bringing the issue to the attention of potential victims as well as those in a position to spot and report it. Documentaries as well as feature films like *Taken* are effective in making people aware of the world of human trafficking. So are actions like placing the phone number for the National Human Trafficking Hotline on soap wrappers in hotels.

- **Identification.** We must take steps to identify victims of trafficking. It is important to educate those who are most likely to come into contact with victims of human trafficking—law enforcement officials, health care providers, teachers, and others. Law enforcement officials in particular need much more training in order to identify victims of human trafficking as well as the traffickers themselves. Here again it is important to educate potential victims. As described above, victims often fear police more than their traffickers, or they identify with their captors.

- **Rescue.** Much work is needed to identify victims and get them out of slavery. Individuals are needed to work with police and prosecutors to raid brothels and rescue victims. Along with rescue, often victims need immediate medical care, trauma counseling, and legal services.

- **Restoration.** Victims of human trafficking do not easily leave that life and integrate into mainstream society. Many suffer from post-traumatic stress disorder and drug addiction. Victims need to be restored through trauma counseling, drug addiction programs, and vocational training.

- **Reforms.** We still need to determine and implement the most effective legal framework to stop human trafficking. And we need law enforcement officials to go after traffickers by all legal means.[98]

Thankfully, many individuals and groups have stepped into the breach to seek an end to human trafficking. Their background and work varies widely, but they are united by a passion to speak on behalf of the abused, oppressed, and enslaved. Here are some examples of these modern-day Wilberforces:

- **Kylla Lanier.** Kylla is a teacher from Broken Arrow, Oklahoma. Kylla, her sisters, and mother decided they needed to do something to make a difference in the lives of others. Although none of them were involved in the trucking industry, they realized that much human trafficking in the United States takes place along interstate highways and at truck stops. They formed the organization Truckers against Trafficking to raise awareness within the trucking community of the buying and selling of women and girls that goes on all around them. They raise awareness through radio shows, internet videos, and wallet cards passed out to truckers. Through their work, and the work of truckers working with them, underage victims have been identified and rescued from a life of slavery.[99]

- **Brad Riley.** Over a decade ago, Brad, who is a former pastor, and a small group of friends became increasingly burdened by the abuse and exploitation of children around the world. He visited southeast Asia, partnering with anti-trafficking groups and meeting trafficking survivors. He "returned to the United States committed to rallying others to join him in efforts to eradicate child exploitation at home and internationally."[100] In 2009 he launched iEmphathize. Through documentary films and training programs, the group seeks to raise awareness and join with partners all over the world to end child exploitation.

- **Neil MacBride.** MacBride was the United States Attorney for the Eastern District of Virginia from 2009 to 2013. He oversaw the prosecution of the Underground Gangster Crips in Fairfax County as well as other traffickers. He is a Christian who decided that he should use domestic prosecution to end slavery. Because of his work and those working with him, over 50 traffickers were prosecuted and some are serving forty-year, fifty-year, and life sentences.[101]

The church has an additional role in the battle against human trafficking. We must affirm the worth and dignity of all individuals, including women and girls. We must affirm that their worth is not found in their sexual usefulness or their physical desirability to men. We must address the ubiquitous use of pornography, including by Christians.

We live in an age when sexual imagery is everywhere. Images in television, movies, advertising, and music are hyper-sexualized and portray women more as objects than as humans with rationality, emotions, and wills. Boys and girls are led to embrace this view from a young age. Girls are taught that they have value as they are attractive and desired. They are trained to objectify themselves.

This view is aggressively promoted through the enormous pornography industry. It is estimated that pornography in all its forms generates between $10 billion and $12 billion each year in the United States.[102] Worldwide, pornography is estimated to be a $97 billion industry.[103] Of all the transferred data across the Internet, 30 percent is pornography.[104] Porn sites get more visitors each month than Netflix, Twitter, and Amazon combined.[105] Largely because of the Internet, cases of child pornography have risen dramatically. In 2006 US attorneys handled 82.8 percent more child pornography cases than they did in 1994.[106]

Pornography is not isolated to one segment of society. In a 2014 survey conducted by the Barna Group, 64 percent of American men acknowledged viewing pornography on a monthly basis.[107] For those between eighteen and thirty, 79 percent of men and 34 percent of women viewed pornography on a monthly basis.[108] Also, 18 percent of American men believed they were addicted to pornography or were not sure whether they were.[109] That is 21 million men nationwide.

The Barna survey found that the rates of pornography viewing are virtually identical among Christian and non-Christian men. Of all self-identified Christian men, 64 percent admitted to having viewed pornography on a monthly basis.[110] This confirmed the findings of earlier studies. An August 2006 "General Social Survey" found that 50 percent of all Christian men and 20 percent of Christian women admitted to being addicted to pornography.[111] A 2002 survey of 1,351 pastors found that 54 percent had viewed Internet pornography within the last year and 30 percent had viewed it in the last 30 days.[112]

We should not be surprised that pornography produces destructive consequences. If people—especially women—are simply objects, they may be degraded, abused, or violated. First, pornography reinforces the view—including to women themselves—that women are simply objects for men's pleasure and use.

> Sexual media, particularly sexualised representations of girls and women, can encourage girls and young women to see themselves primarily in sexual terms, to equate their worth and appeal with narrow standards of physical attractiveness, and to see themselves as sexual objects—to focus on others' sexual interest in and judgment of them rather than their own desires and interests. Both correlational and experimental studies find that adolescents' and young adults' exposure to media which sexualise girls and women is associated with greater acceptance of stereotyped and sexist notions about gender and sexual roles including notions of women as sexual objects.[113]

Second, pornography, having fostered an objectified view of women and girls, is tied to abusive and violent behavior toward them. For example, in a study of Canadian teenagers, "there was a correlation between boys' frequent consumption of pornography and their agreement with the idea that it is acceptable to hold a girl down and force her to have sex."[114] Similarly, a study of Italian teenagers found "associations between pornography use and sexually harassing a peer or forcing someone into sex."[115]

Third, there are direct ties between pornography and sex trafficking. In a study of 854 women in nine countries, 49 percent said that porn had been made of them while they were in prostitution, and 47 percent said they had been harmed by men who had either forced or tried to force them to do things the men had seen in porn.[116]

CONCLUSION

Sexuality is never an easy matter for churches to discuss, but we must discuss it. We must proclaim the biblical truth that *all* human beings are made with inherent—not instrumental—value and dignity. We must proclaim that sex has been designed as a God-given way for husbands and wives to become one flesh and to display the complete love, support, and complementarity that God designed. And we must declare that pornography is not harmless. It facilitates a lust that Jesus describes as dangerous, as "adultery" (Matt 5:28). And our men and boys, and increasingly girls, need to know that by consuming pornography, they are supporting an industry that exploits women and fuels human trafficking and the buying and selling of women and children.

Ending human trafficking will not be a quick or simple matter. We must attack it on many fronts. We need to craft appropriate laws and enforce them effectively. But we need more than legal efforts. We need the involvement of dedicated filmmakers, counselors, vocational trainers, parents, and advocates of all kinds. And we need effective teaching in our churches. It will take all of these efforts for us to truly follow God's command to speak for those who cannot speak for themselves and become Wilberforces of the twenty-first century.

CHAPTER 4:
BIOTECHNOLOGY

What is the value of human life?

No decent society can afford to be callous to human suffering or indifferent to the need to seek cures. No decent society can afford to treat human life, at whatever state of development, as a mere natural resource to be mined for the benefit of others.

—LEON R. KASS,
Chairman of President George W. Bush's Council on Bioethics[1]

I n April 2015, eighteen Chinese researchers led by Dr. Junjiu Huang made a startling announcement: they had edited the DNA of human embryos.[2] DNA—deoxyribonucleic acid—is a molecule that contains the genetic information that organisms use to grow and function. It's basically a blueprint for that organism. Using a technology known as CRISPR-Cas9, Huang's team essentially cut an unwanted section of DNA out of the embryos and pasted a new section in its place.

Scientists had successfully edited human cells before. What made Huang's work so significant—and frightening to many— was that he and his team edited not just ordinary cells, but human embryos. Had these embryos been able to develop and ultimately reproduce, the genetic changes made would not simply affect these embryos; they would be inherited by future generations.

CRISPR

"CRISPR" is an acronym for Clustered Regularly Interspaced Short Palindromic Repeats. It is a biological system that performs a basic cut-and-paste function on DNA. Scientists insert a piece of RNA, "a chemical messenger designed to target a section of DNA," and an enzyme that cuts out the defective gene and pasts in the new one.[3] The system was discovered by professors Jennifer Doudna and Emmanuelle Charpentier in 2012.

"Germline gene therapy," as this process is known, is controversial. Supporters insist that genetic editing of embryos makes possible not just the treatment of individual cases of genetic diseases but the eradication of those diseases altogether. Proponents believe germline gene editing could also be used to boost human intelligence or enhance other inherited traits. Others urge caution, warning that altering the genetic makeup of embryos could have unpredictable and potentially dangerous consequences for future generations.

Huang tried to preempt criticism by insisting that his team had only edited the DNA of non-viable embryos that they had obtained from local fertility clinics.[4] He had selected embryos that could not be born alive (and ultimately reproduce) because they had an extra chromosome.[5]

Huang was unsuccessful in stopping criticism. Instead, additional details that were released about the research only heightened the concern of critics who warned of dangers from germline gene therapy. The team had edited the genes of eighty-four embryos and then waited forty-eight hours to see the results. Seventy-one of the embryos survived. Fifty-four of those were tested, and only a fraction of the embryos contained the replacement DNA. The editing also caused "a surprising number" of other "off-target" and potentially dangerous mutations in other parts of the genome.[6] The failure rate caused Huang and his team to stop their work. Huang said, "If you want to do it in normal embryos, you need to be close to 100%. That's why we stopped. We still think it's too immature."[7]

Some other scientists agree and are calling for a halt to genetic editing of human embryos until the world considers the ethical implications of the research. Leading genetic scientist Edward Lanphier urged, "We need to pause this research and make sure we have a broad based discussion about which direction we're going here."[8]

Despite such calls, the research has not halted. In the same 2015 article about Huang and his team, *Nature* reported that at least four other research teams in China were also pursuing the gene editing of human embryos.[9] On February 1, 2016, Britain's Human Fertilisation and Embryology Authority gave approval for gene editing in human embryos to a UK-based research team from the Francis Crick Institute.[10] Swedish officials have approved similar work at the Karolinska Institute in Stockholm.[11]

Germline gene therapy is just one of many advancements in what is truly a revolution in biotechnology. Science is hurtling forward in areas such as genetic testing, stem cell research, and cloning. Scientists have now cloned several mammals, including a sheep and a monkey. They have also cloned human embryos, though these were destroyed in order to harvest their stem cells.[12] Cloning technology involves human control over the very creation of life itself. Such control leads to a multitude of ethical questions: Should we clone humans? Is it appropriate to create a cloned embryo and allow it to mature and be born? Is it appropriate to create a cloned embryo to use for research purposes?

Lanphier's advice to pause germline therapy research and discuss its ethical implications is wise counsel regarding all of the issues of the biotechnology revolution. Such a discussion cannot be limited to science and its technical successes and failures. Decisions about whether to edit the human genome or clone

humans cannot simply be about costs and benefits. These decisions involve the nature of life, death, and humanity itself. They
involve deeper questions, such as: What is life? What is its purpose? Who controls its beginning, development, and end? These
questions are the subject of this chapter. To answer them, it is
essential to have a right understanding of human nature.

THE BIOTECHNOLOGY REVOLUTION

Genetic research has exploded with the mapping of the human
genome. The Human Genome Project involved scientists from all
over the world who worked to identify and map all of the genes
(collectively known as the genome) of humans. It was one of the
most remarkable scientific advancements ever accomplished.
It identified the organization, structure, and function of all 20,500
human genes.[13] The project essentially unveiled the blueprint for
human life, and it opened up the possibility of not just knowing
but controlling our genetic makeup and destiny.

THE HUMAN GENOME PROJECT

The Human Genome Project was an international research effort that
successfully mapped the complete set of human DNA. The project
began in 1990 and was completed in 2003. The main contributors to
the project were the National Institutes for Health (which created the
National Human Genome Research Institute) and the US Department
of Energy. Research took place at universities in the United States, the
United Kingdom, France, Germany, Japan, and China. The project finished earlier than expected and under budget. One of the reasons for
this was that the project demonstrated that humans have approximately
20,500 genes, far less than the 50,000 to 140,000 expected in some
early estimates.

There are several ways in which scientists are seeking to apply our new genetic knowledge. All promise longer, healthier lives. All also raise significant ethical challenges about the meaning and value of life.

GENETIC TESTING

For many years doctors have conducted prenatal tests that diagnose genetic defects while a child is still in the womb. But with recent scientific advances, prenatal testing can be done earlier and in less-invasive ways.

Traditionally, doctors urged pregnant women who were considered to be at a high risk of having a baby with a chromosome disorder to undergo one of two tests: amniocentesis or chorionic villus sampling (CVS).[14] Both involve extracting fetal cells from the placenta or amniotic fluid. Both involve discomfort and risk to the pregnancy.

Our growing genetic knowledge, however, has opened up a new option: noninvasive prenatal testing (NIPT).[15] NIPT is done through a simple blood test. Researchers have learned that a pregnant woman's blood contains small amounts of fetal DNA, so by testing her blood we can learn a great deal about the genetic makeup of her child. Currently, NIPT is not diagnostic; patients with test results indicating possible genetic defects are urged to undergo invasive tests to confirm the results.[16] Researchers are continuing to work to make NIPT diagnostic, which could be revolutionary in the field of obstetrics. While only 2 percent of pregnant women undergo prenatal testing now, Dr. Hank Seely, a law professor and bioethicist at Stanford University, asserts, "Most in the field believe [NIPT] will be diagnostic in 5 to 10 years, or earlier. That's a revolution."[17]

GENETIC DISEASES

Genetic diseases are caused by an abnormality in a person's genetic makeup. These abnormalities are often inherited from parents, but they can also occur when genetic mutations occur. Among the most common genetic diseases are: cystic fibrosis, Huntington's disease, Down syndrome, Duchenne muscular dystrophy, and sickle-cell anemia.

When it is fully developed, NIPT may be able to diagnose fetal diseases such as Tay-Sachs and cystic fibrosis as early as five to nine weeks after conception (compared with as late as eighteen weeks for amniocentesis).[18] It also may eventually be able to detect risk factors for diseases that develop later in life (like breast cancer and Alzheimer's).[19]

What will be the impact of such testing? Positively, it may help families prepare for the delivery and raising of a child who suffers from a genetic disease. There is, however, a dark side to the increased use of genetic testing: the abortion of many children who test positive for genetic defects. Women currently abort fetuses at very high rates when they learn that the fetus has certain conditions.[20] These abortions have had a dramatic impact on the number of children born with genetic disorders. For example, a 2015 study found that prenatal screening and resulting abortions cut the number of babies born with Down syndrome by 30 percent.[21]

Women who undergo prenatal testing often endure pressure from doctors and others to abort when test results are positive for genetic defects. For example, in 2011, Anne Marie Burgess and her fiancé Jeremy learned through CVS testing that their child had Down syndrome. The testing clinic immediately asked: "Do you want us to look into organising a termination?"[22] Anne Marie and Jeremy decided to take some time before reaching a decision and ultimately chose to have the baby.

Even after Anne Marie and Jeremy made their decision, doctors continued to urge the couple to abort:

> It felt like water torture—there was a constant drip-drip-drip of negativity at every consultation or scan. One doctor told us: "Your lives will never be your own." Another said: "Some people will feel you're being selfish by having this child." Yet another: "Your other child will suffer as a result of this." We were made to feel very naïve.[23]

Pressure continued to mount until the couple decided to find a more supportive hospital.

On April 2, 2012, baby Ella was born. She has Down syndrome, but the family reports that "our lives, although different and sometimes challenging, aren't any less happy because of Ella. ... None of us could imagine life without Ella. I shudder when I think how easy it would have been to give in to the pressure to terminate her."[24]

If prenatal genetic testing becomes routine, we will likely see a more dramatic decrease in the birth of children with genetic defects. For many, this is a triumph—according to some, "NIPT could stamp out some DNA-based conditions almost entirely."[25] But of course the "stamping out" involves the destruction of the lives of children with those disorders. Mark Bradford, president of the Jerome Lejeune Foundation and advocate of those with Down syndrome, says the future is "bleak for children prenatally diagnosed with Down syndrome or some other chromosomal abnormalities."[26]

GENE THERAPY

This chapter began by describing advances in gene therapy, a technique by which scientists alter a person's genetic makeup by replacing defective genes with new, functional genes.[27] Gene therapy holds out the prospect of curing genetic diseases and enhancing the quality of human life.

Scientists most often apply gene therapy to alter somatic cells, or particular body cells that make up organs and tissues like the liver or brain.[28] Much more controversial is when they use gene therapy to modify germ cells—egg and sperm cells. Such gene therapy, known as germline gene therapy, causes all of the body's cells to contain the modified genes, and the genetic modification is passed on to future generations.[29] This second form of gene therapy was the one used by Huang and his team.

Doctors increasingly are using somatic cell gene therapy to successfully combat diseases in patients. The first approved use of this therapy in the United States was in 1990, when Dr. William French Anderson treated four-year-old Ashanti DeSilva for a genetic-based immune system defect.[30] Anderson took DeSilva's blood, altered her own white blood cells, and then returned the blood to her body.[31] The treatment was successful, though the effects were temporary.[32] Scientists now report using gene therapy to successfully treat diseases such as inherited retinal disease, beta thalassemia (an inherited blood disease), HIV, and chronic lymphocytic leukemia.[33] In December 2015, scientists announced a new gene therapy that enabled them to modify prostate cancer cells so that a patient's body attacks and destroys them. The BBC reported that this treatment has improved patient survival by 20 percent.[34]

Proponents of germline gene therapy assert that it holds out the prospect of even greater medical advances. Indeed, because this therapy can make inheritable changes that will impact future generations, proponents hope to eradicate certain genetic diseases altogether, such as cystic fibrosis, Alzheimer's, and Huntington's disease.[35]

Beyond promising long-term cures for disease, germline gene therapy also holds out the prospect of genetically enhancing human capacity and performance. Proponents note that genetic modifications, inheritable by future generations, could include improvements in height, strength, appearance, intelligence, and personality.[36] One could make "your bones so hard they'll break a surgical drill."[37] Bioethicist John Harris from Manchester University insists that employing this technology to make enhancements to human performance is not only possible, it is ethically required: "The human genome is not perfect. It's ethically imperative to positively support this technology."[38]

Such broad claims provoke opposition from germline gene therapy critics: "The fear is that germ-line engineering is a path toward a dystopia of superpeople and designer babies for those who can afford it. Want a child with blue eyes and blond hair? Why not design a highly intelligent group of people who could be tomorrow's leaders and scientists?"[39]

Other critics fear that germline gene therapy may alter the human genome in dangerous and unpredictable ways. In 2015 a group of scientists engaged in somatic cell gene therapy publicly opposed the use of germline gene therapy, arguing that "genome editing in human embryos using current technologies could have unpredictable effects on future generations. This makes it dangerous and ethically unacceptable."[40] Significantly, both *Nature* and *Science* refused to publish the results of the Huang team's research.[41] The Council of Europe's Convention on Human Rights and Biomedicine prohibits genetic modification if it seeks "to introduce any modification in the genome of any descendants."[42]

CLONING

Cloning is a related but functionally different procedure made possible by the biotechnology revolution. In cloning, scientists replicate the genetic makeup of another organism. They do this by removing the nucleus (which contains the DNA) from an unfertilized egg and replacing it with DNA from a cell of the organism being cloned.[43]

After cloning, the DNA of the cloned organism is virtually identical to that of the donor. This does not mean that the cloned organism is an exact replica of the donor. Instead, the cloned organism is essentially the donor's twin.[44]

Scientists have already successfully cloned animals. In 1996, scientists at the University of Edinburgh's Roslin Institute famously cloned Dolly the sheep.[45] More than twenty years later, though, animal cloning is still unpredictable and often unsuccessful. Dolly herself was the only sheep to be born out of 277 embryos cloned at the same time, and she had to be euthanized six years later because of significant health problems.[46] Cloned mammals display a variety of defects in their organs (for instance, the heart, brain, and liver). UNESCO reports that only one to three (at most) out of every 100 experiments produces viable offspring in surrogate mothers.[47] Cloning supporters believe that scientific advances will eventually solve these problems, making human cloning a real possibility.

Human cloning may take one of two forms: reproductive cloning and therapeutic cloning. In reproductive cloning, which has not yet occurred, a human would be created and allowed to be born to live a functioning human life. Like germline gene therapy, reproductive cloning holds out the promise of genetic enhancement. Because reproduction through cloning does not involve the inherent unpredictability of sexual reproduction, with its random genetic combination of attributes from mother and father, parents could select the genetic traits they want their child to have through careful selection of the DNA donor to be cloned.

Because of the poor record of safely cloning mammals, more than thirty nations have banned reproductive human cloning.[48] Even some cloning scientists support such bans. Alan Colman, one of the researchers who cloned Dolly, says, "In the case of humans, it would be scandalous to go ahead given our knowledge about the long-term effects of cloning."[49]

The second form of cloning involving humans is therapeutic cloning, in which scientists clone a human embryo in order to produce embryonic stem cells that can be used in research on diseases and their treatments. Scientists have already successfully carried out human therapeutic cloning.[50] The process of harvesting stem cells (done very early in the embryo's life) destroys the embryo.[51] Thus, the goal of therapeutic cloning is not to produce humans who will be born and live functioning lives; it is to produce cells for research or treatment alternatives to the donor. Therapeutic cloning enjoys more popular support in the United States and Europe than reproductive cloning.[52] England, Israel, Sweden, China, and Singapore allow therapeutic cloning, though they forbid reproductive cloning.[53] As of the writing of this book, the United States has no federal laws on cloning.[54]

STEM CELL RESEARCH

Research on stem cells is closely related to both therapeutic cloning and genetic therapy.[55] Stem cells are "undifferentiated" cells— they are capable of developing into many different cell types as the body grows. As they divide and grow, they can become heart, lung, or skin cells, for example, producing all of the body's cells and organs.[56] Stem cells in adults generate replacements for cells that are damaged or destroyed by aging, injury, or disease.[57]

According to the National Institutes of Health, three key things distinguish stem cells from other cells: "They are capable of dividing and renewing themselves for long periods; they are unspecialized; and they can give rise to specialized cell types."[58] Scientists believe that because of their regenerative nature, stem cells offer the prospect of successfully treating diseases like diabetes, Parkinson's disease, muscular dystrophy, and heart disease.[59]

Stem cell research has proven controversial depending on whether the kind of stem cells used is embryonic or adult. Embryonic stem cells, as their name suggests, are derived from human embryos. Adult stem cells are undifferentiated cells that are found in organs and tissues, including the placenta and umbilical cord, skin, brain, and spinal cord.[60]

There are advantages to using each type of stem cell. Embryonic stem cells can become any cell type found in the body. Adult stem cells are thought to produce a more limited number of cell types, such as brain or heart cells, depending on the source of the adult stem cells. Embryonic stem cells can also survive longer than

adult cells in the laboratory before being deployed for a particular function.[61]

Adult stem cells have a significant advantage for use in therapy.
They are less likely to be rejected if transplanted into a patient
than embryonic stem cells. This is because researchers can take
the stem cells to be implanted from a patient's own body.[62] By contrast, embryonic stem cells have a genetic makeup different from
the patient. As with any organ transplant, the recipient's body may
reject the stem cells of the donor embryo. More fundamentally,
the use of adult stem cells does not require the destruction of a
human embryo. No life is destroyed when harvesting adult stem
cells, while human embryos are always destroyed in embryonic
stem cell research.

Scientists have also begun exploring another alternative to
embryonic stem cells: induced pluripotent stem cells. These can
be derived directly from adult tissues such as skin cells.[63] Like
adult stem cells, these cells possess the same DNA as the donor, but
unlike adult stem cells, they are pluripotent—which means they
can grow into virtually any cell type.[64] As of this writing, there
are still practical hurdles with this technology, but if successfully
developed, it could provide a valuable source of cells that does not
involve the destruction of human embryos.

In 1996 Congress passed the Dickey-Wicker Amendment,
which prohibited the use of federal funds for research in which
human embryos are destroyed, discarded, or "knowingly subjected
to risk of injury or death greater than that allowed for research on
fetuses in utero."[65] This amendment has appeared in the Health
and Human Services appropriations bill in every year since. The
National Institutes of Health nonetheless continue to do research
on embryonic stem cells. They have concluded that, while the
research is conducted on cells that were derived from an earlier
destruction of a human embryo, it does not itself destroy embryos.
This conclusion has been upheld in federal court.[66] Other nations

are split on the practice, with many banning all research done on stem cells taken from human embryos.[67]

HUMAN NATURE AND THE BIOTECHNOLOGY REVOLUTION

The debates over these biotechnologies are not quibbles over minor policy matters. They are rooted in deeply and fundamentally different views of human nature. Indeed, these biotechnologies implicate all three aspects of human nature discussed in chapter 2: we are created with dignity and worth in the image of God; we are fallen; and we are morally accountable agents.

WE ARE CREATED WITH DIGNITY AND WORTH IN THE IMAGE OF GOD

Understanding our origin is key to addressing biotechnology advances. Christianity says not only that we have worth and dignity, but that they come from our Creator—a Creator who still lives and interacts with the people and world he created. The dominant view in the biotechnology community is materialism, which rules out the supernatural and declares that the material world is all that exists. We have merely evolved through a function of time, chance, and matter.

Cornell biologist Dr. William Provine bluntly articulated the implications of the materialist view: "There are no gods, no purposes, and no goal-directed forces of any kind. There is no life after death. When I die, I am absolutely certain that I am going to be dead. That's the end of me. There is no ultimate foundation for ethics, no ultimate meaning in life, and no free will for humans, either."[68] If the materialist view is correct, not only are we the product of natural forces alone, we are fully controlled by them as well. (Chapter 9 will further explore the implications of this view for the possibility of free will and accountability for crime.) Prominent materialist Dr. Richard Dawkins has noted that this view has powerful implications for biotechnology, too: "As a naturalist, in the philosophical sense, I'm committed to the view that there is nothing mystical or supernatural about life, and therefore in principle, it must be possible to construct life either by chemically, making your own by chemistry, or in a computer, and I find that both exciting and a bit alarming."[69]

In a world without God or the supernatural, our lives and futures are in our own hands. If we are merely the products of an evolutionary process, we can use biotechnology to control that process and shape our own genetic future. Some proponents of human cloning and germline gene therapy express this view clearly. One says that these technologies will "allow us to seize control of our evolutionary future."[70] He calls this "the ultimate expression and realization of our humanity."[71] Another says that "science promises to achieve in overnight laboratories the process of natural selection which would otherwise take millions of years in nature."[72] A third asks, why not "control our own biology ... become masters over the processes that created us?"[73]

Beyond the question of human origins, debates over biotechnology raise critical questions concerning the value of human life. The concept of "dignity" is prominently featured in those debates. But what is the source and basis of human dignity? The Christian view is that *all* humans have equal dignity and worth—regardless of age, sex, race, size, wealth, health, or mental condition. This dignity is not based on our achievement or ability. We are not the source of our own dignity; it comes from our Creator.

Some leading bioethicists hold a different view, arguing that merely being human does not ensure dignity and worth. Dr. Joseph Fletcher, for example, declares, "Nobody in his right mind regards life as sacrosanct."[74] Humans gain value only as they satisfy certain criteria, such as self-awareness, self-control, communication capability, and memory.[75]

Peter Singer agrees. Singer is the Ira W. DeCamp Professor of Bioethics at Princeton, one of the most prestigious university professorships in bioethics, and was acclaimed in 2013 as the world's third most influential contemporary thinker in a study conducted by the Gottlieb Duttweiler Institute.[76] Like Fletcher, Singer rejects the notion that all humans are equal in value and dignity: "I do not see any argument in the claim that merely being a member of the species *Homo sapiens* gives you moral worth and dignity, whereas being a member of the species *Pan troglodytes* [chimpanzees] does not give you worth and dignity."[77] There is nothing inherent in a particular species that confers a certain status. "We cannot claim that biological commonality entitles us to superior status over those who are not members of our species. In the case of applying this to people with severe and profound cognitive disabilities, there is also a problem about saying who the 'we' are. What is really important about saying 'us?' "[78]

In fleshing out who "we" are—who is entitled to moral worth and dignity—Singer insists that he would have more in common with an alien with communication abilities "than I do with someone who was of my species but, because he or she is profoundly mentally retarded, has no capacity for verbal communication with me at all."[79] He therefore calls for a graduated hierarchy of moral status that is applied to both humans and nonhumans. He bases the hierarchy on attributes like cognitive ability, self-consciousness, self-awareness, and the ability to suffer or to enjoy life:[80]

I accept the normative view that there is greater significance in killing a being who has plans for the future—who wishes to accomplish things—than there is in killing a being who is incapable of thinking about the future at all but exists either moment to moment or within a very short-time horizon (for example, a time horizon limited to thinking about eating something in the near future).[81]

Armed with this view, Singer advocates for infanticide of infants with hemophilia or severe Down syndrome. Similarly, he supports the involuntary euthanasia of adults with advanced Alzheimer's or who otherwise lack cognitive ability.[82]

The implications of a materialist view for biotechnology are powerful. If Singer is correct, we should have no qualms about research on embryonic stem cells or cloning for research purposes. Human embryos do not yet have cognitive abilities; they have no self-awareness; they feel no pain. Under the Singer approach, they have little moral worth and dignity and few or no rights. Indeed, that human embryos have no rights was the conclusion of a minority of the President's Council on Bioethics that was convened in 2001. They insisted that cloning for research purposes "presents no special moral problems."[83]

WE ARE FALLEN

Christians justly celebrate humans' ability to make creative and meaningful contributions to the world around us when we apply the gifts God has given us as his image-bearers. By his grace we have achieved tremendous breakthroughs in science, technology, and medicine.

We also know, though, that we have the ability to misuse those same breakthroughs to cause destruction and death. While we are made in God's image, we are fallen and often apply good things to evil ends.

This moral realism is essential for living productive and responsible lives. It is too often missing, however, from scientific discussions of biotechnology breakthroughs and applications. Indeed, bioethicists frequently suffer from utopianism as they approach genetic research. Here are some of the claims scientists and writers have made about genetic engineering:

- "We are about to remake ourselves as well as the rest of nature."[84]

- "The great biotechnical transformation is being accompanied by an equally significant philosophical transformation."[85]

- "[CRISPR] raises the possibility, more realistically than ever before, that scientists will be able to rewrite the fundamental code of life."[86]

- "Genetic engineering has given us the power to alter the very basis of life on earth."[87]

Supporters of human cloning and gene therapy promise a world free from genetic disease and filled with humans with selectable hair color, height, build, athleticism, and intellectual ability. One calls this future "the ultimate expression and realization of our humanity."[88]

UTOPIANISM

Utopianism is a belief in the possibility that humans can achieve a perfect (or near perfect) society. For some, utopianism goes hand in hand with scientific advancement: science holds the key for humans to construct and manage an ideal world. Genetic research is particularly susceptible to utopian visions because gene therapy holds out the possibility of not only treating genetic-based diseases, but eradicating them altogether.

While genetic researchers acknowledge that the technology that would bring about this remade world could be misused, they express confidence that we will draw appropriate ethical lines to restrain ourselves. However, human-devised ethical guidelines—especially in a field that has largely abandoned moral absolutes and embraced a materialistic worldview—have very little power to truly restrain evil.

Within the last decade, for example, an international group of scientists, ethicists, and lawyers decided that it is ethical for researchers to create human-animal hybrids (creatures that come from a human sperm and an animal egg or vice versa) as long as the creature is not allowed to breed.[89] Similarly, in the United States, the National Academies of Sciences, Engineering, and Medicine determined that research on human embryos is ethical as long as they are not "grown in culture for longer than fourteen days" and the central nervous system is not allowed to form.[90]

How are such decisions reached? They are not based on a moral view that humans have inherent moral worth and dignity. They are likely based on a pure utilitarian calculus of costs and benefits. That same calculus will certainly be applied to germline gene therapy and human cloning once they are viewed as "safe."

Clear ethical lines should instead be guided by a Christian view of human nature. History warns of the great harm fallen human beings can cause when they run with scientific theories unchecked by moral truth. A great example is the practice of eugenics in the late nineteenth and twentieth centuries.

Eugenics was a social application of Darwin's evolutionary theory of survival of the fittest. It held out the prospect that selective breeding could improve the human species and its survival. Darwin's half cousin Francis Galton coined the term "eugenics" in 1881.[91] He declared, "What nature does blindly, slowly, and ruthlessly, man may do providently, quickly, and kindly."[92] Many others embraced this view; Margaret Sanger, founder of Planned Parenthood, famously asserted, "More children from the fit, less from the unfit."[93]

Eugenics was at one time embraced by the United States Supreme Court. In 1927, in *Buck v. Bell,* the Court authorized the involuntary sterilization of Carrie Buck, a young woman who had been committed to the Virginia State Colony for Epileptics and Feebleminded. In the years following this decision, approximately 60,000 Americans were involuntarily sterilized after being deemed unfit by judges.[94] Hundreds of thousands of women faced the same fate around the world.[95]

BUCK V. BELL (1927)

Buck v. Bell is a 1927 decision of the United States Supreme Court that upheld a Virginia state statute permitting the involuntary sterilization of "mental defectives."[96] The statute specifically authorized state officials to sterilize "feebleminded" individuals (including the "insane, idiotic, imbecile, feebleminded or epileptic") who were inmates of state institutions.[97] By an 8–1 decision, the Supreme Court rejected Buck's claim that the law violated the Fourteenth Amendment to the Constitution, with Justice Oliver Wendell Holmes Jr. infamously declaring: "Three generations of imbeciles are enough."[98] From the time of the decision to 1979, Virginia used this law to involuntarily sterilize approximately 8,000 people.[99]

The Nazis fully embraced eugenics and took it to its logical conclusion. In 1933, the Nazis enacted a sterilization law entitled, "Law for the Prevention of Genetically Diseased Offspring."[100] After a few years, they carried the eugenic program further. In 1939, concluding that some people were "unworthy of life," the Nazis began widespread extermination of disabled individuals.[101] They killed as many as 250,000 disabled individuals by the end of World War II.[102] They did so based on the view that such individuals lacked societal usefulness and were "empty human husks" and "useless eaters."[103] The Holocaust itself was a further application of this eugenic principle as the Nazis killed millions of "useless" and "genetically deficient" Jews, Gypsies, and homosexuals.

Eugenics did not die with the Nazis; its advocates are still among us. In 2012, a Massachusetts probate judge ordered that a thirty-two-year-old pregnant woman who suffered from schizophrenia be forced to have an abortion even if she had to be "coaxed,

bribed or even enticed" into the hospital.[104] This decision was overturned by the Massachusetts Court of Appeals, which held that all
individuals, including those deemed incompetent, have a fundamental right to bear a child.[105] In a 2009 *New York Times* interview,
United States Supreme Court Justice Ruth Bader Ginsburg stated
this about *Roe v. Wade*: "Frankly, I had thought that at the time
Roe was decided, there was concern about population growth and
particularly growth in populations that we don't want to have too
many of."[106] Three years later, NBC's chief medical editor, Nancy
Snyderman, "nonchalantly called the embrace of eugenic abortion
'pro-science' and thought it a 'great way to prevent diseases.'"[107]

There is a strong eugenic push behind germline gene therapy, human cloning, and even genetic testing. Widespread use
of germline therapy and reproductive cloning can—according to
proponents—result in an enhanced gene pool and would eradicate certain diseases altogether. As noted above, many advocates
of making genetic testing diagnostic hope that parents will abort
fetuses that test positive for genetic defects and end, for example,
diseases like Down syndrome.

We are assured that this modern version of eugenics will not
be coercive like its predecessor. This time, all decisions—whether
to abort, to engage in germline gene therapy, or to clone, for example—will be voluntary. But we have been assured of such things
before, and these decisions are necessarily involuntary for the
fetuses and embryos involved. Our fallen human nature should
give us pause when we consider how things like germline gene
therapy, cloning, and genetic testing will be conducted.

WE ARE MORALLY ACCOUNTABLE AGENTS

The materialist worldview embraces the concept that we live in a
deterministic world. We are the products of our genetic makeup
and are often compelled by it to act in certain ways. As will be discussed more fully in chapter 9, Christianity maintains that while

we can be influenced by our genetic makeup, that makeup does not have a determinative role in our lives. We are morally accountable to choose to do right regardless of genetic influences to the contrary.

The revolution in genetic research has prompted many more claims that individuals are not responsible for their actions because they were genetically predisposed to such things as, for example, infidelity or violent crime. Such claims undermine the concept of moral responsibility.

PRESIDENT'S COUNCIL ON BIOETHICS

In 2001, President George W. Bush created an eighteen-member body of leading scholars and medical doctors to advise him on issues emerging from advances in biomedical science and technology. The council met over thirty times from January 2002 until 2009. It produced ten reports on such issues as cloning, stem cell research, genetic screening, and ethical caretaking of the elderly. While some criticized the council for not being practical enough, the council asked core questions about what it means to be human and how to protect the value of human life as new biotechnologies arose. Dr. Leon Kass chaired the council from 2001 to 2005, and Dr. Edmund Pellegrino chaired the council from 2005 to 2009.

Further, the belief that genes determine our lives and behavior fuels the advancement of certain of the technologies discussed above. Reproductive cloning, for example, holds out the prospect of parents making genetic choices for their offspring that will enhance their lives in specific, predetermined ways. As Leon Kass, former chairman of President Bush's Council on Bioethics, has pointed out, however, "There is something deeply disquieting in looking on our prospective children as artful products perfectible by genetic engineering, increasingly held to our willfully imposed designs, specifications, and margins of tolerable error."[108]

LEGAL AND POLICY IMPLICATIONS

According to the Christian view of human nature, any use of biomedical technology should be made with an understanding that humans are morally accountable agents and not simply the predetermined product of a biotechnical process. We should keep in mind two things when evaluating technological advances.

First, we must not reflexively reject all new technologies as dangerous. God made humans stewards over the earth and designed us to be creative problem solvers in that role. Many tremendous advances in science and medicine have been made because individuals and groups have lived out their God-given potential and applied it to benefit society. To that end, we should be "pro-technology."[109] As Michael McKenzie asserts, "We have a mandate to engage in genetic research and therapy, *when it is directed toward the healing end of medicine.*"[110]

Second, in fulfilling this mandate, we must build a moral framework for understanding technology that is based in a biblical view of human nature. As Nigel Cameron, president of the Center for Policy on Emerging Technologies, notes, "Technology isn't the problem. The problem is technology out of context—capacities which we gain to rule this world out of the moral context in which we have been called to do the ruling."[111]

When we look at technological innovations while accounting for our human nature, we notice some clear moral effects:

- Because humans are created in the very image of God, all humans have worth and dignity and must be protected—even the smallest and weakest among us.

- Because we are fallen, we will abuse even the best and most creative technologies if we don't set up clear and appropriate checks and limits.

- Because we are morally accountable agents, we must not embrace a deterministic philosophy or do

anything that downplays human responsibility for
our choices and actions.

In light of these principles, how should we approach specific
innovations in biotechnology? We should pursue some and apply
them with caution—and we should reject others entirely.

GENETIC TESTING: PURSUE WITH CAUTION

The advances in genetic testing are astounding. It is likely that
noninvasive and inexpensive blood tests will be available in the
coming years that will give us tremendous knowledge not only
of fetal genetic defects but also of the likelihood that a particular
fetus will develop certain diseases in adulthood. Christians should
use genetic testing to provide an opportunity for in-womb medical
interventions that may increasingly become available in coming
years as well as to prepare themselves to more effectively parent
children with special needs.

We should use this technology for good while we also hold
firmly to one fundamental principle: every fetus is a human person
at whatever stage of development. Indeed, every human embryo is
a human person. Princeton professor Robert P. George, a member
of President Bush's Council on Bioethics, notes that while not yet
mature, every human embryo is distinct and complete: "It not
only possesses all of the necessary organizational information for
maturation, but it has an *active disposition* to develop itself using
that information. The human embryo is, then, a whole (though
immature) and distinct human organism—a human being."[112]
True, embryos and fetuses cannot yet reason and make choices.
Neither can a four-week-old infant. Yet each embryo is a unique
and complete human organism that will naturally develop into a
human adult if not deprived of the opportunity. Human embryos,
fetuses, and infants all have moral worth and dignity because they
are human.

EMBRYO AND FETUS

Embryos and fetuses are human beings at different stages of development. The Cleveland Clinic states that a developing baby is called an
embryo from conception to the eighth week of pregnancy. After the
eighth week and until birth it is called a fetus.[113]

To hold otherwise is to embrace the view of professors
Fletcher and Singer. They insist that humans do not gain full
dignity and worth until they display—and unless they *still* display—self-awareness and reasoning and communication abilities. If they are right, it is morally acceptable to end the lives not
only of embryos and fetuses, but three-day-old babies, children
with Down syndrome, or elderly adults with Alzheimer's disease.

As Christians, we must reject this view and embrace the value
of all human life at whatever stage of development or functioning. Human life has value not because we have arrived at a certain
level of intellect, rationality, or health, or as a result of our own
achievements, but because God has made all humans—even the
smallest and youngest—in his image.

So how can we embrace genetic testing while also upholding
the value of human life at all stages of development?

First, we should use testing in the service of unborn children.
Early knowledge can help a family prepare—financially, psychologically, spiritually—for a child with special needs. As medical
technology advances, and with the knowledge testing provides,
doctors will be increasingly able to undertake procedures while
the child is in the womb or just after birth to care for and perhaps
even cure genetic diseases.

Second, parents should not be permitted to abort their children because they are the wrong sex, have genetic defects, or for
any other reason. Abortion has been legal—indeed, held to be a
constitutional right—for over forty years. Some have wearied of

the effort to bring the culture and the law to reject abortion. But if a Christian view of human nature is right, this is a battle we must fight. The battle to end slavery took generations, and this likely will as well.

Third, while we work and wait for legal change, we should develop good information and counseling resources for parents who receive news of a child's genetic defects. Too many doctors reflexively—and aggressively—present abortion as the only logical alternative. Just as many states have created informed consent laws for abortion with waiting periods and mandatory information, they should provide comprehensive information about the value of lives of individuals with disabilities and the financial and other resources available for parents of special needs children.

GENETIC THERAPY: PURSUE WITH CAUTION

As with genetic testing, Christians must not immediately dismiss all of the technical advances in genetic therapy. We should pursue gene therapy as long as it does not require experimentation on or destruction of human life. We should also pursue it when it is directed toward healing and not genetic enhancement, which, like performance-enhancing drugs, involves not the healing of disease but the "improvement" of average or less-than-average characteristics.[114] We should be fixing something that is broken as opposed to supercharging a body that is functioning normally.

For example, somatic cell gene therapy (which alters particular body cells that make up organs and tissues like the liver or the brain, rather than egg or sperm cells) offers great hope to individuals suffering from genetic disorders. It does not destroy human embryos, nor does it modify the genetic structure of future generations. Just as we embrace heart and liver transplants to cure disease, we should welcome the genetic equivalent—doctors implanting healthy genes into patients to cure genetic diseases. Somatic cell gene therapy can help us fulfill our role to be stewards of the earth and to care for the hurting around us.

Germline gene therapy is another matter. We should oppose efforts like those of Junjiu Huang and his team to make changes to the genetic structure of embryos that would be passed on to future generations. One reason to oppose such research is that it involves experimenting on human embryos. That researchers use embryos with genetic defects that would prevent them from living past birth does not change that they are experimenting on—and ultimately killing—humans. Germline gene therapy exploits some humans for the potential good of others. Christians' respect for the value of human life counsels us to oppose such research.

Further, our acknowledgment of human fallenness warns that unintended, unknown, and potentially dangerous consequences may follow from changing the human genome for generations to come. Huang's own research—with its many "off-target" mutations—shows how little we know about how a change to one part of the genome may impact others.

EMBRYONIC STEM CELL RESEARCH AND
THERAPEUTIC CLONING: REJECT ENTIRELY

In light of the value of human life at all stages of development, then, we should reject embryonic stem cell research and human therapeutic cloning. Both experiment upon and destroy human embryos. Indeed, therapeutic cloning specifically creates embryos in order to experiment on them and destroy them for the good of others.

Proponents of these techniques argue that embryos are merely collections of cells. Embryos feel no pain; they have no cognitive abilities. They are more akin to tissue than human persons.

In light of the sanctity of human life, however, human embryos, just like fetuses, have moral worth and dignity because they are human. They are unique and complete and will naturally develop into human adults if given the opportunity. Though small and young, they are created in the image of God. Leon Kass puts it well: "No decent society can afford to treat human life, at whatever state of development, as a mere natural resource to be mined for the benefit of others."[115]

Human reproductive cloning does not destroy human embryos as does human therapeutic cloning. However, we should also reject human reproductive cloning.

The first and immediate reason is that medical science does not yet allow cloning to be done safely and without producing harmful consequences. Of course, it is likely that if we were to allow further research on reproductive cloning, our knowledge and techniques would improve. We might well overcome the technical hurdles just as we have overcome many initial hurdles in brain surgery and organ transplantation.

But should we pursue such research? No. To overcome these technical hurdles would require experimenting on unborn and nonconsenting humans. We would create many human embryos only so that the vast majority would die. And we would be essentially experimenting on the children who would be born alive. The development of reproductive cloning technology would by necessity exploit cloned individuals. As in the case of human trafficking, we would be using humans as objects rather than valuing them as persons with inherent worth and dignity.

Second, the cloning process could have negative effects on the clones as their lives develop. Kass asks: "Cloning creates serious issues of identity and individuality. ... What would be the psychic burdens of being the 'child' or 'parent' of your twin?"[116] Undoubtedly, while there is always pressure for children to live up to the expectations of their parents, those pressures will be multiplied when the child is selected to be genetically identical to one parent.

Some have suggested that reproductive cloning might be used by parents of dying children who want that child to live on in some way. Imagine the pressures of the cloned individual who "at a year, 18 months, two years old, it dawns on him that he is not an individual, but someone who has been brought into being as a manufactured copy of another."[117] Another possible scenario is that parents will want to create a genetic copy of a famous athlete or celebrity: "Whether 5,000 of your favorite sports star or singer is quite what you want, think what life will be like for the members of this new class of person who are all monozygotic 'twins.' [118] We do not know the psychological effects of any of these things on cloned individuals.

Third, while we do not know many of the effects of reproductive cloning, as Christians we do know that we live in a fallen world, and the effects of cloning would undoubtedly be colored by human fallenness. As history can attest about human plans, cloning will not proceed according to our best and most noble intentions. It will create unexpected and unintended ills as well.

This reality should give us pause in light of the obvious eugenic aspects of cloning. One of the promises of reproductive cloning is that it gives parents the opportunity to select the exact genetic model for their child. They can use DNA prescribing a certain hair and eye color, intellectual gifting, propensity for disease, and so forth. If reproductive cloning were to become commonplace, we would expect to see healthier and "better" genetic codes passed on.

Given the strong materialist and utilitarian philosophies influencing American culture today, we should be wary of embracing a technology by which we could "purify" the makeup of the human race. It is not unthinkable that, just as it did in our recent past, this seemingly benign goal of improving our DNA could lead us to want to eliminate those who do not meet the standard. Even now, through individual patient decisions (albeit sometimes with strong pressure from doctors) and without government mandate, large numbers of parents choose to end the lives of genetically impaired fetuses. Is it beyond the realm of possibility that we would move from this to permitting infanticide of severely handicapped children or the involuntary euthanasia of elderly people who have lost their cognitive abilities? History would say no. And leading ethicists are already telling us that such actions would be morally acceptable. We should stand against the eugenics of today just as we condemn the eugenics of the early twentieth century.

Finally—and central to our discussion—we should oppose reproductive cloning because of the hubris at its core. Leon Kass calls cloning "inherently despotic."[119]

> The child is given a genotype that has already lived, with full expectation that this blueprint of a past life ought to be controlling of the life that is to come. ... It seeks to make one's children (or someone else's children) after one's own image (or an image of one's choosing) and their future according to one's will.[120]

In his *Atlantic* essay "The Case Against Perfection," Harvard professor Michael J. Sandel agrees, calling genetic engineering "the ultimate expression of our resolve to see ourselves astride the world, the masters of our nature. But that promise of mastery is flawed. It threatens to banish our appreciation of life as a gift, and to leave us with nothing to affirm or behold outside our own will."[121]

Sandel is right. While he does not argue from a Christian point of view, his argument is in line with the foundational Christian understanding of human nature that we are made in the image of God and dependent on him. We are not independent. We are not autonomous. We are not masters of our own universe. We are dependent on God for our worth and dignity—and for our very lives. This recognition counsels humility and wariness of a technology that promises to transfer to us the control of our genetic futures.

CONCLUSION

All of these recommendations will be challenging to enforce. Even if we were to enact legal bans, we should have no illusion that they will stop genetic research from going forward. The CRISPR-Cas9 technology makes it possible for many scientists to do the kind of research pioneered by Huang. In an ideal world, governments would restrict this research not only through legal prohibitions but by cutting off its funding. But because research is going on worldwide, cooperation among nations is necessary. International agreements would be needed to coordinate efforts.

We must be realistic, though, and expect that research will continue. It is essential, then, that we make progress outside of the scientific realm to teach and model an accurate view of human nature. We will be much better equipped to address the dangers from human cloning and germline gene therapy if the dominant worldview is one that values all human life, including that of the youngest and smallest. In our homes, churches, and schools—with everything we have—we must combat the materialistic view of the world and human life.

CHAPTER 5:
GENOCIDE

How does genocide happen, and how can it be prevented?

The victims of these crimes are numbered in the hundreds of thousands. ... For the most part they are nameless dead. To their murderers, these wretched people were not individuals at all. They came in wholesale lots and were treated worse than animals.

−TELFORD TAYLOR,
opening statement in the Nazi Doctors' Trial[1]

Sawela Suliman grew up in the Darfur region of Sudan. In 2004, when she was twenty-two years old, her region was engulfed in a civil war between African tribal groups from the south and west of Sudan and government troops from the Arab north, who were supported by Arab militias known as the "Janjaweed." Sawela and other Africans were hiding in a refugee camp in Geneina, a city in western Darfur, Sudan. Early on a Sunday morning, she and two other young women crept out of the camp to collect straw for their families' donkeys. They thought it would be safe—that the Janjaweed would be asleep. They were wrong. Six men grabbed them, beat them, and raped them. As they did so, the men yelled slurs in Arabic, like "*zurga*" ("black") and "*abid*" ("slave").[2]

JANJAWEED

"Janjaweed" is the name of Arab militia groups operating in Sudan, particularly in the Darfur region, during the genocide that began in 2003. The militias were primarily made up of nomadic Arab tribesmen.

While Janjaweed fighters were not officially part of the Sudanese military, the military armed them and actively supported their efforts. For example, the Sudanese air force would often launch helicopter raids on Darfur villages ahead of Janjaweed raids. The Janjaweed then entered the villages and killed, raped, and kidnapped victims. They burned homes and contaminated wells so that any survivors would be forced to leave. Janjaweed raids killed hundreds of thousands of victims and displaced hundreds of thousands more.

The Sudanese government has denied any involvement in the activities of the Janjaweed.

Two hundred miles east of Geneina, Janjaweed troops raped twenty-two-year-old Aisha Adam as well. Her attackers told her, "Dog, you have sex with me. ... The government gave me permission to rape you. This is not your land anymore, *abid*, go."[3]

The sexual violence Sawela and Aisha endured was not isolated. The rapes were not fundamentally about sexual gratification; they were about violence. They were part of a plan to intimidate and dehumanize the Africans of Darfur, cleansing the region of their presence in the process. One of the rapists told Sawela, "Black girl, you are too dark. You are like a dog. We want to make a light baby. ... You get out of this area and leave the child when it's made."[4]

In Sudan, a child's ethnicity is determined by the father's, so the Janjaweed used rape as a tool to create more Arab babies. One aid worker in Darfur reported, "It's systematic. Everyone knows how the father carries the lineage in the culture. They want more Arab babies to take the land."[5] Another high-ranking international aid worker said: "These rapes are built on tribal tensions and orchestrated to create a dynamic where the African tribal groups are destroyed. It's hard to believe that they tell them they want to make Arab babies, but it's true. It's systematic and these cases are what made me believe that it's part of ethnic cleansing and that they are doing it in a massive way."[6] In short, the Janjaweed, supported by the Sudanese government, used rape as a means of genocide.[7]

GENOCIDE IN THE LAST EIGHTY YEARS

We tend to associate "genocide" with the large-scale killing of human beings. The term is more expansive, though: Genocide is the deliberate destruction of a racial, ethnic, cultural, or religious group.[8] The term was first used in 1944 by Raphael Lemkin, a Polish Jew who escaped the Holocaust and came to the United States.[9] A lawyer, Lemkin wanted to create a word that would command attention and demand action.

While the word "genocide" is relatively new, the crime itself is not. History records many instances of the intentional destruction of people groups. In 146 BC, at the end of the Second Punic War, Rome conquered its great rival, Carthage. Roman soldiers went from house to house, killing 100,000 to 200,000 people. They sold the remaining survivors as slaves.[10] The historian Polybius "noted that 'the destruction of the Carthaginians was immediate and total' so that no Carthaginians were left even to express their remorse."[11]

Nearly 300 years earlier, Athenian soldiers killed all the men of Melos, a Greek island that had remained neutral during Athens' Peloponnesian War with Sparta.[12] The Athenians sold the women and children as slaves, reflecting a "clear intention ... to destroy the Melians as a group and a culture."[13]

It is in the past eighty years, however, that we have seen some of the most egregious and large-scale genocides in history. These genocides are the focus of this chapter. To begin, we'll describe genocide as seen in history and then look at the deeply flawed view of human nature that motivates those who commit it.

THE HOLOCAUST (1939–1945)

The Holocaust is the most horrific example of genocide in recorded human history. The German government carried it out systematically and with ruthless efficiency. It killed an estimated 6 million Jews, nearly two-thirds of the Jewish population living in Europe before World War II.[14] It also targeted and killed numerous other "undesirable" groups:[15]

> Massive deportations of Jews to death camps began in 1942. From all over Europe they were brought by train; and, when the trains arrived, Germans unloaded the prisoners—primarily Jews but also gypsies, homosexuals, and assorted political dissidents—and stood them in lines for inspection by SS doctors. From trainloads of 1,500 people the doctors generally selected 1,200–1,300 for immediate extermination by firing squads or gas chambers. By the end of the war the Germans in the death camps had exterminated an estimated 6,000,000 Jews and nearly that many non-Jews.[16]

As the war came to an end, Allied troops liberated the concentration camps and were shocked by what they found. The world was appalled and vowed: "Never again." The nations of the world formed the United Nations to preserve international peace and security and to protect fundamental human rights. Most nations also agreed to hold a Genocide Convention, at which they pledged to prevent genocide from occurring and to punish offenders if prevention efforts failed.

"Never again." But genocide has happened again. Multiple times. In our lifetimes.

BOSNIA (1992–1995)

In the period following the fall of communism, several republics of the former Yugoslavia declared independence. One of those was Bosnia-Herzegovina. In 1991, Bosnia had a diverse population made up of three major ethnic groups: Bosniaks (predominantly

Muslim; 44 percent), Serbs (predominantly Orthodox Christian; 31 percent), and Croats (predominantly Roman Catholic; 17 percent).[17] Bosnia declared independence on April 15, 1992. Bosnian Serbs opposed this declaration, wishing to remain part of Yugoslavia, which had a majority Serb population. Supported by Yugoslavian national military forces, they launched a military campaign against the Bosnian government. More than just military victory, the Bosnian Serbs sought to rid Bosnia of its Bosniak and Croat populations through ethnic cleansing.

What followed was a brutal war in which Bosnian Serbs engaged in genocide. By the end, an estimated 100,000 people were killed, 80 percent of whom were Bosniaks.[18] Perhaps the event that most horrified the world was the massacre of Muslim men and boys in the town of Srebrenica. Srebrenica is a town in eastern Bosnia that at the time had a population of about 40,000, most of whom were Bosniak. In 1993 the United Nations declared Srebrenica and parts of the neighboring region to be a safe zone, and they deployed troops to guard it. On July 16, 1995, however, Bosnian Serb forces, with no opposition from the Dutch-led UN forces, separated Bosniak men from women, children, and the elderly. They bused the men to a nearby farm and lined them up with their backs to the soldiers, hands tied together. On command, the troops gunned down the civilians hundreds at a time. Bosnian Serb troops executed at least 7,000 Bosniak men.[19]

As in Darfur, Bosnian Serbs also used rape as an instrument of genocide. It is estimated that they raped 10,000 to 60,000 women during the course of the war.[20] Serb forces raped in homes and streets, but they also set up rape camps and "hotels." For example, in May and June 1992, Serb forces detained and raped between 2,000 and 2,500 women and girls in a camp in Doboj.[21]

How was rape used as a form of genocide in Bosnia? First, Bosnian Serb leaders hoped to traumatize Bosniak women and render them unable to have normal sexual or childbearing experiences. A UN Special Rapporteur shared that rape was "intended to humiliate, shame, degrade and terrify the entire ethnic group."[22] Second, based on the belief that ethnicity is determined by the father, the Bosnians sought to impregnate Bosniak women with "Serbian" babies. In some instances, women were raped until they became pregnant.[23]

One Bosniak woman was detained by her Serb neighbor (a soldier) for six months. She reported that she was raped almost daily by three or four soldiers and was told that "she would give birth to a chetnik [a nationalist Serb fighter] boy who would kill Muslims when he grew up. They repeatedly said their President had ordered them to do this."[24] Serb soldiers reportedly raped a seventeen-year-old girl named Marianna up to ten times per day, telling her, "Now you will have Serbian babies for the rest of your life."[25]

RWANDA (1994)

Chapter 1 introduced the story of the genocide that took place in Rwanda in 1994. During this genocide, Hutus brutally murdered 800,000 Tutsis in just three months. Over 200,000 Rwandans may have participated in the killing of their friends and neighbors.

The effort to destroy the Tutsis as a group is almost incomprehensible in its scope. Beyond the killings, the United Nations estimates that 250,000 to 500,000 women were raped.[26] Indeed, University of Alabama at Birmingham professor Lisa Sharlach reports that most women between the ages of thirteen and fifty in the capital city of Kigali who survived the genocide were rape victims.[27]

The rapists in Rwanda were motivated by some of the same things as the rapists in Bosnia. They hoped to frighten, intimidate, and interfere with normal childbearing by Tutsis. They also shared the Sudanese and Serbian view that ethnicity is carried by the father, so by impregnating Tutsi women they believed they were creating Hutu babies. But in Rwanda there was a third motivation, unique to this genocide: rape was a means of killing the victims. "The deliberate transmission of HIV was a unique component of rape as genocide in Rwanda. Survivors report that Hutu men diagnosed with HIV raped Tutsi women during the civil war, then told the women that they would die slowly and gruelingly from AIDS."[28]

DARFUR (2003–)

In the early years of this century, the world stood by again as another genocide took shape in Africa, this time in the Darfur region of Sudan.[29] In 2003, two rebel groups—the Sudan Liberation Army/Movement (SLMA) and the Justice and Equality Movement (JEM)—rose up against the Sudanese government. The government responded with "scorched-earth tactics"[30] that completely destroyed many villages. The government engaged in aerial bombing that was followed by land assaults by Janjaweed or government forces. The air attacks often targeted civilians who were gathered in marketplaces and shops and at wells. The ground forces killed, raped, and tortured those they encountered. By the end of 2005, between 200,000 and 400,000 men, women, and children had been murdered.[31] Around 2.5 million had been displaced, prompting, among other things, the migration of the highly publicized Lost Boys of Sudan. The numbers of those killed and displaced amounted to about half of Darfur's total population.[32]

THE COMPLICITY OF CHRISTIANS IN THE GENOCIDES OF THE PAST CENTURY

In light of the strong biblical witness regarding the nature of human beings, it would be reasonable to assume that at least the Christian church insisted on the worth and dignity of each human being in the midst of these genocides. But it—or large segments of it—did not.

When the core doctrine of the nature of human beings was at stake, significant elements of the church remained silent or even embraced and helped carry out genocide. Germany, Bosnia, and Rwanda each had a strong Christian presence when the genocides occurred. Of 65 million German people in 1933, 41 million identified themselves as Protestant; 21 million identified themselves as Roman Catholic.[33] In Bosnia, the genocide was carried out by those identifying themselves as Orthodox Christians and often in the name of religion. Rwanda was the most Christian nation in Africa—in 1991, 89.8 percent of Rwandans said they were members of the Christian church: 62.6 percent were Roman Catholic, 18.8 percent were Protestant, and 8.4 percent were Seventh-day Adventist.[34] This Christian presence did not stop the genocides.

CHRISTIAN SUPPORT FOR RACIAL AND ETHNIC HATRED

In Germany, Christians largely supported Nazism: they welcomed Nazi opposition to communism and "godlessness" and embraced Adolf Hitler's expressed goal to restore a moral order to the nation.[35] Most Christians, including church leaders, shared the Nazis' anti-Semitism as well. "When Adolf Hitler came to power in January 1933 Protestant churchmen across the country shared in the general enthusiasm for his nationalist, anticommunist, and antisemitic rhetoric. ... Protestant bishops, pastors, and church officials made up a particularly important segment of the group of conservative elites who willingly compromised with Hitler when he first came to power."[36]

A group known as the "German Christians" particularly sought to merge Nazism and anti-Semitism with the Christian faith. They attempted to purge Scripture of Jewish elements, some denying that Jesus was Jewish (pointing out how often Jesus opposed the Jewish religious and political elites of his day).[37] Even many Christians who stayed faithful to the Scriptures considered anti-Semitism acceptable as long as it stayed within "biblical limits."[38] While these Christians opposed cruelty and extermination, they approved of Jews being denied civil liberties or being expelled from Germany.[39]

In 1933, the German Christians, in what was known as the "Brown Synod," essentially took over the Protestant church. They passed the "Aryan clause," which prohibited Christians of Jewish descent from holding positions in the church.[40] The Brown Synod contributed to many faithful Christians breaking away and launching the "Confessing Church." Some Confessing Church leaders, like Dietrich Bonhoeffer, stood bravely against anti-Semitism. Not all did, though. For many, opposition to the Aryan clause stemmed from concern that the state was taking too large a role within the church, not from concern over anti-Semitism.

CONFESSING CHURCH

The Confessing Church was a movement within the Protestant church in Germany that opposed the Nazi takeover of the church. In 1934, led by Karl Barth, Confessing Church leaders drafted the Barmen Declaration, which affirmed orthodox Christian doctrine and stood against efforts to merge Christianity with Nazi philosophy. In one important passage, the Declaration insisted:

> We reject the false doctrine, as though the State, over and beyond its special commission, should and could become the single and totalitarian order of human life, thus fulfilling the church's vocation as well.[41]

German authorities attacked the Confessing Church by taking away financial support for pastors and ultimately imprisoning many Confessing Church leaders or sending them to concentration camps. Dietrich Bonhoeffer was part of the Confessing Church and led the group's efforts to train faithful pastors at a seminary in Finkenwalde, Germany.

In Bosnia, the Serbian Orthodox Church supported hatred of Muslims by portraying them as Christ-killers and race-traitors. The odd notion that Muslims were Christ-killers was rooted in a significant event in Serbian history. In 1389, Serbian King Lazar was defeated by Muslim forces from the Ottoman Empire.

Lazar was viewed as a kind of Christ figure by Serbians. His defeat was secured through the betrayal of a fellow Serb, Vuk Branković, who in Serb minds played the role of Judas in the fourteenth-century drama.[42] Throughout the genocide of the 1990s, the Serbian Orthodox Church supported Serb military power and celebrated Serbian victories as religious triumphs.

In Rwanda, before the genocide, Christians and church leaders were very involved in creating the artificial ethnic distinction between Hutus and Tutsis. The earliest missionaries to Rwanda saw Tutsis as taller, more elegant, and natural rulers, and they supported Tutsi minority rule over Hutus.[43] In the second half of the twentieth century, however, church leaders largely came to support the Hutu cause. Increasingly, they took the position that Hutus were oppressed and supported their efforts to take power.[44] This led to a much closer relationship between the church and Hutu-led governments. In the three years leading up to the genocide, Hutus engaged in a number of attacks against Tutsis. The church stood silent. The silence led many Hutus to conclude that the church supported their actions.[45]

CHRISTIAN INVOLVEMENT IN GENOCIDE

Particularly in Rwanda and Bosnia, Christians contributed to the genocides. First, they failed to protect the victims. During the 1994 genocide, Tutsis frequently sought sanctuary in Rwandan churches. They rarely found it. By some estimates, more people were killed in churches than anywhere else.[46] In one community, 17,000 bodies were dug up from a set of latrines alongside a church.[47] "For centuries the church, or the holy, consecrated ground of the church, has acted as a safe haven from arrest and persecution. This boundary was breached in the genocide as churches served as a holding pen for humans, retaining individuals for mass extermination."[48]

And the role of Christians in genocide involved more than a failure to provide sanctuary; church leaders often supported the killing itself. In Bosnia, Serbian Orthodox clergy frequently stood alongside Serbian troops committing genocide and offered encouragement and support. When soldiers cleared the town of Foča of all Muslims and then destroyed mosques and homes, church officials celebrated with the victors by renaming the town "Srbinje" ("Serb Town").[49] In Trebinje, Orthodox priests led troops as they expelled Muslim families and seized their homes.[50]

In Rwanda, church leaders took part in the genocide in many ways. Catholic priest Anathase Seromba was convicted of genocide and crimes against humanity by the International Criminal Tribunal for Rwanda for his role in bulldozing a church in Nyange. When at least 1,500 Tutsis had taken refuge inside the church building, Seromba encouraged the bulldozer operator to push down the building. He even showed the operator where to begin, pointing out the building's "fragile side."[51] Seromba's explanation? Demons were inside. And when "there are demons in the church, it should be destroyed."[52]

Chapter 1 related some of the story of Adventist church leader Elizaphan Ntakirutimana, who refused to protect Tutsi believers who had cried out to him for help. But his was not only an act of omission. He was found guilty of transporting attackers to multiple locations so that they could kill.[53] Before bringing the killers to a church in Murambi in which Tutsis had taken refuge, Ntakirutimana had ordered the roof taken off the church so that the refuge-seekers would not have shelter.

How could Christians and church leaders have played the role they did in each of these genocides? One thing is clear: most Christians in these cases had adopted the dominant cultural view of race and human nature rather than the biblical one. Those professing to be Christians in these nations failed to affirm the worth and dignity of every human being and instead participated in grave evil. Eric Metaxas, in his biography of Dietrich Bonhoeffer, puts it well: "For many Germans, their national identity had become so melded together with whatever Lutheran Christian faith they had that it was impossible to see either clearly. After 400 years of taking for granted that all Germans were Lutheran Christians, no one really knew what Christianity was anymore."[54]

The same thing happened in each of the genocides. Christians so identified with their nation or ethnic group that they lost their identity as a people of God. And they failed to see the image of God in others.

GENOCIDE AND A FLAWED
VIEW OF HUMAN NATURE

What does genocide show us about human nature? First, it is one of the most powerful evidences of human fallenness. Second, it reflects a failure to see humans as image-bearers of God.

WE ARE FALLEN

It is impossible to hear the accounts of genocide recounted above without confronting the deep darkness of the human heart. In Rwanda, we see this darkness in the number of people who committed murder as well as in the very personal and gruesome methods they used. Up to 200,000 people wielded machetes and nail-studded boards to attack neighbors and coworkers. In a *60 Minutes* episode, journalist Bob Simon spoke with one of the thousands of killers, Alex Ntibirukee, who spent eleven years in prison for killing six of his neighbors. He had known his victims and had worked as a handyman for some of them. When asked why he killed, Ntibirukee responded: "They told me that I would be rewarded with a piece of land and a banana plantation. They told the same to two other people. You see they didn't give me any banana plantation."[55] Asked how he carried out the killings, Ntibirukee responded, "I got my machete and a nail studded-club and started killing."[56]

Philip Gourevitch writes, "Neighbors hacked neighbors to death in their homes, and colleagues hacked colleagues to death in their workplaces. Doctors killed their patients, and schoolteachers killed their pupils. Within days, the Tutsi populations of many villages were all but eliminated, and in Kigali prisoners were released in work gangs to collect the corpses that lined the roadsides."[57] When interviewed as part of the award-winning *Frontline* documentary "Ghosts of Rwanda," one Hutu killer said, "It is as if we were taken over by Satan."[58]

In Rwanda the weapons were low-tech; the killing was personal. The evil of the Holocaust was seen in different ways. In Germany and the nations it occupied, the depth of depravity manifested itself in part in the extensive planning and logistical skill it took to transport and kill six million Jews as well as other individuals who were viewed as expendable. The Nazis spent an unfathomable amount of time perfecting their high-tech killing machine, designing bigger gas chambers and perfecting the poison used to kill.

Human fallenness can also be seen in the sheer cruelty and inhumanity of other acts perpetrated on helpless people. For example, Nazi doctors conducted horrifying medical experiments on fellow human beings. At the Ravensbrück concentration camp, doctors experimented with methods to combat infection. They inflicted battle-like wounds on victims and infected the wounds with bacteria (streptococcus, tetanus, and gangrene).[59] At Dachau, doctors conducted high-altitude experiments on victims. They placed victims into low-pressure chambers that simulated altitudes as high as 68,000 feet. One doctor dissected victims' brains while the victims were still alive to see the effect that altitude sickness had on blood vessels.[60] These experiments reflect, as do all of the things that human hearts devised during these genocides, our deep depravity.

WE ARE MADE IN THE IMAGE OF GOD

Genocide involves a second element relating to human nature. In addition to human depravity, genocide especially reflects a failure to see all human beings as created in the image of God with worth and dignity. None of these genocides sprang up *ex nihilo*. Each was the fruit of a past racial hatred and the devaluing of certain human lives. In every genocide, perpetrators treated victims as less worthy of dignity or even as nonhuman.

In Germany, Nazis called Jews names like "killers of Christ," "people of the curse," and "alien blood" that would poison the pure Aryan race.[61] Most often they were described as parasites and disease carriers: leeches, lice, bacteria, or rats—especially rats.[62] As David Livingstone Smith writes in his book *Less Than Human*:

> The Nazis were explicit about the status of their victims. They were *Untermenschen*—subhumans—and as such were excluded from the system of moral rights and obligations that bind humankind together. It's wrong to kill a person but permissible to exterminate a rat. To the Nazis, all the Jews, Gypsies and others were rats: dangerous, disease-carrying rats.[63]

In 1943 Adolf Hitler brazenly articulated the view that Jews threatened to bring disease on the German people: "International Jewry is the ferment of decomposition of peoples and states, just as it was in antiquity. It will remain that way as long as people do not find the strength to get rid of the virus."[64]

Germans had been prepared to embrace such a dehumanized view of Jews and other undesirables. In the early twentieth century, influential Germans were quick to expand Darwin's theories on the survival and thriving of certain species over others into social Darwinism and eugenics, just as Oliver Wendell Holmes Jr. had done in the United States. Such thinking fostered the development of concepts like *lebensunwertes leben* ("lives unworthy of life").[65] In 1922, university professors Karl Binding and Alfred Hoche penned an influential article calling for the killing of people with disabilities.[66] They described such individuals as "empty human husks" or "useless eaters."[67] "Their life is absolutely pointless, but they do not regard it as being unbearable. They are a terrible, heavy burden upon their relatives and society as a whole. Their death would not create even the smallest gap—except perhaps in the feelings of their mothers and their loyal nurses."[68] In 1933, Germany enacted the Law for the Prevention of Genetically Diseased Offspring, which provided for the sterilization of such unworthy lives as those suffering from dementia, schizophrenia, manic-depressive disorder, genetic deafness, genetic blindness, genetic epilepsy, severe physical deformity, and chronic alcoholism.[69]

The Holocaust extended the concept of "lives unworthy of life" and "useless eaters" to other human beings: the disabled, homosexuals, Gypsies, and Jews. Such dehumanization is a hallmark of all of the genocides of the last hundred years.

In Yugoslavia, propaganda from popular culture portrayed Muslims as "treacherous, coldblooded murderers."[70] Serbs not only killed but humiliated their victims. Arnold Krammer reported that in the town of Bratunac, a Muslim cleric was dragged to a soccer stadium, tortured, and forced to drink alcohol, eat pork, and make the sign of the cross before he was executed.[71]

Dehumanizing propaganda played an even clearer role in Rwanda. In the months and years leading up to the genocide, Hutu leaders consistently spoke in terms that denied the humanity of Tutsis. About a year before the genocide began, a close friend and advisor to President Habyarimana gave a speech urging Hutus to "wipe out this scum."[72] At consciousness-raising meetings, local leaders described Tutsis as devils—"horns, hoofs, tails, and all."[73] As mentioned in chapter 1, a radio station promoting Hutu power, Radio Télévision Libre des Mille Collines, played a particularly important role, consistently calling Tutsis "cockroaches" and urging Hutu listeners to exterminate them.[74]

Hutus viewed Tutsi men, women, and even children as less than human. James Orbinski, a Canadian doctor who remained in Rwanda through the genocide, traveled to an orphanage hoping to rescue children. A Rwandan military officer met Orbinski and said, "These people are POWs, and as far as I'm concerned they're insects, and they'll be crushed like insects."[75]

The perpetrators of genocide in Darfur employed similar techniques of dehumanization. Sudanese military personnel and Janjaweed militants did all they could to not only kill and rape but to humiliate and treat their victims as less than human. Attackers most commonly called their victims "black," "slave," and "dog."[76] The victims were merely objects to be cleared off the land.

If you ever wonder how a man could do a thing like attack his long-time neighbors with a machete, the answer is: If he believed his neighbors weren't fully human. Like the Nazis before him, he was merely ridding the world of disease-carrying pests.

LEGAL AND POLICY IMPLICATIONS

What is needed to ensure that the world's vow of "never again" is truly fulfilled? From the perspective of law and policy, the main problem of addressing genocide is not one of inadequate legislation; it is one of inadequate enforcement.

In response to the Holocaust, many of the world's nations agreed to the Convention on the Prevention and Punishment of the Crime of Genocide (Genocide Convention). Ratifying states agreed to enact laws prohibiting and punishing genocide, as well as ensuring that perpetrators of genocide will be criminally tried.[77] At the time of writing, 146 states are parties to this convention. "States" are entities with duties and legal authority under international law. A community is considered an independent state when it has: "a) a permanent population; b) a defined territory; c) government; and d) capacity to enter into relations with the other states."[78] So genocide has a clear and accepted legal definition, and nations of the world have embraced anti-genocide laws, enforcement mechanisms, and penalties for both states and individuals. This legal framework generally reflects a proper view of human dignity.

GENOCIDE CONVENTION

The Genocide Convention is one of the first and most important treaties created in the wake of World War II and the Holocaust. The UN General Assembly enacted the Convention on December 9, 1948–the day before it affirmed the Universal Declaration of Human Rights–and the Convention entered into force on January 12, 1951. The Convention clearly defines "genocide" and importantly declares genocide to be a crime for which individuals may be held criminally responsible. It also imposes the duty on ratifying nations to prevent and punish genocide. The United States is a party to the Convention, though it did not ratify the treaty until 1988.

THE ISSUE OF ENFORCEMENT

But because confronting genocide requires a significant response from states that have agreed to prevent and punish it, states often hesitate before declaring actions to be genocide or intervening to stop them. One of the deeply troubling aspects of the Rwandan genocide, for example, was the role of the United States. From early to mid-April 1994, credible reports made clear that genocide was taking place.[79] The Clinton administration, however, strongly opposed intervention by the United States or the United Nations. A year earlier, in Mogadishu, Somalia, American troops had been killed in a public and humiliating way (captured in the film *Black Hawk Down*) as they brought food and supplies to the Somalian people as part of a peacekeeping mission. President Clinton concluded that the American public was unwilling to intervene in another violent, African war zone.

Knowing that the United States, as a contracting party to the Genocide Convention, had responsibilities under that convention if it was aware that genocide was occurring, the Clinton administration went out of its way to avoid characterizing the situation in Rwanda as genocide. One Defense Department memorandum from the time instructed: "Be careful ... genocide finding could commit USG [the US government] to actually 'do something.' "[80] Consequently, administration officials engaged in awkward and painful linguistic gymnastics when discussing Rwanda. An example is this excerpt from a press conference with State Department spokeswoman Christine Shelley from June 1994, the third month of the genocide:

> **Christine Shelley**: We have every reason to believe that acts of genocide have occurred.
>
> **Alan Elsner** (Reuters correspondent): How many acts of genocide does it take to make genocide?
>
> **Christine Shelley**: Alan, that's just not a question that I'm in a position to answer.
>
> **Alan Elsner**: Is it true that the—that you have specific guidance to not use the word "genocide" in isolation, but always to preface it with this—these words "acts of"?
>
> **Christine Shelley**: I have guidance, which—to which I—which I try to use as best as I can. I'm not—I have—there are formulations that we are using that we are trying to be consistent in our use of.[81]

From the perspective of law and policy, one of the most significant steps to prevent genocide is for states to speak truth. When genocide is occurring, it must be identified as such and addressed through the legal mechanisms that exist.

Of course, this oversimplifies the situation. What should a state do if it speaks truth about genocide and the rest of the world refuses to listen or act? The United States found itself in this position during the Darfur genocide. Both Congress and the Bush administration identified as genocide what was taking place in Darfur.[82] The United States, along with other nations, appealed for action by the UN Security Council, the group tasked by the UN Charter with preserving international peace and security. Russia and China thwarted that appeal, however, refusing to approve anything other than limited sanctions against Sudan.[83]

As a result, in 2006 President Bush imposed a variety of economic sanctions on Sudan.[84] Should the United States have done more? Should it have considered military intervention either by itself or with other willing nations? Under the principles of international law as articulated in the UN Charter, the answer appears to be no. A state should act militarily only in self-defense; any international intervention is left to the UN Security Council.[85]

However, there is disagreement about whether the charter continues to accurately set forth the current state of the law on this issue. In 1999, for example, the North Atlantic Treaty Organization (NATO) bombed targets in the former Yugoslavia without Security Council approval in an effort to head off a possible genocide in Kosovo. As described in more detail below, the world's response to this effort—including the response of the Security Council itself—shows some uncertainty over whether such a military intervention violates international law.

If the charter does accurately state the law, this is a situation in which it appears that the law may conflict with higher principles of justice. From Augustine on, Christian thinkers have explored when it is permissible—or at times even required—for nations to use force to combat injustice. The result of this exploration forms what is known as "just war theory."

JUST WAR THEORY

Just war theory is an ethical doctrine that addresses when and how wars may be fought in a just manner. It is very much intertwined with Christian theology. The doctrine began with the writing of Augustine in the fifth century, but it was Thomas Aquinas in the thirteen century who really developed the doctrine into the main categories we still embrace today.

Just war theory has two main components. The first is *jus ad bellum* ("right to war"), which addresses when it is just for a nation to go to war. The second component is *jus in bello* ("right in war"), which addresses how a just war should be fought, such as the need to protect civilians and other noncombatants.

Just war theory has influenced both the conduct of nations and the development of law. Just war principles are reflected in, for example, the Geneva Conventions and the Rome Statute of the International Criminal Court.

WHAT MAKES A LEGITIMATE USE OF FORCE

Some Christians, and those within the Anabaptist tradition in particular, have questioned whether any war can be "just" in light of Jesus' instruction that individuals should endure injustice, walk the extra mile, and turn the other cheek. Historically, the church has not viewed these instructions on individual behavior to require national pacifism. As the late just war scholar Jean Bethke Elshtain noted, leading Christian thinkers such as Augustine, Ambrose, and Aquinas "knew that in a fallen world, filled with imperfect human beings, we cannot achieve perfection in earthly dominion, in religious life, or in anything else, and that—even more important—we all have a responsibility to and for one another to serve and to love our neighbors. If our neighbor is being slaughtered, do we stand by and do nothing?"[86]

The just war tradition, while opposing violence, recognizes that force is sometimes necessary to promote justice and even peace itself. For Augustine, what we now call genocide would have been a clear example of when "a resort to force may be an obligation of loving one's neighbor."[87] So if a nation is certain that a genocide will take place in another nation, "the first country may be justified in coming to the aid of the targeted group and using force to interdict and punish their would-be attackers."[88]

Just war theory has other requirements for the just use of force besides a just cause. One is that war must be declared by a lawful authority acting with the right intention. In addition, there must be an appropriate proportion between the goals sought and the costs, a likelihood of success, and war must be a last resort.[89] But within these parameters, a Christian understanding of love for neighbor and human fallenness may permit the use of force by states confronting genocide.

A good example of states putting these principles into action occurred in 1999 in Kosovo. As noted above, NATO conducted bombings of military targets to stop the Serbian government from committing atrocities on ethnic Albanians living in Kosovo. Albanians comprise the majority of Kosovo's population, and many sought independence in the early and mid-1990s as Yugoslavia dissolved into a number of independent republics. The Serbian government, led by Slobodan Milošević, responded brutally. It fought against separatist forces but also severely repressed ethnic Albanians.[90] Serbian forces killed, raped, and displaced thousands of Albanian Kosovars.[91]

Before NATO intervened militarily, there were a number of efforts to bring about a negotiated settlement of the conflict. In March 1998, the UN Security Council condemned Serbia's use of excessive force against Albanian Kosovars and imposed an arms embargo.[92] That September, the Security Council issued another resolution demanding that Serbian troops withdraw from Kosovo. It called for "additional measures" if Serbia refused to comply, but it did not identify those measures. The United States and others pushed for a UN-approved military intervention, but Russia and China threatened to veto any such resolution that might be brought before the Security Council.[93]

Groups of states also tried to intervene diplomatically. In February 1999, the United States, Russia, the United Kingdom,

France, Germany, and Italy met in Rambouillet, France, and crafted a proposed settlement for the conflict. While the Kosovo Liberation Army accepted the terms, Serbia did not.[94]

NATO began bombing on March 24, 1999. It deployed no ground troops. The airstrikes ended on June 10, 1999, when Serbia accepted NATO's conditions for an end of the conflict. On the same day, the UN Security Council adopted a resolution that essentially ratified NATO's conditions.[95]

The UN's view of NATO's intervention is complicated. While the Security Council refused to authorize military intervention, it also refused to condemn NATO's actions. During the bombing, the Security Council voted twelve to three to reject a resolution proposed by Russia to condemn NATO's intervention.[96]

Although opinions are mixed, many see NATO's humanitarian intervention in Kosovo as morally justified and an appropriate application of just war principles. It was carried out by a legitimate authority: states that acted collectively through NATO. They united around a just cause: preserving the lives of Kosovar Albanians who were enduring atrocities and were threatened with more. A chief NATO concern was that Serbia would begin a campaign of ethnic cleansing like the one it had conducted in Bosnia a few years earlier.[97] On the campaign's first day, the United Kingdom's permanent representative to the United Nations told the Security Council:

> The action being taken is legal. It is justified as an exceptional measure to prevent an overwhelming humanitarian catastrophe. Under the present circumstances in Kosovo, there is convincing evidence that such a catastrophe is imminent. Renewed acts of repression by the authorities of the Federal Republic of Yugoslavia would cause further loss of civilian life and would lead to displacement of the civilian population on a large scale and in hostile conditions.

Every means short of force has been tried to avert this
situation. In these circumstances, and as an exceptional
measure on grounds of overwhelming humanitarian necessity, military intervention is legally justified.[98]

It could be contended that NATO acted with a right intention.
NATO and its member states did not seek territorial conquest.
They acted on behalf of oppressed people. As Czech President
Václav Havel insisted at the time, "If one can say of any war that
it is ethical, or that it is being waged for ethical reasons, then it is
true of this war."[99]

NATO's intervention also appears to have met just war theory's other requirements. It was an action of last resort; negotiations and UN sanctions had failed. Russia and China would
almost certainly have prevented any further intervention. NATO
also directed its airstrikes at military installations in an effort to
minimize civilian casualties and satisfy the requirement that the
goal sought must be proportionate to the costs. And the action was
indeed successful—ending the conflict in less than three months.

There is still disagreement about the legal status of the intervention in Kosovo, particularly because it was not authorized by
the Security Council. Interestingly, the Independent International
Commission on Kosovo concluded that the intervention was "illegal but legitimate."[100] How can that be? Because the intervention
did not follow the letter of the law but met the moral standards
for the use of force under just war theory.

THE RESPONSIBILITY TO PROTECT

The success of NATO's intervention in Kosovo played a significant
role in the development of an international legal doctrine known
as the Responsibility to Protect. In 2001, following the failures in
Bosnia and Rwanda and the successful Kosovo intervention, the
International Commission on Intervention and State Sovereignty

(ICISS) concluded that intervention should be considered a responsibility of other nations under the following circumstances:

- Where there is a just cause—a large-scale loss of life, ethnic cleansing, or genocide, etc.

- Where there is a right intention of the intervening group to protect others;

- Where the intervention is a last resort and all other efforts, such as diplomacy, have been tried;

- Where the intervener uses proportional means (the level of force used is appropriate to the objective pursued); and

- Where there are reasonable prospects that the intervention will successfully accomplish its purpose.[101]

The legal status of the Responsibility to Protect is uncertain, though it was approved unanimously by the UN General Assembly at a 2005 World Summit for use in cases of genocide, crimes against humanity, war crimes, and ethnic cleansing.[102] Importantly, the doctrine as approved at the summit (which took place after the United States' invasion of Iraq) requires any intervention to be approved by the Security Council.[103] Some commentators believe that the Responsibility to Protect is now an established norm of international law that provides a legal framework for protecting individuals and groups from large-scale atrocities occurring within sovereign states. Princeton professor Anne-Marie Slaughter has called the Responsibility to Protect "the most important shift in our definition of sovereignty ... since the Treaty of Westphalia in 1648."[104]

How should Christians view this developing doctrine in light of the nature of human beings? On one hand, the Responsibility to Protect provides a basis to not just speak about human dignity but act on its behalf. It views as a duty the protection of individuals threatened with genocide and crimes against humanity.

On the other hand, we must be careful when analyzing the doctrine not to forget human depravity. Because of our fallenness, good intentions do not always assure good results. The results of US interventions in Iraq and Afghanistan are instructive. Initial military success and regime change have not guaranteed long-term stability or the protection of human rights.

Some fear that the Responsibility to Protect ignores human fallenness and embodies an almost utopian vision of nation-building. They note that the Responsibility to Protect doctrine as often articulated goes well beyond just war theory and charges intervening parties with not only a responsibility to stop genocide and preserve lives, but also the responsibility to rebuild the victim nation in the spheres of security, justice, and economic development.

From the beginning, the ICISS recognized that a responsibility to rebuild was daunting because of "the cost of such an operation for the necessarily long time it would take to recreate civil society and rehabilitate the infrastructure in such a state."[105] It expressed concern that the responsibility to rebuild "might be an altogether unrealistic concept."[106]

Subsequent commentators have agreed and warned of the dangers that the responsibility to rebuild poses. Roland Paris warns that "the requirements for terminating such a mission [a humanitarian intervention based on the Responsibility to Protect] are different—and more expansive—than the initial goal of preventing mass killing. As a result, humanitarian intervention appears to have a built-in propensity toward mandate-expansion."[107]

My colleague Eric Patterson, Dean of Regent University's Robertson School of Government, goes further and worries about the Responsibility to Protect's push for Western-led economic rebuilding:

Whereas R2P [Responsibility to Protect] begins with a noble aspiration, to save human life, the "responsibility to rebuild" shows its true colors—it is a grand scheme for nation building, financial transfers from Western donors, and political transformation. It is not, on paper at least, characterized by the just war presupposition of restraint.[108]

The next chapter explores how such a utopian vision led by well-intentioned human rights advocates will ultimately fail and can even cause unintended harm because it fails to recognize the fallenness of human actors.

Thus, a Christian approach to policy in this area calls for truth-speaking on behalf of victims made in the image of God. It also calls for keeping promises we have made in agreements like the Genocide Convention. This may require forceful intervention with or even without UN sanction in order to combat the consequences of human fallenness. And it counsels for wisdom, restraint, and care. Force should be the last, rather than the first, resort. Many other options, including diplomacy and nonmilitary sanctions, should be explored first. And any use of force should serve justice and not be a pretext for wars of aggression or part of a utopian vision that could lead to disappointment or even abuse.

IMPLICATIONS FOR THE CHURCH

The suggestions above are largely directed to government officials. Is there any role for Christians who are not involved in setting national policy? Absolutely. We all have an important role to play in bringing attention to genocide taking place and holding government officials accountable.

But we have an even more important role to play that is unrelated to public policy. Laws to prevent and punish genocide are on the books. Absent more effective enforcement of these laws, legal change will not have the greatest impact in preventing genocide.

Hearts and minds must change as well. This is an area where the church must lead. We have to get race relations right and model it.

One of the most sobering aspects of the genocides in the last eighty years is the role of the church in fostering racial and ethnic divides—and even promoting genocide itself—rather than in combating them. In Germany, Bosnia, and Rwanda, many Christians identified more as a member of their own racial or ethnic group than they did as a member of Christ's kingdom, where "there is neither Jew nor Greek, there is neither slave nor free, there is no male or female, for you are all one in Christ Jesus" (Gal 3:28).

While it is tempting as American Christians to insist that what has occurred in Africa and Europe could not happen here, our history suggests otherwise. Discrimination, abuse, and slavery occurred in this nation with the active support of both state and (large segments of) the church. While Christians did lead the abolition movement and segments of the church called for the end of slavery, many Christians and some entire Christian denominations defended slavery. Even today, "the degree of racial segregation within religious congregations remains high."[109] While the situation is slowly improving, the Pew Research Center reports that "eight-in-ten American congregants still attend services at a place where a single racial or ethnic group comprises at least 80% of the congregation."[110] We cannot draw the conclusion that this segregation is caused only by racism in the church; there are many factors that contribute. However, we have no room for overconfidence.

What is God's call to his people today? Christians, of all people, should affirm the worth and dignity of every human being. We serve a God who created all people in his own image. He consistently upholds and rescues the poor and oppressed. The picture of the heavenly worshiping community is of people "from every tribe and language and people and nation" (Rev 5:9). We must be the model for the world in embracing respect, love, and unity in the midst of racial and ethnic diversity.

As I write, the United States is embroiled in a passionate national debate over race relations. The debate was ignited by controversy over the role of race in policing, but it has much broader implications. To date, that debate has produced more heat than light. The church could make an enormous contribution to a productive and peaceful dialogue about race by serving in a mediating role. It is uniquely suited to do so with our belief in the dignity and worth of all human beings and Jesus' explicit call for his followers to be peacemakers. This may be a wonderful opportunity for the church to live out Dr. Martin Luther King Jr.'s call for the church to be a thermostat—and not merely a thermometer—in the culture.[111]

CONCLUSION

How do we end genocide? How do we fulfill the post-Holocaust promise of "never again"? Nations must speak truth about genocide and act to fulfill their obligations to prevent and punish it. They must create and enforce laws that affirm the dignity and worth of all human beings.

But courts, laws, and international organizations cannot end genocide. As Jesus noted, it is out of the heart that come evil thoughts, immorality, theft, and murder. Hearts and minds need to change for there to be an end to race-based hatred and violence. And the church must take the lead. We must proclaim the worth and dignity of every human being. More than that, we must model it ourselves.

CHAPTER 6:
HUMAN RIGHTS

Do our basic human rights originate from our humanity—or are they conferred on us by human institutions?

Unless man's proper nature, unless his mind and spirit are brought out, set apart, protected and promoted, the struggle for human rights is a sham and a mockery.

–CHARLES MALIK[1]

As the Soviet Union began to crumble in 1991, the Salvation Army returned to Moscow with joy and the motto "Heart to God—Hand to Man."[2] It was sixty-eight years after the government had dissolved its Moscow branch as an "anti-Soviet organization."[3] The Salvation Army began serving the poor and homeless in Moscow and at one point was serving 6,000 Russians during the winter months.

This changed in 1997. That year, Russia enacted a law tightening government control over religious groups. The Law on Freedom of Conscience and Religious Associations required all religious organizations that had been given legal status to re-register with the government. When the Salvation Army filed its paperwork, it almost immediately met opposition from local government officials. Years of struggle and legal wrangling followed. Ultimately, the government rejected the registration petition and ordered the Moscow branch of the Salvation Army to again dissolve.

The government offered many reasons for its decision. One was that the Salvation Army was a "foreign" religious organization, since its headquarters were in London. Another was that the Salvation Army was actually a paramilitary organization that threatened the security of the state. After all, it is called an "army," its members wear uniforms, and it is organized hierarchically.[4]

The Salvation Army's inability to register and obtain legal status limited its work. Local officials often thwarted food delivery efforts. Employees were unable to obtain registrations needed for their work. Negative publicity hurt contributions and caused some landlords to refuse to rent to the group.[5]

After exhausting all remedies in the Russian legal system, the Salvation Army turned to the European Court of Human Rights (ECtHR) in Strasbourg, France. The ECtHR is the main enforcement body of a regional human rights system that was established shortly after World War II. It permits any individual or group suffering a denial of human rights within Europe to petition the court for relief.[6]

In 2006, the ECtHR ruled that Russia had violated two key human rights protected by the European Convention on Human Rights: freedom of thought, conscience, and religion (Article 9) and freedom of peaceful assembly and association (Article 11).[7] It ordered Russia to pay the Salvation Army 10,000 euros in damages.[8]

In 2009, on the eve of Orthodox Easter, the Moscow branch of the Salvation Army learned that it had officially been registered by the Russian Ministry of Justice. The leader of the Salvation Army in Eastern Europe, Commissioner William van der Harst, announced, "My friends, this is a proud and joyous moment, this is a new beginning."[9]

This moment and others like it were dreamed of by the people who joined together after World War II to establish an international system that would affirm and enforce fundamental human rights—even against powerful governments that opposed those rights. This vision—of basic human rights, both articulated and enforced—would seem to offer an antidote to the horrors described in the previous chapter. The modern human rights movement was motivated by the notion that all individuals have worth and dignity.[10] And indeed, it has had many important achievements.

HUMAN RIGHTS

Human rights are universal and fundamental rights that belong to every person simply because they are human. These rights do not vary based on time, place, or culture. They do not depend on a person's race, sex, national origin, wealth, power, or influence. It does not matter if a particular government, elite, or majority chooses not to protect such rights; they are human rights nonetheless.

Despite its promising beginning, however, the international human rights movement suffers from a failure to fully grasp a robust and complete view of human nature. And that failure endangers not only the movement but the very rights it seeks to protect. In the rest of this chapter, I will lay out the origins of the international human rights movement, its successes, and some of its dangers, and close with law and policy implications.

ORIGIN OF THE HUMAN
RIGHTS MOVEMENT

When the nations of the world proclaimed "never again" at the end of World War II, part of their resolution was that there should be no more aggressive wars. Thus, the international system created in the aftermath of that war was designed first to protect peace and security. It was also designed to promote and protect human rights. The UN Charter that entered into force on October 24, 1945, begins:

We the Peoples of the United Nations determined to save succeeding generations from the scourge of war, which

twice in our lifetime has brought untold sorrow to mankind, and to reaffirm faith in fundamental human rights,
in the dignity and worth of the human person, in equal
rights of men and women and of nations large and small.[11]

Chapter 5 told of the creation of the Genocide Convention, one
of the first major treaties to be created at the end of World War II.
The day after the Genocide Convention was approved, the UN
General Assembly approved the Universal Declaration of Human
Rights. The declaration insists that all humans—regardless of race,
sex, national origin, wealth, influence, or power—have fundamental rights that must be affirmed and secured.[12]

The declaration's first article roots these rights in the dignity
of each person: "All human beings are born free and equal in dignity and rights."[13] The rights include the rights to life, to freedom
of speech and religion, to not be enslaved, and to be free from
arbitrary arrest. Most of the rights are civil and political—protecting individuals' freedom from infringement by governments,
individuals, and groups. Others are economic, social, and cultural.
These include the right to work, the right to rest and leisure, and
the right to education.[14]

A diverse group of nations approved the declaration with no
dissents and eight abstentions.[15] It is justly celebrated as one of the
most important statements of human rights in world history. Law
professor Mary Ann Glendon calls it "the single most important
reference point for cross-cultural discussion of human freedom
and dignity in the world today."[16]

The Universal Declaration of Human Rights was not passed
as a binding legal document. It was approved with the understanding that later binding treaties would elaborate and enforce
the rights enumerated in the declaration. These include the
International Covenant on Civil and Political Rights (ICCPR) and
the International Covenant on Economic, Social and Cultural
Rights (ICESCR), both of which took effect in 1976.[17] As their

names indicate, these are broad, binding treaties in which ratifying nations agree to respect and enforce key human rights.

Besides these two core treaties, the United Nations has facilitated the creation of many others dealing with issues such as torture, slavery, and the rights of children and women. The United Nations has also created entities and offices to further protect human rights, such as a Human Rights Council and a High Commissioner for Human Rights. These bodies and others like them seek to enforce the rights articulated in the Universal Declaration of Human Rights and treaties that have followed it.[18]

REGIONAL HUMAN RIGHTS SYSTEMS

The United Nations plays an important role in enforcing human rights, but it is not the only international body dedicated to protecting human rights. After World War II, nations in several regions of the world decided that they could better–and perhaps more quickly–protect rights if they acted regionally, rather than waiting for UN action. The United Nations is a notoriously slow-moving organization. Its first comprehensive human rights treaties were not in force until 1976.

In 1949, the nations of Europe formed the Council of Europe, dedicated to promoting human rights, democracy, and the rule of law. This is not to be confused with the European Union, which has a more varied focus and has significantly fewer member states. The European system has become the most comprehensive and powerful human rights enforcement system in the world, built around a full-time court, the ECtHR, and the European Convention of Human Rights, which came into force in 1953.

Regional systems also exist in the Americas (the Organization of American States) and in Africa (the African Union). These systems have spurred the enactment of many regional human-rights treaties, and work alongside the United Nations to promote the enforcement of human rights.

From a Christian perspective, there is much to admire about the beginnings of the human rights movement. First, it stood for human worth and dignity. Charles Malik was the Lebanese ambassador to the United Nations and a member of the Human Rights Commission that drafted the Universal Declaration of Human Rights.[19] A devoted Christian, Malik was one of the most important voices urging adoption of the declaration. He said this about the origin and nature of human rights:

> By what title does man possess them? Are they conferred upon him by the state, or by society, or by the United Nations? Or do they belong to his nature so that apart from them he simply ceases to be man? Now if they simply originate in the state or society or the United Nations, it is clear that what the state now grants, it might one day withdraw without thereby violating any higher law. But if these rights and freedoms belong to man as man, then the state or the United Nations, far from conferring them upon him, must recognize and respect them, or else it would be violating the higher law of his being.[20]

The declaration included this notion of inherent rights in its first article, and the conventions that followed similarly reaffirmed the worth and dignity of all human beings. The preamble attached to both the ICCPR and the ICESCR asserts: "Recognition of the inherent dignity and of the equal and inalienable rights of all members of the human family is the foundation of freedom, justice and peace in the world."[21] Similarly, the preamble of the American Convention on Human Rights begins: "Recognizing that the essential rights of man are not derived from one's being a national of a certain state, but are based upon attributes of the human personality, and that they therefore justify international protection."[22]

Second, the early human rights movement declared that there is moral right and wrong. It stood against the evil that had taken place in World War II. It proclaimed the rights of all humans against the backdrop of Nazi and Japanese regimes that had treated some humans as animals. The Nazis had done so bolstered by a legal philosophy known as positivism, "the view that 'law was law' and that Hitler's racist laws had the character and quality of law as much as the benevolent law of any democracy."[23] Positivism opposes the concepts of natural law and natural rights. To the extent that rights exist, they come from the state and can be taken away without moral consequence. Thus, while positivists certainly would not sanction Nazism, they argue for a strong separation between morality and law.[24]

LEGAL POSITIVISM

Legal positivism is a legal philosophy that believes the legitimate source of law is the positive law—human-made statutes, regulations, and case law. It generally opposes looking to morality to decide if a particular legal norm is right or wrong. As leading positivist scholar Hans Kelsen put it, "It endeavors to answer the question, What is the law? but not the question, What ought it to be?"[25] Historically, positivism has stood in opposition to natural law theory, which believes that moral principles are essential to determine the validity of law.

The early human rights movement rejected the positivist view. Indeed, its assertion that individuals have fundamental human rights that must be protected even against their own government is an assertion of moral truth. There is moral right and wrong. Governments have a duty to treat their peoples with justice.

Third, the early human rights movement stood for the poor and powerless against powerful institutions and individuals. In so doing, it acted in accord with scriptural admonitions like these:

> Open your mouth for the mute,
>   for the rights of all who are destitute.

Open your mouth, judge righteously,
> defend the rights of the poor and needy.
> (Prov 31:8–9)

Cease to do evil,
> learn to do good;
seek justice,
> correct oppression;
bring justice to the fatherless,
> plead the widow's cause. (Isa 1:16–17)

SUCCESSES OF THE HUMAN RIGHTS MOVEMENT

Before I criticize aspects of the human rights movement, I first want to point out that the movement has achieved great good. Human rights norms as moral standards are openly promoted and influence policy. Each year, the US State Department prepares country reports on how each nation protects human rights. Human rights violations are tracked and discussed. The United States and other Western governments often request compliance with human rights standards as a condition before they will give international aid. The European Union has made membership conditional on achieving a certain level of human rights protection.[26] The transition of former Eastern bloc nations to regimes protecting human rights and promoting the rule of law was hastened by leverage applied by the human rights movement.[27]

States have changed laws in response to the human rights movement. Many now have strong prohibitions against human trafficking. South American states have worked hard through legislation and enforcement to combat the vexing long-term challenge of forced disappearances of individuals.[28]

In Europe, all individuals have a right to petition the ECtHR to seek relief for human rights violations. As seen in the Salvation Army case, religious liberty is better protected in Europe because

the ECtHR exists. And beyond its impressive body of decisions, the
ECtHR has a strong record (among international bodies) of state
compliance with its judgments.[29]

When I look at the successes of the human rights movement,
I agree with this statement of Harvard law professor David W.
Kennedy:

> Over the past half century, we have amassed an enormous
> library of legal norms and aspirational declarations. A com-
> plex institutional practice has grown up in the shadow
> of those pronouncements to promote, defend, interpret,
> elaborate, implement, enforce, and simply to honor them.
> There is no question the human rights movement has done
> a great deal of good, freeing individuals from harm, and
> raising the standards by which governments are judged.
> It has cast light on catastrophic conditions in prisons
> around the world. Human rights advocacy became at once
> a professional practice and a movement.[30]

DANGERS OF THE HUMAN
RIGHTS MOVEMENT

While we should celebrate the achievements of the human rights
movement, we should also be wary of it. The movement poses dangers to its own vitality and to the protection of rights itself because
it does not have a proper view of human nature. First, while the
movement proclaims human dignity, it has an understanding of
the nature and source of that dignity that is not in accord with
the Christian understanding. Second, it fails to fully acknowledge
human sinfulness.

HUMAN DIGNITY

The human rights movement's understanding of the basis of
human dignity and rights is not rooted in the image of God, the
transcendent, or indeed anything lasting or stable. It is rooted

purely on human agreement or political will. This endangers human rights and the movement.

CHARLES MALIK (1906-1987)

Charles Malik was an extraordinary diplomat and world leader. He served as Lebanon's foreign minister and ambassador to the United States. It was at the United Nations, though, where Malik had perhaps his greatest achievements. He headed the most powerful United Nations bodies in the postwar world, serving as president of the General Assembly and the Economic and Social Council, and as chairman of the Commission on Human Rights.

Malik was one of the drafters of the Universal Declaration of Human Rights, and he used his personal credibility and diplomatic skills to shepherd the declaration through the General Assembly without a single dissenting vote.

Despite all of his achievements, Malik found his ultimate identity in Jesus Christ. He declared: "Jesus Christ is my Lord and God and Savior and Song day and night. I can live without food, without drink, without sleep, without air–but I cannot live without Jesus."[31]

When presenting the Universal Declaration of Human Rights to the General Assembly, Charles Malik warned that understanding the basis of human rights was critical:

Where do they come from? Are they conferred upon me by some external visible power such as the state or the United Nations, so that what is now granted me may someday be conceivably withdrawn from me? Or do they belong to my essence so that if they are violated in any way I cease to be a human being at all? If they did belong to my essence, should they not also be grounded in a Supreme Being who,

by being the Lord of history, could guarantee their meaning and stability? ...

The most important issue in the order of truth today is
what constitutes the proper worth and dignity of man. ...
Do not tell me you are going to settle Korea, and Germany,
and Palestine, and atomic energy, and leave this central
issue unsettled! For what is the use of peace in a settlement
in which man is left ambiguous, estranged from himself
and from the truth?[32]

Despite Malik's warning, there was and is no agreement on
the proper basis for rights. Scholar Louis Henkin notes that while
the founders of the human rights movement shared an intuition
that human beings have dignity, they did not agree on the source
of that dignity:

The international expressions of rights themselves claim
no philosophical foundation, nor do they reflect any clear
philosophical assumptions; they articulate no particular moral principles or any single, comprehensive theory
of the relation of the individual to society. That there
are "fundamental human rights" was a declared article of faith, "reaffirmed" by "the peoples of the United
Nations" in the United Nations Charter. The Universal
Declaration of Human Rights, striving for a pronounce-
ment that would appeal to diverse political systems governing diverse peoples, built on that faith and shunned
philosophical exploration.[33]

Lack of Agreement on What Rights Should Be Protected

The results of this lack of agreement on a basis for human dignity
and human rights are seen in important ways. First, there is no
agreement—or way to reach an agreement—on what rights should

be protected. This shows itself, for example, in battles over how human rights are to be interpreted.

One example of such a battle relates to rights to religious liberty and freedom of speech. From the beginning of the international human rights movement, these were seen to be core human rights. According to the Universal Declaration:

> Article 18. Everyone has the right to freedom of thought, conscience and religion; this right includes freedom to change his religion or belief, and freedom, either alone or in community with others and in public or private, to manifest his religion or belief in teaching, practice, worship and observance.[34]

> Article 19. Everyone has the right to freedom of opinion and expression; this right includes freedom to hold opinions without interference and to seek, receive and impart information and ideas through any media and regardless of frontiers.[35]

These protections for religion and speech are affirmed in greater detail in the treaties that followed.

It is surprising, then, to see the interpretation of religious freedom currently put forward by the fifty-seven-member Organization of the Islamic Conference (OIC). The OIC has relentlessly sought to use the framework of human rights to forbid speech that it deems critical of Islam, Muhammad, or Muslims. Many OIC states prohibit proselytizing or even conversion to religions other than Islam. And they seek to use human rights institutions to restrict proselytizing in non-Muslim nations.

This effort bore fruit for the OIC in 2008 when the UN Human Rights Council passed a resolution condemning what it calls "Defamation of Religions." The resolution asserts that speech critical of Islam undermines human rights, and calls on states to limit free speech in order to protect religions from contempt.

Article 8 "Urges States to take actions to prohibit the dissemination, including through political institutions and organizations, of racist and xenophobic ideas and material aimed at any religion or its followers that constitute incitement to racial and religious hatred, hostility or violence."[36] The resolution passed 21–10 (with 14 abstentions). While this resolution speaks broadly of "any religion," it only addresses one by name: Islam.

Two years later, the UN Human Rights Council passed a similar resolution, this time by a closer 20–17 vote (with 8 abstentions). This resolution mentions Christianity and Judaism as well as Islam.[37] While these resolutions are phrased in terms of tolerance and freedom, they restrict speech and religious liberty. They might be used to ban Christian missionaries from urging Muslims to embrace Christianity or even investigative journalists from writing openly about Islamic fundamentalism.

A second example of the impact of the failure to agree on the origin and meaning of human rights is seen in the American human rights system. The American Convention on Human Rights provides very strong protections for the unborn. Article 4 states: "Every person has the right to have his life respected. This right shall be protected by law and, in general, from the moment of conception."[38] Despite the clear language, the Inter-American Commission on Human Rights interprets this provision to be consistent with abortion rights; a provision that on its face protects the lives of unborn children thus is used to permit their destruction.[39]

This inability to agree on the origin and meaning of human rights is perhaps most evident in the European human rights system. There the ECtHR has struggled greatly in deciding how to interpret and understand the rights provided for in the European Convention on Human Rights. Far from taking a view that human rights are fixed, universal, and fundamental, the ECtHR openly embraces what it calls an "evolutive approach" to human rights: "Since the Convention is first and foremost a system for the protection of human rights, the Court must have regard to the changing conditions within the respondent State and within Contracting States generally and respond, for example, to any evolving convergence as to the standards to be achieved."[40] In other words, the ECtHR is committed to interpreting the meaning of fundamental human rights in a changing way based on social changes taking place within Europe.

The fruit of this evolutive approach to human rights is seen in a series of cases that the European Court decided between 1986 and 2002. These cases involved claims by transgender people that the United Kingdom violated their right to "respect" for "private and family life" under Article 8 of the European Convention on Human Rights by refusing to allow them to change their birth certificates to reflect their new sexual identity. In three separate cases between 1986 and 1998, the ECtHR ruled in favor of the United Kingdom, finding that the United Kingdom had a "wide margin of appreciation" in structuring and implementing its birth certificate system.[41]

In the 2002 case of *Goodwin v. United Kingdom*, however, the ECtHR found that the United Kingdom *had* violated the applicant's fundamental right to respect for family and private life by not allowing her to change her birth certificate.[42] It did not reach this conclusion because the text of the European Convention or its list of protected rights had changed. It did so because society had changed—or, more accurately, because society was changing. A key component of the ECtHR's analysis of this and previous cases was determining whether there was a "European consensus" on whether transgender individuals should be permitted to change their birth certificates. In *Goodwin*, as in the previous cases, the court found that such a consensus did not exist. It nonetheless ruled in favor of the applicant:

> While this [the lack of a European consensus] would appear
> to remain the case, the lack of such a common approach
> among forty-three Contracting States with widely diverse
> legal systems and traditions is hardly surprising. ... The

Court accordingly attaches less importance to the lack of evidence of a common European approach to the resolution of the legal and practical problems posed, than to the clear and uncontested evidence of a continuing international trend in favour not only of increased social acceptance of transsexuals but of legal recognition of the new sexual identity of post-operative transsexuals.[43]

The ECtHR found this "international trend" by looking at developments in Australia and New Zealand, not at activity within Europe. Again, the ECtHR did not base its decision—a decision determining the scope of a fundamental human right—primarily on the language of the European Convention. It based its decision on social developments in nations thousands of miles away.

Such an evolutive approach to human rights is deeply troubling. It makes it impossible for individuals and governments to know the content and scope of rights, which will inevitably be uncertain whether the ECtHR looks at international trends or a consensus within Europe. Even worse, the evolutive approach undermines the universal and fundamental nature of human rights. As Louis Henkin writes, "Human rights are universal: they belong to every human being in every human society. ... To call them 'human' implies that all human beings have them, equally and in equal measure, by virtue of their humanity."[44]

The ECtHR's approach to human rights has moved far from this view of human rights as fundamental and universal. This poses a grave danger: If the existence of rights depends on the consensus of individuals or states at a particular time and place, rights are fragile indeed. Rights by their very nature are intended to protect individuals against societal consensus—against the tyranny of the majority or the will of a particular regime or powerful interest group.

Defenders of the evolutive approach insist that it does not endanger human rights. They say that the ECtHR consistently uses a changing standard to expand, rather than contract, rights. It is not reasonable, however, to assume that this standard will always expand rights. In 1978, the ECtHR applied a consensus standard in granting Germany greater leeway to open and inspect mail and telegraph messages in order to protect against a rising tide of terrorism.[45] Similarly, consider the "defamation of religions" resolution mentioned above. Representatives on the Human Rights Council have reached a consensus that the "right" to not have one's religion criticized requires restricting freedom of speech and religion. In its effort to expand one right, it has contracted others.

Lack of Rights Enforcement

Along with a lack of agreement on what rights are or how to interpret them, there is a second danger that arises from lacking an understanding of the origin and scope of human rights. While we have expanded the number of rights claims, we have not expanded the enforcement of rights.

The ECtHR's approach offers a revealing glimpse into the method of the modern human rights movement, which often puts its greatest emphasis on public policy advocacy to expand the number of asserted rights. This can come at the expense of critically needed efforts to thoroughly enforce core, universally agreed-upon rights, such as the rights to life, freedom of speech and religion, and to be free from torture or detainment without due process of law. Since 1945, the number of declarations, conventions, and resolutions has exploded. Jacob Mchangama and Guglielmo Verdirame, cofounders of the Freedom Rights Project, count sixty-four human-rights agreements under the United Nations and Council of Europe:

> A member state of both of these organizations that has ratified all these agreements would have to comply with 1,377

human rights provisions (although some of these may be technical rather than substantive). Add to this the hundreds of non-treaty instruments, such as the resolutions of the UN General Assembly and Human Rights Council (HRC). The aggregate body of human rights law now has all the accessibility of a tax code.[46]

David Smolin agrees: "It is an odd feature of the human rights movement that although it has failed to successfully implement principles with broader acceptance, such as the bans on genocide, slavery, and torture, it continues to define ever more specific and controversial additional rights."[47]

Claims identified as "human rights" now include the right of individuals to leisure, to "periodic holidays with pay," to "social security, including social insurance," the right of "peoples" to "a general satisfactory environment favorable to their development," and the "Right to Peace."[48] While most core civil and political rights primarily protect individuals against government interference, many other asserted rights, like those above, necessarily require extremely broad and aggressive action by government for their fulfillment. Consider this expansive mandate from the Convention on the Elimination of All Forms of Discrimination against Women (CEDAW):

> States Parties shall take all appropriate measures: (a) to modify the social and cultural patterns of conduct of men and women, with a view to achieving the elimination of prejudices and customary and all other practices which are based on the idea of the inferiority or the superiority of either of the sexes or on stereotyped roles for men and women.[49]

One problem with this expansion of asserted rights is that it can cause individuals and nations to lose respect for human rights in general. This is the international equivalent of the domestic phenomenon that enacting unenforceable laws can actually lead to disrespect for law and greater lawlessness. It is easy for nations to ratify human rights conventions with no intention of fulfilling their obligations. North Korea, Sudan, and Iran have ratified the ICCPR, the ICESCR, and many other human rights conventions, yet they regularly infringe freedom of speech and religion and detain individuals without due process of law. Law professor Eric Posner notes that "each of the six major human rights treaties has been ratified by more than 150 countries, yet many of them remain hostile to human rights. This raises the nagging question of how much human rights law has actually influenced the behaviour of governments."[50] Governments ratify conventions with no intention of fulfilling them in order to receive foreign aid or to score political or diplomatic points. This diminishes respect for human rights and the ability to enforce them.

Another problem is that some states actually use the language and apparatus of human rights in order to cloak abuses of rights or to advocate for "rights" that undermine other core, accepted rights. According to Mchangama and Verdirame, "There is also a darker agenda behind the expansion of human rights law. Put simply, illiberal states have sought to stretch human rights law to give themselves room to hide behind it."[51] For example, "China cites 'the right to development' to explain why the Chinese government gives priority to economic growth over political liberalization. Many countries cite the 'right to security,' a catch-all idea that protection from crime justifies harsh enforcement methods. Vladimir Putin cited the rights of ethnic minorities in Ukraine in order to justify his military intervention there."[52]

Through all these means, nations are able to use human rights terminology and processes as a smokescreen to hide abuses and to deflect attention, time, and resources away from true human rights enforcement.

HUMAN FALLENNESS

The modern human rights movement displays more than an improper understanding of human dignity. It also lacks a full understanding of human fallenness.

One sign of this is the extent to which the movement embraces a utopian vision that, in the Christian view, is not attainable in this fallen world. It continues to call for the recognition of more rights while failing to recognize how far short we fall in enforcing even the most fundamental core rights. In his book *The Last Utopia: Human Rights in History*, Samuel Moyn writes:

> When people hear the phrase "human rights," they think of the highest moral precepts and political ideals. And they are right to do so. They have in mind a familiar set of indispensable liberal freedoms, and sometimes more expansive principles of social protection. But they also mean something more. The phrase implies an agenda for improving the world, and bringing about a new one in which the dignity of each individual will enjoy secure international protection. It is a recognizably utopian program.[53]

This utopian language is perhaps inevitable—and is at times even inspiring. But it can be dangerous as well. As the number of asserted rights has exploded, and as there is less agreement on what core rights are, there is a danger that the human rights movement may become purely aspirational and utopian. David Smolin writes: "The language of human rights has in many respects already been reduced to the role of vacuous platitudes which evoke warm feelings and high ideals but are not intended to contribute to the hard work of settling disputes or governing peoples."[54] Rather than focusing on clear, agreed-upon, and fundamental values, "some of the rights articulated in the documents are highly controversial even within the West, and represent essentially the wish list of certain elites which has never been implemented in any society."[55]

Human rights advocates too often act as if simply articulating the right aspirations will cause international organizations and nations to work effectively toward their enforcement. They display a strong faith in the basic goodness of humans and of the institutions that we create. University of Chicago Law School professor Eric Posner writes, "Human rights treaties are not so much an act of idealism as an act of hubris."[56] Smolin warns of the danger of such hubris: "Human rights are left to depend on human constancy—indeed, upon a world governed by consistent human goodness. Yet, what ground has history given us to believe that human beings would ever bring such a world of consistent goodness into existence? When has goodness and power been consistently joined in this world?"[57]

Of course, the answer is that they have never been so joined. Only look at the role of the UN Security Council under Chapter VII of the UN Charter to see a good example of the failure of utopian aspirations. Under the charter, states are not to engage in armed conflict except in cases of self-defense.[58] The assumption is that in cases of armed conflict, the Security Council will act—including authorizing, even mandating, military action if necessary—to restore international peace and security.

Reality has been far different. In 2006, the Heritage Foundation reported that between 1945 and 2006, there were 300 wars that had killed 22 million people. Despite those wars, the UN Security Council authorized the use of military force to combat aggression only twice (in response to North Korea's invasion of South Korea and Iraq's invasion of Kuwait).[59]

A second sign of the human rights movement's lack of understanding of human fallenness is the way international institutions are constructed and governed—with few checks and little accountability. In the cases mentioned above, the ECtHR finds itself unbound by the text of the European Convention on Human Rights and is guided by its own view of consensus and trends within Europe and the world as it determines the scope of rights.

The UN Human Rights Council provides another example. It was formed in 2005 after the failure of its predecessor body, the Human Rights Commission. The commission, the former drafter of the Universal Declaration of Human Rights, had by 2005 become an ineffectual and intensely political organization. It consisted of fifty-three member states elected by the UN General Assembly. In 2001, the General Assembly voted the United States off the commission while electing the following "Rogues' Gallery of Abusers"[60] as members: Cuba, Libya, Saudi Arabia, Sudan, and Zimbabwe. Libya was elected—by secret ballot—to chair the commission in 2003.[61] With this membership, the commission "ignored atrocities in Sudan, Myanmar and North Korea."[62] It chose not to look into the suppression of women's rights in Saudi Arabia or journalists in Iran; it decided not to examine the intense political repression in Zimbabwe.

Things were so bad that UN Secretary General Kofi Annan acknowledged: "The Commission's capacity to perform its tasks has been increasingly undermined by its declining credibility and professionalism. In particular, States have sought membership of the Commission not to strengthen human rights but to protect themselves against criticism or to criticize others."[63] One nation that was unprotected from criticism and censure was Israel. According to Brett Schaefer of the Heritage Foundation, "The number of country-specific resolutions against Israel was equivalent to the combined total adopted against all other countries, and emergency special sessions and special sittings were frequently dedicated to condemning Israel."[64]

Differences between the Human Rights Council and the commission it replaced are largely cosmetic. The United States and other states advocated for criteria restricting membership to nations that display a genuine commitment to human rights enforcement. The General Assembly rejected this effort and created no meaningful membership criteria. It also decided to continue to make membership based only on a majority vote.

The result? "Even countries with deplorable records can run and win seats on the UN's premier human rights body."[65]

With no meaningful limitations on membership, the focus and actions of the council have been little changed from its predecessor. For example, the number-one target for censure continues to be Israel. The council has "condemned Israel more times than all of the other 192 member states combined. The total number of UNHRC condemnations of Israel from the UNHRC's inception in 2006 through 2015 so far is 61, as compared to 15 for Syria."[66]

This resistance to accountability does not only affect human rights organizations. Because of human sinfulness, any organization—large or small—is susceptible to corruption and abuse. But without a clear understanding of human fallenness and without effective checks and limitations on power, it is unrealistic to expect human rights enforcement bodies to operate with efficiency, transparency, and accountability. And it is unreasonable to look for the human rights system to fulfill its highly aspirational claims.

LEGAL AND POLICY IMPLICATIONS

The critique above does not mean that the human rights movement should be abandoned or that Christians should decline to participate in it. Christian involvement is crucial. In a world that increasingly rejects the transcendent, the human rights movement grasps after transcendent standards. It rightly stands at odds with the positivist notion that all law and rights come from government. It operates within a framework of moral right and wrong. The real question is what direction the movement should take. I suggest that we must do three things.

ESTABLISH A STRONG BASIS FOR HUMAN RIGHTS

First, and most fundamentally, we must articulate a proper understanding of the basis for human rights. Human rights must be acknowledged as universal and fundamental claims that are basic to being human. They must not vary based on time, place, or culture. Unless rights are seen in this way, they will disappear. Human rights will not last if they depend on current political will or contemporary consensus, and they cannot be merely the wish list of a cultural elite.

It is high time that the human rights movement revisits the questions that Charles Malik asked at the framing of the Universal Declaration of Human Rights. Malik labeled the key question, "the question of the nature and origin of these rights." Answering the question of the nature and origin of rights, of course, will not be a simple task. The nations of the world were unable—or chose not—to do so when they created the Universal Declaration. And we are no closer to a common understanding of rights today. If we are to make any progress, it must be by embracing a right understanding of human nature. Malik understood this well. He insisted: "Unless man's proper nature, unless his mind and spirit are brought out, set apart, protected and promoted, the struggle for human rights is a sham and a mockery."[67] Similarly, when discussing the Universal Declaration, Malik maintained that it "must define the nature and essence of man. ... It will, in essence, be an answer to the question: what is man? It will be the United Nations' answer to this question. It will, in short, give meaning to the phrase, 'worth and dignity of man,' which is found in the preamble of the Charter."[68]

Malik was right. The human rights movement desperately needs to be based on a proper view of human nature. First, it needs a proper view of human dignity. Our dignity comes from our Creator and our dependence on him. It is not rooted in human will or autonomy. If it were, both it and human rights themselves would be limitless and ultimately useless. As John Witte notes:

> The very ubiquity of the principle of human dignity today threatens its claims to universality. And the very prolif-eration of new human rights threatens their long-term

effectiveness for doing good. Human dignity needs to be assigned some limits if it is to remain a sturdy foundation for the edifice of human rights. Human rights need to be founded firmly on moral principles like human dignity, lest they devolve into a gaggle of wishes and wants.[69]

We should be stirred by the language of human rights. We should be moved by the movement's aspirations—but in order to view these aspirations properly, a true anthropology of human rights must, second, acknowledge human fallenness. "Most of the human rights standards in the major conventions are simply one way of voicing common human hopes for peace, prosperity, justice, and the conditions of political, economic, social, and cultural life under which human beings most easily flourish."[70] But we cannot be fooled into thinking that human rights will transform the world into a utopian paradise, nor can we be fooled into thinking that the international institutions we create for this purpose will naturally work efficiently, effectively, and without corruption.

One implication of having a proper understanding of both human dignity and human fallenness is that we should focus our attention on fewer, more core rights. We should proclaim those rights that are most foundational to human dignity and most crucial for justice—and then work diligently for their enforcement. Our time and efforts should be devoted to such fundamental rights as the right to life, freedom from slavery and torture, freedom from arbitrary arrest, and freedom of speech and religion.

A second implication of having a proper understanding of both human dignity and human fallenness is that our efforts to champion human rights must be tempered with realism. We must insist upon accountability and transparency in the human rights institutions we establish. In the United States, we know that individual liberty cannot thrive unless government power is limited. It is the same with international institutions:

Controls, such as the checks and balances of the U.S. Constitution, are necessary in any system of limited powers. Without them, restrictions as they appear in an organization's charter are liable to disappear, and the organization is likely to take actions either in violation of its allocated authority ... or for a purpose for which that authority was not granted.[71]

Our institutions will not achieve their noble objectives unless we demand accountability and transparency. Instead, they will squander resources or even foster corruption.

All institutions—especially international institutions—should work with clear governing structures. Membership criteria should be clear, identifiable, and contingent on human rights compliance. No authority should be given without accountability. International institutions, like national ones, should implement checks, limits, and divisions of power.

PROMOTE THE RULE OF LAW

Effective protection for human rights also requires that the human rights movement and the nations of the world promote the rule of law. Individual states may be able to enact detailed and well-crafted laws. They can ratify elegant and comprehensive human rights conventions. But without basic law enforcement, those laws and conventions will do nothing for the average person on the street.

In 2008, the United Nations reported that "most poor people do not live under the shelter of the law, but far from the law's protection."[72] While we are making progress on reducing poverty worldwide, around 2.5 billion people continue to live on less than two dollars per day.[73] In their book *The Locust Effect,* Gary Haugen and Victor Boutros conclude that the poor are "by the hundreds of millions—threatened every day with being enslaved, imprisoned, beaten, raped, and robbed."[74]

THE RULE OF LAW AND THE POOR

When the rule of law is missing, the world's poor suffer most. They lack access to just and effective policing and court systems. Indeed, in many nations, police pose one of the greatest threats to the poor. In a large-scale study of poverty, the World Bank concluded: "Particularly in urban areas, poor people perceive the police not as upholding justice, peace and fairness, but as threats and sources of insecurity."[75] While there are many fine and hardworking police officers worldwide, too many engage in extortion, sexual assault, and abusive detention.

The lack of the rule of law undermines effective law enforcement by prosecutors and judges as well. Too often, underpaid and overworked prosecutors and judges languish under overwhelming caseloads. This allows violent criminals to go free and innocent people to sit in jails for years waiting for trials. Bribery and extortion thrive.

Enforcing the rule of law is vital for all people, but it is desperately needed by the world's poor.

As will be more fully discussed in the next chapter, the rule of law requires not simply that the law exist, but also that it determine what happens in a society. The rule of law requires rulers to rule by the law and to themselves be under the law. In too many places, the rule of law fails because police, prosecutors, and judges ignore the law or set themselves above it. For those caught in such a dysfunctional—and often abusive—system, the existence of a burgeoning body of human rights treaties is meaningless. Haugen and Boutros conclude: "There are billions for whom the promise of the human rights revolution remains a check they cannot cash."[76]

The next generation of human rights advocates must focus their attention on combating violence through effective law enforcement. Real, on-the-ground enforcement of core human rights is more important than seeking to expand the list of rights with ever-more-debatable claims. And we need to apply what we learn throughout the world.

IMPLICATIONS FOR THE CHURCH:
NONGOVERNMENTAL ORGANIZATIONS

Much of the discussion so far has focused on top-down approaches to human rights protection. However, a biblical understanding of fallen human nature warns us of the difficulty of bringing Christian principles to bear on national—and especially international—policy. That does not mean, however, that Christian human rights advocates cannot make a difference. Our call is to protect the poor, oppressed, and enslaved whether or not we wield political power. While important work is done through organizations like the United Nations and the Council of Europe, one other way in which the church at large is accomplishing critical work is through individual nongovernmental organizations—large and small—that daily are making a real difference in lives of oppressed men and women. Here are two.

INTERNATIONAL JUSTICE MISSION

International Justice Mission (IJM) describes itself as "a global organization that protects the poor from violence in the developing world."[77] IJM was founded by Gary Haugen in 1997. Haugen had served with the US Department of Justice, focusing on police misconduct.[78] In 1994, he directed the United Nations's investigation into the Rwandan genocide. The evidence he and his team gathered helped bring the genocide's perpetrators to justice.

Haugen's Washington, DC-based organization now employs over six hundred staff and operates in twenty communities in thirteen nations around the world. It focuses its work on these key areas: (a) Rescuing victims of violence; (b) bringing criminals to justice; (c) restoring survivors; and (d) strengthening justice systems.[79]

In the section on promoting the rule of law above, I discussed Haugen's conviction that human rights will best be protected by working to make the rule of law and effective law enforcement a reality for the poor of the world. IJM seeks to do this in six areas where violence is prevalent: slavery, sex trafficking, sexual violence, police brutality, property grabbing, and abuse of citizen rights.

IJM does not just talk aspirationally about rights. It is not pushing to have more rights enshrined in more treaties. It works on the ground to make sure that core rights are realized, and the results are staggering and encouraging. In 2014 alone, IJM freed over 2,600 individuals from forced labor bondage in India. It rescued 258 people from sex trafficking in Cambodia. And it secured property rights for 361 widows and orphans in Africa.[80]

JUBILEE CAMPAIGN USA

The Jubilee Campaign works to promote the religious liberty of ethnic and religious minorities in nations around the world. It advocates on behalf of refugees and those who are persecuted for their faith, sometimes seeking religious asylum in the West for persecuted individuals and families.

Jubilee Campaign USA, led by Ann Buwalda, has consultative status with the United Nations, which allows them to advocate before the UN Human Rights Council, the UN High Commissioner for Refugees, and other bodies.

The group, in partnership with others, helped obtain the release of Pastor Youcef Nadarkhani from imprisonment in Iran. Nadarkhani was arrested in 2009 when he objected to mandatory Islamic indoctrination for his children. He was held incommunicado and tortured in prison for three years. His wife and children were threatened. His lawyer was suspended from law practice and sentenced to nine years in prison for his advocacy for religious liberty.

The Jubilee Campaign and many other groups advocated loudly and widely on Nadarkhani's behalf. They obtained 20,000 signatures demanding Nadarkhani's release and delivered them to the Iranian Embassy in The Hague. Finally, in 2012, the Iranian government withdrew the charge against Nadarkhani, and his sentence was commuted to time served. He was released to his family.

The Jubilee Campaign, by advocating for the powerless before the powerful, is making a meaningful difference in protecting religious freedom around the world.[81] The group ensures that persecuted believers have a voice before key international bodies and at times provides a means of escape for those who can no longer live and worship in their home country.

CONCLUSION

The human rights movement began with great promise. It still has great promise, but it must embrace a Christian view of human nature in order to fulfill that promise. By articulating a firm basis for rights, protecting the rule of law, and embracing a bottom-up approach, Christians can do much to fulfill God's charge to speak for the mute and defend the rights of the poor and needy.

The rule of law is not just important for international human rights. It is critical for national legal systems, too, as we will see in the next chapter. Using examples from both history and today's headlines, chapter 7 illustrates the profound consequences of embracing or ignoring the rule of law.

PART 3
DOMESTIC ISSUES

CHAPTER 7

RULE OF LAW

How does sin affect
the role of government?

Power tends to corrupt, and absolute power corrupts absolutely.

—LORD ACTON[1]

The nation of Zimbabwe was born in 1980. Formerly known as Rhodesia, the newly independent nation began with great optimism. Though it had endured British colonial rule, it boasted great physical beauty, abundant natural resources, and one of the strongest economies in Africa.

In the nation's first democratic election, Robert Mugabe was chosen as prime minister.[2] Despite having come to power through a popular vote, Mugabe increasingly maintained his power through corruption, exploitation, and a disregard for the law. In 1987, the constitution was amended, and Mugabe took on greatly expanded powers as executive president.[3] In the early 2000s, he undertook land "reform" by seizing large farms from primarily white landowners and giving them to his supporters, most of whom lacked any farming experience. The landowners challenged this action in court. The Supreme Court of Zimbabwe ruled in their favor, holding that the Mugabe government had violated the fundamental rights of property owners. Mugabe did not care: "Whatever the courts might say on the matter, the land is ours and we will take it."[4] He had similarly ignored legal requirements during an earlier debt crisis, choosing to simply default on Zimbabwe's obligations.[5]

Mugabe continued to flout the law and to maintain power by rigging elections. In elections in 2002, 2008, and 2013, he not only distorted vote counts but also used violence against opposition leaders. In the 2008 election, human rights groups documented 350,000 election-related injuries, including rape and torture, most of which were perpetrated by Mugabe's supporters.[6]

Mugabe's increasing lawlessness has been devastating to the nation. Zimbabwe's once-thriving economy collapsed. By 2008, his government's mismanagement of the currency caused hyperinflation. In November of that year, a loaf of bread cost 1 billion Zimbabwean dollars.[7] Prices doubled every 24.7 hours.[8] The inflation rate reached an unfathomable 500 billion percent when the government finally abandoned their currency and foreign currencies, such as the US dollar, euro, and South African rand became accepted as legal tender in Zimbabwe.[9] Only by conducting transactions using foreign currencies could the hyperinflation be stopped. The formal unemployment rate reached over 90 percent as most individuals completely dropped out of the traditional economy and began surviving through black market barter.[10]

Life expectancy by 2006 had fallen to thirty-four years for women and thirty-seven years for men.[11] Government lawlessness led to increased lawlessness throughout society.

The people of Zimbabwe have experienced what happens when a nation abandons the rule of law and substitutes rule by a person or party. Their experience is a powerful reminder of how much good governance and the rule of law matter to any nation. It is also a reminder that the rule of law is constantly under threat. The importance of the rule of law and threats to its achievement— including in the United States today—is the subject of this chapter. As with the subjects of earlier chapters, we will see that key to establishing the rule of law is having a right understanding of human nature.

GOOD GOVERNANCE AND
THE RULE OF LAW

Robert Mugabe is not the first ruler to govern through fear, power, and corruption rather than law. The biblical book of 1 Kings tells the story of the evil and corrupt rule of King Ahab and Queen Jezebel over the northern kingdom of Israel. At one point, Ahab covets a vineyard next to his palace. The vineyard's owner, Naboth, refuses to sell it, leaving Ahab frustrated and discouraged. When Ahab relates the story to Jezebel, she responds: "Do you now govern Israel? Arise and eat bread and let your heart be cheerful; I will give you the vineyard of Naboth the Jezreelite" (1 Kgs 21:7). Jezebel fulfills her word by having "worthless men" falsely accuse Naboth of cursing God and the king, having Naboth stoned, and seizing his property. "Aren't you the king? Use your power to take what you want." This has been the philosophy of many kings, dictators, and ruling parties throughout history.

It was the philosophy of General Augusto Pinochet, who in 1973 became Chile's dictator through a military coup. He ruled through a four-man military junta—and later as president—until 1990. Investigators after his death found that his government had killed over 3,000 people and tortured as many as 29,000.[12] He used his unchecked power not just to retain political control but to profit personally. Investigators found ten tons of gold worth $160 million in Pinochet's name in a Hong Kong bank.[13]

Another example of such a nation is North Korea. In 2014, the United Nations released a four-hundred-page report on North Korea based on firsthand testimony of victims and witnesses to what it described as "systematic, widespread and gross human rights violations."[14] It found that the state used "an all-encompassing indoctrination machine" to "manufacture absolute obedience to the Supreme Leader."[15]

> The key to the political system is the vast political and security apparatus that strategically uses surveillance, coercion,

fear and punishment to preclude the expression of any
dissent. Public executions and enforced disappearance to
political prison camps serve as the ultimate means to ter-
rorize the population into submission.[16]

North Korea is perhaps the greatest example in the early twenty-
first century of the results of unchecked power and ruling through
fear and coercion rather than law.

Unchecked power can bring corruption even to democratic
states. A century ago, Argentina was a nation on the rise. It had a
new democracy and was one of the ten richest nations on earth.[17]
Its gross domestic product per person was higher than Germany's,
France's, or Italy's.[18] It boasted tremendous natural resources. But
since then, it has undergone great political instability and economic
decline. In 2014, *The Economist* declared, "Their country is a wreck."[19]
The magazine attributed Argentina's decline to many factors, but
the most important was the lack of good government. Political leaders over the last century have interfered with membership on the
Supreme Court, tampered with the constitution to allow them to
serve longer terms, falsified important statistics, and interfered with
property rights.[20] The president can change the budget at will without parliamentary approval. *The Economist* concluded: "The lesson
from the parable of Argentina is that good government matters."[21]

Good government does matter. All governments exercise
power; power is necessary to protect us from murder, theft, and
other wrongs. But history reveals that it is also necessary to limit
the power granted to governments and to hold government officials and entities accountable. A critical feature of good governance is adherence to the rule of law.

THE ANGLO-AMERICAN POLITICAL
TRADITION AND THE RULE OF LAW

A hallmark of English and American history has been the never-
fully-achieved quest to establish government by the rule of law.

One of the most fundamental and influential statements of the rule of law comes from thirteenth-century English judge and legal scholar Henry de Bracton. He wrote: "The King himself ought not to be subject to man, but subject to God and to the law, for the law makes the King."[22] Although the king is very powerful, he is not the law, nor is he superior to the law. He, like his subjects, must submit to the law.

THE RULE OF LAW

The rule of law holds that the law—and not individual rulers or parties—is the ultimate authority in a state. It compels government officials to rule by law (and not by whim or power) and under law (they are subject to the law, just as the citizens they govern are subject to the law). Following the rule of law means more than just having law; the Soviet Union, for instance, had a constitution and a sophisticated legal system, but the ultimate authority in the state was the Communist Party. The party, not law, truly determined policy.

The rule of law provides accountability for all institutions and entities—all government officials and offices—under law. It provides freedom and protection of individuals from their rulers. Citizens can appeal to law to protect themselves from arbitrary decisions and acts. It also provides for equal justice under the law. All individuals are subject to the same laws, whether rich or poor, favored or disfavored, influential or not. The rule of law provides stability and predictability for behavior because legal rules are known and predictably enforced.

Less than fifty years before Bracton wrote these words, King John had been forced to acknowledge the rule of law when confronted by a group of English barons at Runnymede. John had regularly ruled through arbitrary power. He supported his wars with France through arbitrary and exorbitant fines and fees.[23] He engendered fear and insecurity through extortion and murder.[24]

A contemporary famously declared of John: "Foul as it is, hell itself is defiled by the fouler presence of John."[25]

In 1215, led by Archbishop Stephen Langton, the barons insisted that John sign what has become one of the most important documents in English and American constitutional history—the Magna Carta. In it, John agreed to end such arbitrary royal actions as stealing the corn, wood, carts, and horses of his barons. He agreed to establish standard weights and measures and a court system that would meet at fixed places and times. In some ways, the Magna Carta was very much rooted in its medieval context, but it also contains broad principles of justice that form the basis for the rule of law today. Most important and influential was paragraph 39: "No free man shall be taken or imprisoned or disseised, nor will we go or send against him, except by the lawful judgement of his peers or by the law of the land."[26]

Over the years, some English kings tried to renege on John's agreement. Probably the greatest challenge to the principles of the Magna Carta and the rule of law came in the seventeenth century. The Stuart kings James I and Charles I, like many rulers of that era, believed in the divine right of kings. Under this theory, kings had almost unlimited power over their nation and subjects. James I explained his views in stark terms during an address to Parliament:

> Kings are justly called gods, because they exercise a manner or resemblance of divine power on earth, for if you consider the attributes of God, you will see how they are found in the person of a king. ... Now a father of a family may dispose of his inheritance to his children at his pleasure. ... He may make them beggars or rich at his pleasure. He can restrain them, or banish them from his presence if he finds them offensive, or he may restore them to favor again like penitent sinners: so may the King deal with his subjects.[27]

James and his son Charles tried to rule by this philosophy. James acted authoritatively toward Parliament, lecturing them rather than working with them. Charles was even worse. He raised money without parliamentary approval and quartered troops in the homes of free citizens.

In response, Parliament drew up the Petition of Right in 1628, which called for the king to abide by four key principles: (1) no taxation without Parliament's consent; (2) no imprisonment without cause; (3) no forced billeting of soldiers; and (4) no martial law in peacetime.[28]

Charles agreed to this document, but grudgingly. Eventually, he grew frustrated, dismissed Parliament, and ruled for eleven years without it.[29] When he ran out of money in 1640, he was forced to call Parliament back and the stage was set for civil war. From 1642 to 1646 the king and his troops battled Parliament and its troops. Parliament eventually triumphed, and in 1649 Charles was beheaded for treason against his own people.[30] Fueling the revolution was the rejection of the divine right of kings—and arbitrary rule itself. In victory, Parliament insisted that no one was above the law.

Ultimately the monarchy was restored, and Charles II and then James II reigned. It was restored, though, with the understanding that the king must rule under law and with a recognition and respect for the power of Parliament and other government officials. In 1689, after the Glorious Revolution peacefully overthrew James II and brought an end to the revolutionary period, Parliament conditioned its offer of the crown to William III and Mary II on their acceptance of the Bill of Rights and parliamentary limits on their power.

THE ENGLISH BILL OF RIGHTS

The English Bill of Rights was passed by Parliament in 1689 and accepted by William and Mary as they took the English throne. It again articulated the rule of law and insisted that specific liberties—such as freedom of speech, trial by jury, no excessive bail, and no cruel and unusual punishment–be protected.[31] It rehearsed violations of these principles by the Stuart kings and took the form more of a "bill of limitations" than a modern statement of rights.[32]

This English experience very much influenced the framers of the United States government. They believed that the rights protected under English common law and declared in documents like the Petition of Right and the Bill of Rights were crucial and part of America's legal heritage. Three years after the Constitution was ratified, many of these rights were enshrined in the US Bill of Rights. For example, the First Amendment protects the freedom of speech, assembly, and religion; the Eighth Amendment prohibits cruel and unusual punishment; and the Fifth Amendment, as did the Magna Carta, forbids the government from taking life, liberty, or property except by due process of law.[33]

Significantly, though, the rule of law is not just—or even most effectively—protected through the Bill of Rights. As late Supreme Court Justice Antonin Scalia said in 2015:

> Every tin horn dictator in the world today, every president for life, has a Bill of Rights. That's not what makes us free; if [34] it did you would rather live in Zimbabwe. But you wouldn't want to live in most countries in the world that have a Bill of Rights. What has made us free is our Constitution. Think of the word "constitution"; it means structure.[35]

The key to the Constitution's structure is its separation of powers, by which the Constitution's framers carefully limited powers they granted to different branches and government officials. An example of the separation of powers is seen in the legislative process. Article I of the Constitution grants "all" legislative power of the national government to Congress.[36] Congress is divided into House and Senate with different terms of office for members of each. A bill may not become law unless both bodies approve it and the president signs it. The president may veto a bill, but Congress may override that veto by a two-thirds vote of both chambers.

This complex process sometimes creates gridlock. However, as Scalia noted, the process also makes abuse of power much more difficult and less likely: "The genius of the American constitutional system is the dispersal of power. Once power is centralized in one person, or one part [of government], a Bill of Rights is just words on paper."[37]

The separation of powers shows itself in more than the legislative process. Treaties negotiated by the president do not become effective without Senate approval. Similarly, the president may appoint federal judges, but only with the advice and consent of the Senate.

It is important here to note that such constitutional protections do not guarantee that the rule of law will be achieved. Indeed, the United States has had egregious violations of the rule of law in our treatment of racial and ethnic minorities, particularly Native Americans and African Americans. From lawless stripping of property rights to legally mandated segregation to the legalized enslavement of millions, our country has at times failed to rule through the equal application of law. This history serves as an important reminder that while we should justly celebrate the rule of law and the many benefits it brings, we should also remember that merely having divided government and limited power does not guarantee that we will faithfully follow the rule of law.[38] It counsels continued and increased vigilance to make sure that the benefits of the Constitution are applied to all.

THE RULE OF LAW AND HUMAN NATURE

Embrace of the rule of law is not simply a product of historical progress. It is rooted in a Christian view of human nature that humans are both created in the image of God and flawed by sin.

The rule of law reflects our creation in God's image by the way it treats all humans with dignity, worth, and equality under the law. As my colleague Craig Stern notes: "As all humans equally bear the image of God, so all are to enjoy equality before the law."[39] In this way, the rule of law reflects how God treats us, his image-bearers. For example, Job 34:19 notes that God "shows no partiality to princes, nor regards the rich more than the poor, for they are all the work of his hands."

God insisted that ancient Israel apply the same equality principle in its civil justice system. A good example is found in Deuteronomy 1:17, in which Israelite judges were directed: "You shall not be partial in judgment. You shall hear the small and the great alike." Under the rule of law, all have a right to be heard, whether rich or poor, powerful or weak. The law protects all as equally valuable.

The rule of law also reflects an understanding of human fallenness. People marred by sin will naturally promote their own self-interest and grasp for power. As British historian Lord Acton stated in the epigraph to this chapter, "Power tends to corrupt, and absolute power corrupts absolutely."[40] The acknowledgment of sin is of critical importance to establishing good government. On the one hand, sin makes necessary the existence of states—we need the state's protection from the sinful acts of individuals and other nations. But we must also guard against the sinfulness and abuse of our rulers. Dutch theologian and statesman Abraham Kuyper put it well: Christianity's "deep conception of sin" has two important implications:

> First—that we have gratefully to receive, from the hand of God, the institution of the State with its magistrates, as a means of preservation, now indeed indispensable. And on the other hand also that, by virtue of our natural impulse, we must ever watch against the danger which lurks, for our personal liberty, in the power of the State.[41]

The American constitutional framers held the same view. They, too, acknowledged both the dignity and sinfulness of humans and believed that having a proper understanding of human nature was critical to having a proper separation and allocation of powers under the Constitution. The framers regularly turned to discussions of human nature—especially human fallenness, which was the prime motivation for the separation of powers. For example, James Madison wrote the following in *The Federalist Papers* when discussing the size of the House of Representatives: "As there is a degree of depravity in mankind which requires a certain degree of circumspection and distrust: So there are other qualities in human nature, which justify a certain portion of esteem and confidence."[42] Again, Madison wrote in Federalist 48: "It will not be denied, that power is of an encroaching nature, and that it ought to be effectually restrained from passing the limits assigned to it."[43] Finally, he added this in Federalist 51:

> Ambition must be made to counteract ambition. The interest of the man must be connected with the constitutional rights of the place. It may be a reflection on human nature, that such devices should be necessary to controul the abuses of government. But what is government itself but the greatest of all reflections on human nature? If men were angels, no government would be necessary. If angels were to govern men, neither external nor internal controuls on government would be necessary. In framing a government which is to be administered by men over men, the great difficulty lies in this: you must first enable the government to controul the governed; and in the next place, oblige it to controul itself.[44]

Madison, along with Alexander Hamilton and John Jay, emphasized human sinfulness relentlessly throughout their defense of the Constitution in *The Federalist Papers*. Their recognition of that sinfulness counseled them to support, for example, the following propositions:

- The Articles of Confederation did not sufficiently constrain the power of individual states: ("Has it been found that bodies of men act with more rectitude or greater disinterestedness than individuals?");[45]

- The Senate should be required to approve presidential appointments (the Senate provides "a considerable and salutary restraint upon the conduct of that magistrate");[46]

- The president should have a four-year term (such a term provides an incentive for the president to hold office with the proper "firmness" but is not so long as "to justify any alarm for the public liberty");[47]

- There should be a Senate as well as a House of Representatives (the Senate's purpose is "first to protect the people against their rulers: secondly to protect the people against the transient impressions into which they themselves might be led")[48]

THE FEDERALIST PAPERS

The Federalist Papers were a series of essays written following the Constitutional Convention of 1787 defending the draft Constitution and encouraging states to ratify it. The essayists wrote under the pseudonym of "Publius," but the authors' real names were later made known to the world: James Madison, John Jay, and Alexander Hamilton.

The essays, which originally appeared in newspapers, were published in a book in 1788. *The Federalist Papers* are widely used today by lawyers, judges, political leaders, historians, and many others to understand the intention of those who wrote the Constitution.

The framers constructed a system of government that they believed would both have sufficient power to enable the government to function effectively and enough checks, limits, and divisions of that power to prevent it from falling into tyranny. In doing so, they strongly supported both the rule of law and the biblical view of human nature.

But the framers' view of human nature—and its centrality to protecting the rule of law—is not universally held. Other nations and regimes have tried to build on a very different understanding of who humans are. Those that lacked the framers' distrust of human nature, such as revolutionary France and Cambodia under the Khmer Rouge, have reaped a harvest of violence, abuse, and tyranny.

REVOLUTIONARY FRANCE

The French Revolution began in 1789, just a year after the United States ratified its Constitution. Many factors led to the revolution, including deep anger over inequality and aristocratic privilege and tensions with the Roman Catholic Church.

The revolution was also the intellectual fruit of certain Enlightenment ideas, especially the philosophy of Jean-Jacques Rousseau. Two ideas of Rousseau played a central role. First, Rousseau believed that humans are basically good; it is society and its institutions that corrupts them. He famously wrote that "man was born free, and he is everywhere in chains."[49]

Rousseau's second influential idea was that of the social contract, which said that individuals form civil society by becoming parties to a contract. As part of this contract, people give up their individual rights and submit to what Rousseau called "the general will." The general will promotes the welfare of the people as a whole and also determines moral standards. Rousseau wrote that the "general will, which tends always to the preservation and welfare of the whole and of every part, and is the source of the laws, constitutes for all the members of the State, in their relations to

one another and to it, the rule of what is just or unjust."⁵⁰ Similarly,
"the voice of the people is, in fact, the voice of God."⁵¹

JEAN-JACQUES ROUSSEAU

Jean-Jacques Rousseau was a Swiss-born eighteenth-century
Enlightenment philosopher. He moved to France to study music but
was drawn into a group of philosophers beginning to have influence in
Paris. He became a contributing writer to an important Enlightenment
encyclopedia that is now known simply as the *Encyclopédie*.

Rousseau's most famous work is *The Social Contract*, written in
1762. In it he asserted his belief that humans in the state of nature
are basically good, but they are corrupted by society and its institutions. *The Social Contract* and an earlier work, *Discourse on Inequality*
(1754), had a powerful role in shaping the thinking of those who led
the French Revolution.

The French revolutionaries embraced this philosophy, acted
on its principles, and reaped its fruit. The view that humans are
basically good was seen in the revolutionaries' optimism about
what humans could do if they were freed from the institutional
corruption around them.

In the Revolution's second phase, especially in 1792–1793, the
revolutionaries, led by the Jacobin party, began seeking the total
transformation of society. "The goal of French radicals was to
reconceive and reorganize the political, legal, and social structure of the nation, to overthrow the nation's institutions, to break
with a thousand years of history."⁵² They abolished aristocratic
titles, seized property for the benefit of the poor, and even created
a new calendar—dating the new year from September 22, 1792,
the birth of the new republic. The calendar divided up days and
months so as to eliminate the Christian Sabbath.⁵³ The revolutionaries seized church property and tried to abolish Christianity and

substitute the worship of Reason instead.[54] They closed churches and destroyed religious images. The Jacobin revolutionaries took Rousseau's view of human goodness and embarked on a utopian program to remake humanity itself.

Rousseau's views regarding the general will and its supremacy in all things was equally impactful. "His idea of the general will was particularly suited to be exploited by tyrants."[55] At all points, the French Revolution rejected the notion that power needed to be carefully limited and divided and instead embraced the idea that the people's will had to triumph.

Again, this was particularly clear during the radical phase of the Revolution in 1792–1793. At that time, power was concentrated in the hands of twelve individuals known as the Committee of Public Safety. The committee was headed by radical leaders Georges Jacques Danton and Maximilien Robespierre, and was tasked with enforcing the general will. What followed was a dictatorial "reign of terror" in which tens of thousands of individuals were arbitrarily arrested and imprisoned, and over 17,000—including eventually Danton and Robespierre themselves—died by guillotine.[56]

Ultimately the revolutionary period ended with the embrace of a military dictator, Napoleon Bonaparte. At no point in this period did the French embrace the rule of law. Instead, they optimistically concentrated almost unchecked power in the hands of those who would further the general will.

CAMBODIA UNDER THE KHMER ROUGE

Nearly two centuries later, from 1975 to 1979, there was another attempt to totally transform a society believing that a utopia could be built on earth: the Khmer Rouge regime in Cambodia, led by dictator Pol Pot.

In a transformation reminiscent of the French Revolution, Khmer Rouge leaders tried to throw off all that came before and to remake society altogether. They created a new calendar,

beginning anew at year zero. They abolished capitalism and confiscated all private property. They also abolished money, religion,
and family life, and they resettled residents of cities into rural
collective farms.[57]

Why? The Khmer Rouge regime embraced a Rousseau-like
philosophy that people are naturally good but are corrupted by
social institutions around them. Pol Pot, the General Secretary
of the Communist Party of Kampuchea, had studied Rousseau
and other Enlightenment thinkers in France in the 1950s. He and
his fellow Khmer Rouge leaders believed that if corrupt institutions were removed, people would thrive. They viewed capitalism as a source of vanity, rank, boastfulness, individualism, and
authoritarianism. The Khmer Rouge "convinced themselves that
by abolishing private property these human traits were erased
from society."[58] Similarly, the regime was certain that if peasants
were freed from distractions like religion and family obligations,
"they could devote their days to work in fields and factories and not
be required to market, clean, cook, raise children, or worry about
their upbringing and education. The country would experience
an economic miracle. This stark, 'modern' restructuring of society
would unleash the people's hidden potential."[59]

Cambodia's social experiment was a horrific, bloody failure.
With no concern for human sinfulness, the Communist Party of
Kampuchea assumed all power. There were no checks, balances,
or limitations. Like the French Committee for Public Safety, it
exploited that power and ruled through terror. It killed the "ene-
mies of the revolution," which included not only political figures
from the previous regime, but also many professionals and educated persons—such as teachers, engineers, and doctors—who
were thought to pose a danger to the state. In the end, the party
tortured and executed hundreds of thousands of middle-class
Cambodians. It is estimated that approximately 1.7 million
Cambodians lost their lives before the regime fell in 1979.[60]

After the fall of the Khmer Rouge, Cambodia struggled with war and instability. In 2006, Cambodia and the United Nations created a tribunal to try Khmer Rouge leaders for crimes committed during the 1970s. The tribunal combined both Cambodian and international elements in an effort to preserve Cambodia's sovereignty while bringing to bear international expertise.

The tribunal has received significant criticism. After a decade of work and the expenditure of almost $300 million, the tribunal has convicted only three people: the regime's number-two man, its chief of state, and the former commander of a prison.[61] All were convicted of crimes against humanity and sentenced to life in prison.[62]

CHALLENGES TO THE
RULE OF LAW TODAY

As the previous chapter described, one of the most important steps in the protection of human rights is to promote the rule of law worldwide. There is a desperate need for nations not only to enact good laws, but to build political structures and accountability so that those laws are faithfully enforced. Only with such structures and accountability will vulnerable individuals be protected from human trafficking and ethnic minorities be safe from genocide.

Though the United States has a constitution with divided powers and a historical commitment to the rule of law, the danger of government officials exercising unchecked power is as relevant today as ever. Indeed, one could argue that it is more relevant today given the powerful tools that the government now has at its disposal, from mass data collection to electronic surveillance to the ability to target terror suspects via drones.

The remainder of the chapter will focus on two areas in modern American life where the rule of law is being significantly challenged: executive orders and judicial policy making.

EXECUTIVE ORDERS

In March 2014, President Barack Obama unilaterally made important changes to the operation of the Affordable Care Act (ACA), also known as Obamacare. The ACA had been controversial, bitterly fought over, and the subject of multiple lawsuits. Nonetheless, President Obama used his executive power to extend congressionally set deadlines for enrollment in qualified plans as well as deadlines for compliance with mandates put on employers.[63] He did so using a tool known as an executive order.

EXECUTIVE ORDERS

An executive order is a directive with the force of law made by the president to executive officials. The term is found nowhere in the Constitution, but executive orders are appropriate when they are based on authority that comes from the Constitution or existing laws. Indeed, they are necessary for the functioning of the executive branch.

Of much greater concern are those executive orders that displace or circumvent the legislative process. These orders have implications for the separation of powers. The Constitution's framers were very careful to delegate "all" legislative power of the national government to Congress.[64] They did so in order to foreclose legislative action by the executive branch. "The framers of the Constitution feared executive power the most. ... Having endured the tyranny of the king of England, the framers viewed the principle of separation of powers as the central guarantee of a just government."[65]

Presidents throughout American history have attempted to exert executive power that usurps congressional power. For instance, during the Civil War, Abraham Lincoln suspended the ability of courts to issue writs of habeas corpus. Franklin Delano Roosevelt created the National Labor Board and took the country off the gold standard through executive orders.[66] And Harry

Truman used an executive order to seize most of the nation's steel mills to head off a steel strike during the Korean War.[67]

Recent presidents, however, have used executive orders more regularly. President Clinton turned to executive orders when legislation became stalled in Congress. For example, on Earth Day 1997, Clinton took provisions from the Children's Environmental Protection Bill that was pending before the Senate and issued them as an executive order.[68] Similarly, when Congress refused to pass a law prohibiting employers from hiring permanent replacements for striking workers, Clinton declared this to be law through executive order instead.[69]

President Bush issued a number of executive orders relating to the War on Terror, asserting that his actions were based on the fairly broad authority that the Constitution grants the president as commander in chief. He also used executive orders in ways that more obviously substituted for the legislative process. For example, he issued a directive blocking funding of international family planning groups that provided abortion-counseling services.[70]

President Obama used executive orders with even greater frequency than his predecessors. In addition to several orders modifying the requirements of the ACA, he effectively nullified the No Child Left Behind Act through executive waivers.[71] One of Obama's most sweeping and controversial executive orders relates to immigration law. As a candidate, he expressed strong support for immigration reform, including the Dream Act, which would have provided residency to some undocumented individuals who were brought to this country while minors. When Congress refused to pass the Dream Act, the president simply ordered executive agencies to implement key portions of the unpassed act administratively.[72]

In the first months of his presidency, President Trump showed his willingness to continue in the tradition of his recent predecessors by issuing a large number of executive orders. For example, on May 4, 2017, he issued a widely publicized executive order on religious liberty. One part of the order directs the Treasury Department to "not take any adverse action against" churches and other religious organizations who engage in political speech.[73] This appears to be targeted at the Johnson Amendment to the tax code, which prohibits tax-exempt churches, for example, from directly or indirectly participating in political campaigns.[74] In his 2017 National Prayer Breakfast address, President Trump had vowed to "get rid of and totally destroy the Johnson Amendment and allow our representatives of faith to speak freely and without fear of retribution."[75] As I write, Trump appears to have chosen to bypass legislative efforts to address the Johnson Amendment and to instead resort to executive action.

Why is it so tempting for presidents to make extensive use of executive orders? First, presidents are often frustrated by the gridlock that so often accompanies the legislative process. This has become increasingly true in recent years as the country has become more polarized, with very little common ground between left and right, blue and red. In contrast to the legislative process, executive action is quick and easy. As Clinton advisor Paul Begala remarked: "Stroke of the pen. Law of the land. Kind of cool."[76]

Obama was explicit in his second term that he intended to act unilaterally on certain key matters where Congress had failed to act. In his 2014 State of the Union address, he declared: "America does not stand still—and neither will I. So wherever and whenever I can take steps without legislation to expand opportunities for more American families, that's what I'm going to do."[77]

Second, executive orders are hard to overturn. One would think that Congress has the greatest incentive to oppose the use of executive orders. But members of Congress, too, are often frustrated with lack of legislative progress, and those affiliated with the president's party or agenda are pleased to see progress made even if it is through executive action. Further, even if there is bipartisan opposition to the president's action, it is very difficult to undo an executive order. Congress can pass a law undoing the executive order, but the president can veto that law, and it takes a two-thirds vote of each house to override such a veto.

Executive orders may be overturned by courts, but this, too, occurs infrequently. Federal courts are often hesitant to make decisions on what they consider to be political questions. Further, the law is fairly restrictive on who has legal standing to challenge government actions in court.

So what should be done to take a stand against the use of executive orders in which presidents are effectively usurping legislative power? We must remember and articulate why the Constitution's framers were so concerned to separate and limit governmental power. As Jonathan Turley explained in testimony before Congress, this increasing use of executive orders represents "a massive gravitational shift of the authority of the Executive Branch that threatens the stability and functionality of our tripartite system."[78] The Constitution delegated "all" federal legislative powers to Congress, yet legislative actions are increasingly being taken by the executive branch.

Human nature has not changed. Just as in the framers' day, we face the danger of abuse of power and even corruption when government branches and officials overstep their constitutional boundaries. We must still be wary of human fallenness. This calls for restraint on the part of presidents. It also calls for vocal opposition and action by members of Congress and the public.

This means we need to oppose executive orders even if we support their substance. For reasons discussed in chapter 4, I was sympathetic with the intent behind President Bush's executive order on abortion funding. It is possible that Congress, through its cumbersome processes, would not have reached the same result. But that matter should have been left to legislation rather than executive order. By celebrating executive orders that we like and opposing only those with which we disagree, we embolden future presidents to continue to assume legislative powers through executive action. Journalists, bloggers, and ordinary citizens should bring attention to and oppose unlawful executive action as we speak, write, and participate in the political process.

It is also incumbent on Congress to challenge illegal executive orders through legislative efforts and actions to defund illegal executive initiatives. Courts also must uphold the separation of powers and strike down illegal executive orders. These other branches must heed James Madison's *Federalist* warning that "power is of an encroaching nature, and ... it ought to be effectually restrained from passing the limits assigned to it."[79]

JUDICIAL POLICY MAKING

Another threat to the rule of law in the United States is the creation of policy on the part of the courts. It is surprising in some ways to talk about a threat to the rule of law coming from the judiciary branch. The Constitution's framers saw the executive—like John, Charles I, or Robert Mugabe—as the greatest threat to the rule of law. They viewed the judiciary as the "least dangerous" branch of government since it "may truly be said to have neither Force nor Will."[80]

It is true that, historically, common-law judges exercised a great deal of humility and restraint as they approached cases. They did so based on a biblical view of human nature.

> Judges, as they discerned the customs and rules that composed the common law, had no discretion to alter the law, or even to depart from precedents unless clearly erroneous. This principle not only stabilized law, ... but also checked indulgence of any judicial impulse to pursue passion rather than law.[81]

Judges were to interpret the law, not to make it. They were to exercise judgment, not force or will.

Increasingly, though, courts have rejected the humility and restraint of their predecessors and embraced a policy making role. This is dangerous, especially given that federal judges are

appointed for life and that the judicial branch is least accountable
to the people. While it is beyond the scope of this chapter to examine the judiciary as a whole, I will take as an example the way the
United States Supreme Court has created policy in high-profile
cases dealing with privacy and personal autonomy.

One tool the Supreme Court has used to create policy is a
doctrine known as substantive due process. The Constitution's
Fourteenth Amendment states: "nor shall any State deprive any
person of life, liberty, or property, without due process of law."[82]
This provision was deeply rooted in the common-law history of
England and finds its origin in Article 39 of the Magna Carta. The
Due Process Clause insists, in short, that appropriate legal procedures must be followed before the government may interfere with
life, liberty, or property.

The Supreme Court now reads this clause much more broadly
than it once did. Not only must the government follow a particular process, it may not (except in the rarest instances) interfere with certain fundamental rights no matter what process
it follows.

For example, in 1973 the Supreme Court declared in *Roe v. Wade*
that a woman has a constitutional right to abort a fetus, subject to
some state regulation in the later stages of pregnancy.[83] Nineteen
years later, in *Planned Parenthood v. Casey* (1992), the Court reaffirmed *Roe* and again endeavored to explain why the decision
to have an abortion is a fundamental right under the Fourteenth
Amendment's Due Process Clause. Yet it struggled mightily to root
its finding in anything concrete; the Court pointed to no clear basis
in the Constitution's text. And it insisted there was no simple formula to determine what is a fundamental right. The best the Court
could do, it said, is use "reasoned judgment."[84] It acknowledged
that in applying this judgment, it must look to history and tradition. But, significantly, it declared that this "tradition is a living
thing."[85] In other words, the Court must view the Constitution as
a living and evolving document.

In the end, the Court determined that the decision of whether to have an abortion—like that of whether to marry, have children, or how to educate them—involves "the most intimate and personal choices a person may make in a lifetime, choices central to personal dignity and autonomy."[86] It declared that such choices

> ... are central to the liberty protected by the Fourteenth Amendment. At the heart of liberty is the right to define one's own concept of existence, of meaning, of the universe, and of the mystery of human life. Beliefs about these matters could not define the attributes of personhood were they formed under the compulsion of the State.[87]

Those looking for textual interpretation or clear legal categories and lines—things we might expect from law and judicial opinions—are doomed to disappointment. Indeed, much of the Court's language focused on philosophies about life and its meaning, and political judgments about what values ought to be affirmed. Justice Scalia in his dissent blasted the majority for this very thing: "The best the Court can do to explain how it is that the word 'liberty' *must* be thought to include the right to destroy human fetuses is to rattle off a collection of adjectives that simply decorate a value judgment and conceal a political choice."[88]

This policy-making focus of the Court is perhaps most clearly—and boldly—demonstrated in its 2015 opinion in *Obergefell v. Hodges.*[89] There the Court resolved as a matter of constitutional law the debate over same-sex marriage that was taking place in state legislatures throughout the country. Preempting further state legislative action, the Court resolved once and for all that laws prohibiting same-sex marriage violate the Due Process and Equal Protection clauses of the Fourteenth Amendment. In setting forth its opinion, the Court spent most of its time on the Due Process Clause, again interpreting it in a substantive way.

Throughout the opinion, the Court emphasized that marriage, while a "keystone of our social order,"[90] is also an institution of change and evolution. This theme of evolution became critical to the Court's substantive due process analysis. As in *Casey*, the Court noted that deciding that a particular claimed right is a "fundamental liberty" protected by the Constitution "has not been reduced to any formula."[91] And the Court must not make that determination simply by interpreting the meaning of the Constitution's words as the framers likely would have understood them:

> The generations that wrote and ratified the Bill of Rights and the Fourteenth Amendment did not presume to know the extent of freedom in all of its dimensions, and so they entrusted to future generations a charter protecting the right of all persons to enjoy liberty as we learn its meaning. When new insight reveals discord between the Constitution's central protections and a received legal stricture, a claim to liberty must be addressed.[92]

In other words, the Constitution's framers invited us to determine new meanings of their words based on our own values and desires over time.

The Court insisted that this process of applying new meanings to the constitutional text must be done with the issue of marriage: "The right to marry is fundamental as a matter of history and tradition, but rights come not from ancient sources alone. They rise, too, from a better-informed understanding of how constitutional imperatives define a liberty that remains urgent in our own era."[93]

Having claimed for itself the role to reinterpret fundamental rights and constitutional protections, it was fairly easy for the Court to determine that same-sex marriage is required by the Constitution. After all, our understanding of homosexuality and same-sex unions has changed dramatically in a short time. And the choice of same-sex couples to marry is just as intimate, personal, and central to personal autonomy as the right to have a child or abort a fetus. Significantly, in order to reach this decision, the Court had to take sides on the very nature of marriage itself rather than merely decide whether to extend the right to marriage to a new group of people.

OBERGEFELL V. HODGES (2016)

In *Obergefell v. Hodges,* the United States Supreme Court found unconstitutional state laws barring same-sex couples from marrying or refusing to recognize same-sex marriages permitted in other states. The case was a collection of a number of individual cases coming from Michigan, Kentucky, Ohio, and Tennessee. They were brought by fourteen same-sex couples and two men whose same-sex partners had died. Plaintiffs in all cases alleged that state officials had refused to permit them to marry or to give full recognition to a marriage that had been performed in another state.

For example, one of the plaintiffs was James Obergefell, an Ohio man who had married fellow Ohioan John Arthur in Maryland, where same-sex marriage was legal. When Arthur died, Obergefell sought to be listed as a surviving spouse on the death certificate, something forbidden by Ohio law.

The Supreme Court ruled that the Fourteenth Amendment's Due Process and Equal Protection clauses require states to recognize same-sex marriage.

We should be just as concerned over the jurisprudential approach in the above Supreme Court cases as we are with the European Court of Human Rights' evolutive approach to interpreting fundamental human rights. As eloquent as the Court's opinion is, and as persuasive a policy determination it is to some, the Court has overstepped its constitutional role. The Constitution's framers assigned judicial power to the judiciary. This is the power to interpret law, not to make it. As *The Federalist Papers* put it, courts have the power of judgment, not will. Will was left to Congress through the Constitution's Article I, which grants it legislative powers. And in matters reserved to the states, will is left to the state legislatures.

Even a cursory glance at the *Obergefell* opinion makes it painfully obvious that the Court is exercising a quasi-legislative function. Rather than waiting for a decision about same-sex marriage to be made by the states one by one—with different states perhaps reaching different results—the Court made the legislative call for the nation as a whole. Justice Scalia pointed this out in his dissent: "This is a naked judicial claim to legislative—indeed, *super*-legislative—power; a claim fundamentally at odds with our system of government. Except as limited by a constitutional prohibition agreed to by the People, the States are free to adopt whatever laws they like, even those that offend the esteemed Justices' 'reasoned judgment.' [94] In another dissent, Chief Justice Roberts agreed: "The majority's decision is an act of will, not legal judgment. The right it announces has no basis in the Constitution or in this Court's precedent."[95]

As I have been arguing, the Court's policy making overreach is more than just an unfortunate constitutional faux pas. It poses a threat to the rule of law itself because of the ambiguity it introduces. Crucial to the rule of law is that law is clear and predictable, including as it is interpreted and explained in judicial decisions. Clarity and predictability are necessary for individuals and entities subject to the law to know what it requires and what it forbids. They give freedom for action and freedom from hesitation.

Under the Court's substantive due process analysis, it is difficult for any state, individual, or entity to know what constitutes a fundamental right. It certainly cannot be determined by looking at the Constitution's text. What rights are and how we understand them will differ based on changing times in society and changing judicial philosophies of the majority of the court—and with the changing makeup of the court.

Obergefell opens up a host of additional questions. For example, will polygamy be found to be a fundamental right? Historically, polygamy has been viewed as illegal, and laws banning it have been held to be constitutional.[96] But presumably polygamist relationships can be just as intimate, personal, and central to personal autonomy as monogamous relationships. The majority in *Obergefell* is careful to emphasize that marriage is a two-person union. But if the definition of marriage can be judicially rewritten to allow same-sex couples to marry, could not a future Court change the definition to allow more than two parties to marry? Nothing in the Court's analysis suggests that this could not—or even should not—occur. This uncertainty and lack of clear legal principle is a strong indication that the rule of law is lacking.

The *Obergefell* dissenters also took up the constitutional framers' warning of danger whenever a government branch or official takes on powers beyond those delegated. Justice Alito declared, "Today's decision will also have a fundamental effect on this Court and its ability to uphold the rule of law. If a bare majority of Justices can invent a new right and impose that right on the rest of the country, the only real limit on what future majorities will be able to do is their own sense of what those with political power and cultural influence are willing to tolerate."[97] Chief Justice Roberts agreed: "The majority's understanding of due process lays out a tantalizing vision of the future for Members of this Court: if an unvarying social institution enduring over all of recorded history cannot inhibit judicial policymaking, what can? But this approach is dangerous for the rule of law."[98]

THE SUPREME COURT AND SUBSTANTIVE DUE PROCESS

In *Casey* and *Obergefell*, the Supreme Court applied the Due Process Clause of the Fourteenth Amendment to protect certain "fundamental rights" from state restriction. In recent decades, the Supreme Court has used the doctrine of substantive due process mainly to assert the existence of fundamental rights in matters relating to contraception, marriage, procreation, medical decisions, abortion, and so on. Most such decisions have been praised by liberal commentators and criticized by conservative commentators.

It has not always been so. In the early part of the twentieth century, politically conservative judges used substantive due process to strike down state laws because they interfered with economic rights. For example, in *Lochner v. New York* (1905),[99] the Supreme Court struck down a law limiting the work hours of bakers to no more than ten hours per day or sixty hours per week. The Court held that this law violated the fundamental right to freedom of contract. The Court continued to strike down a number of labor laws until it rejected this approach in 1937 in the case of *West Coast Hotel v. Parrish*,[100] which upheld a Washington-state minimum wage law against the claim this the law violated the Due Process Clause.

What is to be done? The nation—and our judiciary—must embrace a proper view of human nature. We must recognize that the judiciary can suffer from the same hubris and certainty of its own good intentions as the French revolutionaries or the Stuart kings in the era of the divine right. It is vital that they exercise restraint and return to the role—the robust and important role of exercising legal judgment and not political will—allocated by the Constitution.

This means, in part, that the judiciary ought to exercise restraint when faced with policy questions that ought to be resolved by legislatures, rather than by judges finding "rights" in the Fourteenth Amendment that are found nowhere in the Constitution's text or history. They should heed the eloquent appeal of Chief Justice Roberts:

A much different view of the Court's role is possible. That view is more modest and restrained. It is more skeptical that the legal abilities of judges also reflect insight into moral and philosophical issues. It is more sensitive to the fact that judges are unelected and unaccountable, and that the legitimacy of their power depends on confining it to the exercise of legal judgment.[101]

This understanding that judges are to exercise legal judgment and not political will should also play the central role in all Senate judicial confirmation hearings. Too often, hearings are dominated by questions seeking to learn how the nominee might vote in cases of particular interest to the questioner. Does the nominee support abortion rights? Does the nominee support the government's use of the eminent domain power to seize private property? By asking such questions, senators perpetuate the falsehood that judges are appointed to the bench to vote the "right way" on important policy issues. Instead, presidents should select and senators should confirm nominees who are committed to interpreting the law and rejecting the role of judicial policymaker.

As ordinary citizens, we too must resist the temptation to see the courts as a means to effect social change. We must remember the fallen nature of all human beings and protect the rule of law. Many of us live in states where citizens directly elect their judges. In these states, we should vote for judicial candidates who embrace a philosophy of judicial restraint and reject the notion that they are to shape the state's social policy in a certain direction. In many other states and in the federal system, judges are appointed by other elected officials. As we vote for and lobby these officials, we should call for the appointment of judges who reject the policy-maker role. We must resist the temptation ourselves to seek judges who will vote the "right way" on certain issues.

CONCLUSION

The rule of law is critical in any society. It was desperately needed in thirteenth-century England, eighteenth-century France, and twentieth-century Cambodia. It is critical today to people around the world, including the citizens of Zimbabwe and citizens of the United States.

A biblical view of human nature calls for all governments and government officials to rule by law and under law. Insisting on the rule of law is the only way to hold governments accountable and to protect the liberty and equality under law of all of God's image-bearers.

CHAPTER 8

CRIMINAL PUNISHMENT

How and why do we punish?

To be punished, however severely, because we have deserved it, because we "ought to have known better," is to be treated as a human person made in God's image.

—C. S. LEWIS[1]

I n the early hours of June 12, 1983, Karla Faye Tucker and her friend Danny Garrett secretly entered the home of Jerry Dean. Dean was the estranged husband of Tucker's close friend Shawn Dean. Tucker was twenty-three years old, a drug addict, and a former prostitute. She had been partying for three days, consuming large amounts of alcohol, cocaine, and amphetamines.[2] While partying, Tucker had seen Shawn, who had a broken nose and a fat lip from Jerry's abusing her. Tucker was enraged. She already hated Jerry from previous encounters, and now she and Garrett planned to avenge Shawn's injuries.

Tucker and Garrett entered Jerry Dean's apartment that morning with the intent of stealing his motorcycle. While they were in the apartment, however, Dean and his girlfriend, Deborah Thornton, woke up—and robbery turned to murder. Garrett attacked Dean with a hammer, and Tucker attacked both Dean and Thornton with a pickax.

When their bodies were discovered later that morning, Dean and Thornton had each been struck by the pickax over twenty times. The pickax was left embedded in Thornton's chest. In the days following the murder, Tucker bragged to friends about what she had done and claimed to have gotten a sexual thrill with each strike of the pickax. Tucker and Garrett were arrested, each charged with and convicted of murder, and sentenced to death.[3]

In jail, Tucker's life changed dramatically. By the time of her trial, Tucker had become a Christian. She admitted responsibility for the murders and began to care for others around her. While on death row, Tucker became a counselor to fellow inmates and was very active in prison ministry. According to one of her attorneys, Tucker "offer[ed] herself to anyone who needed a compassionate and wise listener" and "actively counseled scores of people struggling with their own issues of sin and forgiveness."[4]

Stories of jailhouse conversions are not new and are often met with skepticism. But everyone who knew Tucker insisted that hers was real—that she truly had become a new person. Many began calling for clemency, arguing that it would be unjust to execute the new Karla Faye Tucker. One of the prosecutors in the Garrett case (Garrett and Tucker were tried separately) argued, "The Karla Tucker who killed Jerry Dean and Deborah Thornton cannot be executed by the state of Texas because that person no longer exists. The Karla Tucker who remains on death row is a completely different person who, in my opinion, is not capable of those atrocities."[5] Others agreed, including prison guards and a juror who had voted to sentence her to death in the first place.[6] Support for commutation of Tucker's sentence came from such diverse voices as Pope John Paul II, Sister Helen Prejean (author of *Dead Man Walking*), Italian Prime Minister Romano Prodi, and evangelical leaders Pat Robertson and Jerry Falwell.[7]

In the end, however, the Texas Board of Pardon and Parole rejected Tucker's clemency application, a decision that then-Governor George W. Bush allowed to stand.[8] Tucker was executed on February 3, 1998. She was the first woman to be executed in Texas since 1863.[9]

Much of the controversy over Tucker's sentence and clemency application centered on various views of whether the death penalty is appropriate. But the controversy also reflected widely differing views on why we punish at all. To some, punishing Tucker was pointless. By all accounts, Tucker had been rehabilitated. She was a new person; she was not the woman who had killed Dean and Thornton. From a public safety perspective, she no longer posed a danger to society. One attorney insisted: "I am comfortable enough in this belief [that Tucker was no longer dangerous] that, if possible, I would welcome Karla into my house to meet my family."[10]

For others, however, Tucker's punishment was appropriate because it was deserved. It was a just application of retributive justice. Though Tucker had changed, death was an appropriate response to the crime she had committed. Others argued that even if Tucker was no longer a danger to society, her execution could serve as a deterrent to others.

How should we evaluate these competing claims? Which of these theories should take precedence in determining when and how to punish an offender? In this chapter, I will examine varying views of criminal punishment. In light of human nature, I will then make the case that retribution provides the most appropriate basis on which to punish offenders.

HOW AND WHY DO WE PUNISH?

The widely varying reactions to Karla Faye Tucker's clemency petition provide a good introduction to several prominent bases for criminal punishment that lay behind them.

One of the most prominent bases is that punishment acts as a deterrent—punishment of one offender may induce others to refrain from criminal activity out of fear of being punished themselves. This is known as general deterrence. Another form of deterrence is known as specific deterrence—punishment that deters *this* offender from committing crime again. Closely related to deterrence is incapacitation. Punishment of the offender (by imprisonment or death) renders him or her incapable of committing further crimes.

A second basis for punishment is rehabilitation. Rehabilitation advocates focus their attention on changing the offender. Many do so largely in order to protect society. A changed offender is one who will no longer commit criminal acts. Others support rehabilitation out of concern for the well-being of the offender.

A third basis for punishment is retribution. Retributivists believe punishment is appropriate when it is deserved. Punishment should not be based primarily on concerns over future offenses or over the future condition of the offender. Instead, punishment should be focused on the offense and the appropriate penalty for the wrong done.

The popularity of these bases for punishment has waxed and waned at different times. In the United States during the first half of the twentieth century, much of the focus was on rehabilitation. At that time, criminal justice reformers had great faith in science and social science. They believed they could discover scientifically the causes of crime and take appropriate steps to change the mindset and ultimately the actions of offenders. Indeed, by 1949, the Supreme Court declared, "Retribution is no longer the dominant objective of the criminal law. Reformation and rehabilitation of offenders have become important goals."[11]

Rehabilitation's ascendance did not last long, however. The data did not support the early faith in rehabilitation's ability to change hearts and actions. By the late twentieth century, rehabilitation went "from the top of most scholars' and reformers' lists of the purposes of punishment to the bottom. The dominant goal of criminal punishment changed almost in an instant, and the first became last."[12] With concern over rising crime rates, sentences grew longer. The focus of the criminal justice system turned from rehabilitation to incapacitation and deterrence.[13]

Today we have multiple theories of punishment at work both in the United States and abroad. At times, this has made the sentencing of criminals more creative—and controversial. An example of such creative sentencing came from Cleveland Municipal Court Judge Pinkey S. Carr, who received national attention with her sentence of Shena Hardin. Hardin had driven her car on a sidewalk to get around a stopped school bus. She was sentenced to stand on a street corner holding a sign saying, "Only an idiot drives on the sidewalk to avoid a school bus."[14] Shawn Gementera received a similar sentence after his conviction for stealing letters from San Francisco mailboxes. A federal judge sentenced Gementera to stand outside the post office wearing a sign reading: "I stole mail. This is my punishment."[15]

The Hardin and Gementera punishments are part of a trend to inflict punishment that shames victims. Judges hope the shame of such punishments will succeed in deterring similar acts—by this offender and other potential offenders (both specific and general deterrence).

Other sentences are clearly motivated by general deterrence—inflicting a severe punishment in hopes of keeping others from committing similar offenses. Such a sentence was handed down following riots in England during August 2011. A judge sentenced two men to four years each in prison for setting up Facebook events calling on friends to join the riots. Twenty-one-year-old Jordan Blackshaw from Manchester set up a Facebook event called "Smash Down Northwich Town." A post written by Blackshaw read: "We'll need to get this kickin' off all over."[16] Twenty-two-year-old Perry Sutcliffe-Keenan created a similar event called "Let's Have a Riot in Latchford."[17] No one showed up for either event. In sentencing Blackshaw and Sutcliffe-Keenan, the judge stated that the prison terms should act as a deterrent. A fellow Manchester judge opined: "The courts should show that outbursts of criminal behaviour like this will be and must be met with sentences longer than they would be if the offences had been committed in isolation."[18]

Some judges focus their efforts on changing offenders to keep them from repeating criminal acts (rehabilitation). One example is the 2004 sentence given to James Lee Cross, who was convicted of misdemeanor domestic assault. Judge Larry Standley sentenced Cross to one year of probation—and yoga. Standley explained the unusual sentence this way: "It's part of anger management. For people who are into it, it really calms them down."[19]

Some sentences that are exclusively focused on rehabilitation can be controversial, especially if they appear to focus on the perpetrator while ignoring the victim. For example, in 2013, Montana state court judge G. Todd Baugh provoked outrage when he sentenced a former teacher to thirty days in jail for the statutory rape of a fourteen-year-old student. The original sentence was fifteen years in prison, but Judge Baugh suspended all but thirty-one days of the sentence and gave the teacher, Stacey Rambold, a one-day credit for time served. One of the judge's prime justifications was that Rambold "had no prior record and [was] a low risk to re-offend after spending more than two years in a sex-offender treatment program."[20]

Often, judges try to accomplish multiple purposes with sentencing. A great example is the sentence in the Oscar Pistorius trial in South Africa. Pistorius, an amputee sprinter, was the first athlete to compete in both the Olympic and Paralympic games. Judge Thokozile Masipa sentenced Pistorius to five years in prison for killing his girlfriend, Reeva Steenkamp. In explaining the sentence, Judge Masipa asserted that a sentence must reflect a balance of retribution, deterrence, and rehabilitation. She called her sentence "fair and just, both to society and to the accused."[21] She continued, "A non-custodial sentence would send the wrong message to the community. On the other hand, a long sentence would not be appropriate either, as it would lack the element of mercy."[22]

Penal codes often reflect a similar desire to achieve multiple goals through punishment. For example, the state of Texas declares the following objective for criminal punishment:

(1) To insure the public safety through:

(A) the deterrent influence of the penalties hereinafter provided;

(B) the rehabilitation of those convicted of violations of this code; and

(C) such punishment as may be necessary to prevent likely recurrence of criminal behavior.[23]

Interestingly, while the Texas code specifically identifies deterrence and rehabilitation as appropriate goals, it identifies as an additional goal furthering retribution's principles of desert and proportionality: "(3) To prescribe penalties that are proportionate to the seriousness of offenses."[24] New York's penal code is similar.[25]

EVALUATING COMPETING PUNISHMENT THEORIES

While judges and penal codes refer to many different bases for punishment, as seen above, they can be grouped into two main—and starkly competing—theories: utilitarianism and retribution. Utilitarianism encompasses a variety of bases for punishment, including general and special deterrence, incapacitation, and rehabilitation. These varying bases share important characteristics that distinguish them from retribution.

The first major difference between utilitarian and retributive theories is that utilitarianism is future-focused while retribution focuses on the past. To the utilitarian, an evil has occurred. The law should ensure that future good comes from this evil. The appropriate punishment should prevent the recurrence of this evil or amend the offender—or it should do both.

The retributivist counters that we cannot look to the future until we appropriately address the evil that has occurred. Rather than focusing on preventing future crime, retributivism focuses on just desert. Retribution is not about issuing harsh or long sentences; it is committed to meting out a just penalty for the crime that has already occurred. Because the offender deserves punishment, imposing it is justified.

There is a second major difference between the two theories. To a utilitarian, punishment is an evil—at times a necessary evil, but an evil nonetheless. As eighteenth- and early nineteenth-century philosopher and social reformer Jeremy Bentham famously stated, "All punishment is mischief: all punishment in itself is evil. Upon the principle of utility, if it ought at all to be admitted, it ought only to be admitted in as far as it promises to exclude some greater evil."[26] By contrast, to a retributivist, punishment that is just and appropriate is good.

In light of these basic differences, it is important to examine in more detail the case for each punishment theory.

THE CASE FOR A UTILITARIAN PUNISHMENT THEORY

Historically, utilitarian theory has been most closely identified with the British Enlightenment philosopher Jeremy Bentham. Bentham believed that the object of criminal law and punishment, like all laws, was "to augment the total happiness of the community; and therefore in the first place, to exclude, as far as may be, every thing that tends to subtract from that happiness."[27] Bentham equated happiness with pleasure and unhappiness with pain. Crime causes pain. So does punishment. As noted above, punishment is an evil—a necessary evil. In sentencing, the most effective and least painful sanction should be used.[28]

JEREMY BENTHAM

Jeremy Bentham was a British philosopher and economist whose career spanned the late eighteenth and early nineteenth centuries. He sought to bring an empirical and rational approach to philosophy and law.

He was a strong critic of natural rights theory, instead embracing utilitarianism, which is grounded in the idea that we should maximize pleasure and minimize pain for the community as a whole. He applied this theory not only to criminal punishment but all of political life. In fact, he worked on drafting legal codes built on his theories and offered his legal reform advice to political leaders around the world.

Modern adherents of utilitarianism build upon Bentham's foundation of maximizing happiness and minimizing pain for the community as a whole. This is the express goal of deterrence, for example. As stated well by legal scholar Joshua Dressler, "D's [Defendant's] punishment serves as an object lesson to the rest of society; D is used as a means to the desired end of a net reduction in crime."[29]

Rehabilitation is viewed in the same way. The offender is transformed so that he or she no longer commits crime and causes pain. While this benefits the offender, it benefits society even more. Judge Richard Nygaard of the United States Court of Appeals for the Sixth Circuit expresses this view well: "Rehabilitation? Perhaps we should dust this concept off and try it again. I am not talking about the goody-goody rehabilitation of the fifties and sixties. I do not bleed for the criminal. I bleed for the society which must reassimilate him after he has served his time."[30]

Utilitarianism is a kind of consequentialism, which is "the view that the value of an action or course of conduct is to be assessed from its consequences. A consequentialist theory of punishment would justify punishment on the basis of the good consequences promoted by punishment."[31] Because of its view that the worth of an action can be measured by its consequences, utilitarianism lends itself to scientific analysis—calibrating the costs and benefits of criminal sentencing options. For this reason, it has often been embraced by economists, psychologists, and others. Some who advocate the application of economic principles to law argue that the appropriate sentence for a particular crime should be determined through a straightforward calculus. In other words, the cost of committing a crime must be made to exceed its expected benefit. The criminal justice system should "choose a combination of probability and severity of punishment that will impose that cost on the would-be offender."[32]

From a utilitarian perspective, calculating the costs and benefits of crime often involves understanding the underlying motivations for committing a crime. Psychiatrist Karl Menninger found the utilitarian approach attractive. In his book *The Crime of Punishment*, he urges that we see crime and punishment as a doctor would: "The question doctors might ask is not what would be *just* to do to this dangerous fellow or this dishonest woman, but as in the case of a patient with compulsions, what would be effective in deterring them!"[33] Science should ask: "Why? What was behind the discovered act which brought the matter to our attention? What pain would drive a man to such a reaction, such a desperate outbreak, and such a deliberate gamble?"[34]

Judge Nygaard agrees. After years of seeing repeat offenders come through his courtroom, Nygaard urges: "We cannot effect cures unless we discover causes. ... Behavior can be studied scientifically. Antisocial behavior can be modified. I suggest that criminals be treated like dreaded diseases and examined just as closely to see what caused them to err. We must 'discover' why one commits crimes before we set about any deliberate fashion to develop appropriate remedies."[35]

Utilitarians reject retributive theory for several reasons. First, they argue that retribution is irrational. It is based on emotion, not reason.[36] Second, they argue that punishment is senseless and cruel if it does no good for the future. Third, retribution glorifies anger and hate.[37] As Judge Richard Nygaard expresses it, retribution primarily addresses society's anger at the crime, not the criminal's rehabilitation: "Retribution only provides a fertile bed for the malignant growth of hatred."[38] Equating retribution with a futile vengeance, Nygaard argues instead that "all sentences take a view towards the future, towards change, towards correction."[39]

THE CASE FOR A RETRIBUTIVE PUNISHMENT THEORY

Retribution has been most closely identified historically with the philosophy of Immanuel Kant. He argued that the sole legitimate basis for punishment is that it is deserved. Punishment can never be inflicted solely because it is useful to others or to society: "[The offender] must first be found to be deserving of punishment before any consideration is given to the utility of this punishment for himself or for his fellow citizens."[40] Kant argued strenuously that when punishment is deserved, it must be imposed: "If legal justice perishes, then it is no longer worthwhile for men to remain alive on this earth."[41]

IMMANUEL KANT

Immanuel Kant was an eighteenth-century German philosopher. He grew up in a devout Pietist Christian home, then studied at the University of Königsberg and went on to become a leading Enlightenment thinker. In 1781 he published his *Critique of Pure Reason*, one of the most influential works in Western philosophy.

One of his most important philosophical contributions is the notion of the "categorical imperative," which he viewed as a universal ethical principle: "Act according to a maxim which can be adopted at the same time as a universal law of human conduct."[42] Kant was a leading proponent of retributive justice, believing that if a crime is not punished, society becomes an accomplice to that crime.

Kant also argued that punishment should be strictly proportional to the offense. He did so based on his principle of equality: "Any undeserved evil that you inflict on someone else among the people is one that you do to yourself. If you vilify him, you vilify yourself; if you steal from him, you steal from yourself; if you kill him, you kill yourself. Only the Law of retribution (*jus talionis*) can determine exactly the kind and degree of punishment."[43]

Following Kant, modern retributivists unite around several principles. First, they reject the utilitarian view that pleasure is the only intrinsically good thing. There are other intrinsic goods, like fulfilling moral duties and protecting moral rights.

Second, punishment itself—when based on desert (what a person deserves)—is a moral good. This is true in a number of important ways. For one, as Kant maintained, it is desert itself that ties punishment to justice. C. S. Lewis agreed: "The concept of Desert is the only connecting link between punishment and justice. It is only as deserved or undeserved that a sentence can be just or unjust."[44] He further explained,

> I do not here contend that the question "Is it deserved?" is the only one we can reasonably ask about a punishment. We may very properly ask whether it is likely to deter others and to reform the criminal. But neither of these two last questions is a question about justice. There is no sense in talking about a "just deterrent" or a "just cure."[45]

DESERT

"Desert" is a term meaning that which one deserves. Retributivists believe that this is the appropriate basis for all punishment. The law should only punish those who are responsible for a crime. In addition, the amount of punishment should be proportional to the level of responsibility. Thus, the decisions of whether and how much to punish are both based on desert.

Punishment is also good because it speaks truth in an important way. Through crime, the offender degrades and dishonors the victim. "Punishment, in contrast to crime, speaks the truth. ... Punishment is thus our way of censuring or condemning the wrongdoer's wrong, of annulling the false message he implicitly conveys through his wrongdoing, and of vindicating the moral worth and standing of his victim."[46]

Finally, punishment is good in that it restores a moral balance to society when a wrong has been done. Crime leaves a deficit of justice that requires punishment to remedy. The biblical law text Numbers 35:33 seems to refer to this: "You shall not pollute the land in which you live, for blood pollutes the land, and no atonement can be made for the land for the blood that is shed in it, except by the blood of the one who shed it."

The third major principle on which retributivists agree is that humans are persons with value and rights. This includes not only the victim, who needs to be affirmed as a person with value and dignity, but the offender as well. C. S. Lewis made this point strongly in the epigraph to this chapter: "To be punished, however severely, because we have deserved it, because we 'ought to have known better,' is to be treated as a human person made in God's image."[47] Retributivists insist that all humans—including criminal offenders—are persons; they are not mere objects of the law.

A fourth principle of retributive justice is that punishment should be proportional to the crime committed. It is not appropriate to impose either a milder or harsher penalty than deserved simply to produce a desired effect. Contrary to the view that it is synonymous with harshness, retributivism is dedicated to limiting punishment to no more than what is deserved.

Each of these four principles rejects the implications of utilitarianism. One of these implications, in particular, provokes a strong reaction from retributivists: If individuals may be punished to promote the good of society as a whole, what is to stop us from punishing an innocent person if by doing so we deter crime and increase the overall pleasure and happiness of society? For a consistent utilitarian, there may be situations where the net gain to society of punishing an innocent person (who fits the perpetrator's description and lacks an alibi) may outweigh the harm to the individual being punished. To a retributivist, such a scenario would be morally unthinkable.

LEGAL AND POLICY IMPLICATIONS

Both utilitarian and retributive advocates marshal strong arguments in favor of their positions. How should we evaluate them? Human nature again provides the key.

I believe that the retributive approach to punishment better fits a Christian view of human nature. All aspects of human nature highlighted in this book support this view: the moral accountability of humans, their creation in the image of God, and their fallenness. Focusing on these core aspects of human nature will make it possible to provide judges and legislatures with guidance on how to appropriately punish criminals.

MORAL ACCOUNTABILITY

Earlier in this chapter, I described the shift in the early twentieth century toward a utilitarian, and especially a rehabilitative, view of punishment. That shift took place largely because of a particular scientific perspective on human nature. As Professor Albert Alschuler puts it, "Twentieth-century reformers gave up on retribution largely because they gave up on human autonomy, a concept they believed science had discredited."[48] He explains further:

> Many twentieth-century reformers doubted their ability to blame. They saw people as the far-from-divine products of heredity, social circumstances, random breeding, and Darwinian struggle. They and others also insisted that blame was functionless and that society should direct its efforts to more constructive goals. Like the rest of law, criminal punishment should look forward, not backward.[49]

This strong deterministic perspective motivates more recent utilitarian thinkers as well. For example, psychiatrist Karl Menninger has objected to retribution's focus on what is "just":

> Behavioral scientists regard it as equally absurd to invoke the question of justice in deciding what to do with a woman who cannot resist her propensity to shoplift, or with a man who cannot repress an impulse to assault somebody. This sort of behavior has to be controlled; it has to be discouraged; it has to be *stopped*. This (to the scientist) is a matter of public safety and amicable coexistence, not of justice.[50]

Likewise, Judge Richard Nygaard is direct in his rejection of retributive justice, advocating instead for a punishment system based on the rejection of the concept of free will. The notion that people, no matter their background, are free to change, he writes, "is almost totally inapplicable to sentencing as we approach the 21st Century."[51]

This deterministic view of human behavior flies in the face of the biblical notion described in chapter 2 that humans are morally accountable agents. As chapter 9 will discuss more fully, while we can be influenced by cultural and genetic factors, they do not cause our behavior. Our actions are not simply the product of blind determinism; rather, humans have moral choice and accountability.

A retributive view of justice aligns much better with the biblical view of human nature than a utilitarian one. The retributive view depends on the proposition that humans are morally accountable for their choices and actions. The just punishment in a retributive system is based on what the offender deserves as a result of those choices and actions.

CREATED IN THE IMAGE OF GOD

More than utilitarianism, retributivism also supports the notion that we are created with worth and dignity in the image of God. Kant insisted that humans be treated as persons with rights and value. We "can never be confused with the objects of the Law of things."[52] Because of retribution's notion that human beings are punished because they deserve it, C. S. Lewis supported a retributive view "in the interests of the criminal."[53]

In a utilitarian system, by contrast, criminals are not holders of rights. "Instead of a person, a subject of rights, we now have a mere object, a patient, a 'case.' [54] Professor Michael Moore describes it this way: "Utilitarianism treats a free, subjective will as an object. It is a refusal to admit that the rest of humanity shares with us that which makes us most distinctively human, our capacity to will and reason—and thus to be and do evil."[55]

Indeed, the utilitarian view permits manipulating criminal defendants for the good of others. Justice Oliver Wendell Holmes Jr. explains it well: "If I were having a philosophical talk with a man I was going to have hanged I should say, I don't doubt that your act was inevitable for you but to make it more avoidable by others we propose to sacrifice you to the common good."[56] Retributivists object strongly to this notion that individuals should be punished for the good of society in general. As Kant wrote, "A human being can never be manipulated merely as a means to the purposes of someone else and can never be confused with the objects of the Law of things."[57]

The utilitarian theory of justice inevitably treats criminals as objects instead of persons. They are punished to increase society's collective happiness, sacrificed to the common good. By contrast, retribution affirms humans as having rights, worth, and dignity as individuals made in the image of God.

FALLENNESS

The fallenness of humans supports the retributive theory as well. One of the most thoughtful expressions of this view is found in C. S. Lewis's essay "The Humanitarian Theory of Punishment," which I have already quoted several times in this chapter. In it, Lewis responded to the criticism that retribution is vindictive and harsh. According to such critics, retribution should be replaced by a more humanitarian theory that is focused on deterrence and rehabilitation.

Lewis argued that the utilitarianism of this kind of theory is dangerous even if those who seek to deter us or cure us are prompted by the best possible motives. Once desert is removed from the decision of how to punish, the door to abuse is open. Under this "Humanitarian theory," confinement is not limited by justice or desert. Instead, we are confined until we are deterred or cured. Lewis wrote:

> My contention is that good men (not bad men) consistently acting upon [the Humanitarian theory] would act as cruelly and unjustly as the greatest tyrants. They might in some respects act even worse. Of all tyrannies a tyranny sincerely exercised for the good of its victims may be the most oppressive. It may be better to live under robber barons than under omnipotent moral busybodies. The robber baron's cruelty may sometimes sleep, his cupidity may at some point be satiated; but those who torment us for our own good will torment us without end for they do so with the approval of their own conscience. They may be more likely to go to Heaven yet the same time likelier to make a Hell of earth.[58]

Lewis went on to recognize that people, of course, are not good. And this led to an ominous note:

> And when they are wicked the Humanitarian theory of punishment will put in their hands a finer instrument of tyranny than wickedness ever had before. For if crime and disease are to be regarded as the same thing, it follows that any state of mind which our masters choose to call "disease" can be treated as crime; and compulsorily cured. It will be vain to plead that states of mind which displease

government need not always involve moral turpitude and do not therefore always deserve forfeiture of liberty. For our masters will not be using the concepts of Desert and Punishment but those of disease and cure.[59]

Under this "Humanitarian theory" of punishment, even religious persecution could be justified by the seemingly benign desire to cure people. An acknowledgement of human sinfulness should make us hesitant to put in fallen hands a punishment theory not rooted in desert but in the dubious scientific view that government or experts can fix crime or cure criminals.

THE BIBLICAL CASE FOR RETRIBUTION

Scripture consistently supports a retributive theory of justice. It does so throughout all of redemptive history: creation, fall, and redemption.

In the narrative of creation in Genesis 1–2, we are introduced to the foundational principle that humans are created in the image of God. That concept informs all of the passages that follow. Even after the fall, God's instructions on how to live consistently support a retributive view of justice. For instance, God gave the following instructions to Noah after the flood:

And for your lifeblood I will require a reckoning: from every beast I will require it and from man. From his fellow man I will require a reckoning for the life of man. Whoever sheds the blood of man, by man shall his blood be shed, for God made man in his own image. (Gen 9:5–6)

Because humans are image-bearers of God, the taking of a life is a most serious offense. God instituted a deserved punishment that is proportionate to the offense.

The Mosaic law also reflected this retributive principle. Consider this command from Exodus 21:23–25, an example of the *lex talionis* ("law of retaliation"): "But if there is harm, then you shall pay life for life, eye for eye, tooth for tooth, hand for hand, foot for foot, burn for burn, wound for wound, stripe for stripe." When someone harmed another person, there was a punishment based on desert. The important thing to remember about the law of retaliation in the Mosaic law is that it was not intended to be harsh; it was designed to prevent individuals from taking revenge. Punishment was limited. It was to be *no more than* an eye for an eye, *no more than* a tooth for a tooth.

LEX TALIONIS

The *lex talionis* (Latin for "law of retaliation") is a principle of justice that punishment should fit the crime. This principle is found in the Mosaic law's statement about what punishment should be imposed upon an individual who harms another. Some look at this text from Exodus 21:23–25 as evidence of the harshness of the law. But this principle, rooted in desert, actually puts a limitation on criminal punishment. Individuals may not be punished more than an eye for an eye or a tooth for a tooth. Punishment must be proportionate to the severity of the offense. This was also not an authorization of private vengeance; the *lex talionis* was guidance for judges.[60]

This concept is central to Deuteronomy 25's discussion of punishment. It details what would happen if an individual was found guilty in the Israelite justice system:

> The judge shall cause him to lie down and be beaten in his presence with a number of stripes in proportion to his offense. Forty stripes may be given him, but not more, lest, if one should go on to beat him with more stripes than these, your brother be degraded in your sight. (Deut 25:2–3)

Again we see the concept of desert. The number of stripes was to be proportionate to the severity of the offense, but there was a limit. Because humans, including criminals, are image-bearers of God, criminal punishment may not degrade offenders.

It is in the New Testament story of redemption, though, that we most powerfully see a retributive theory of justice displayed. The ultimate solution to the problem of sin comes through the life and death of Jesus Christ. Knowing that we are helpless to save ourselves, Jesus Christ came to earth, assumed human form, and died a criminal death on our behalf. His life satisfied the law's righteous demands, and his death paid the punishment for the sins that we have committed.[61]

Could God simply have absolved humans of our sin? No. To do so would have violated his own character—his holiness and justice. In Romans 3, Paul says Jesus' atoning sacrifice "was to show his righteousness at the present time, so that he might be just and the justifier of the one who has faith in Jesus" (Rom 3:26). Yes, God justifies sinners and forgives our sins. But that does not mean our deserved punishment simply went away. God is not only a justifier, but he is just. The penalty had to be paid. This was a just penalty based on desert, and Jesus paid that penalty; he was punished for our sins. Both Old and New Testaments make this clear:

> But he was pierced for our transgressions; he was crushed for our iniquities; upon him was the chastisement that brought us peace, and with his stripes we are healed. (Isa 53:5)

> He himself bore our sins in his body on the tree, that we might die to sin and live to righteousness. By his wounds you have been healed. (1 Pet 2:24)

God's application of retributive justice as he deals with our sin—meted out on his own Son—is powerful evidence that retribution is central to the very nature of justice. Human judges, too, should apply retributive principles when sentencing.

LINGERING QUESTIONS

This brief overview of punishment theory has covered some basics, but it leaves unanswered questions as well. Here I will answer two of the most common objections to preferring the retributive vision of justice.

If retribution is the core of a just system of punishment, does deterrence have any role?

Yes. Scripture makes clear that a just penalty based on desert often will have a deterrent effect. Deuteronomy 17:8–13 describes how judges and priests were to make just decisions and the people were to obey them. People who refused to obey the decision were to be punished, to the effect that "all the people shall hear and fear and not act presumptuously again" (Deut 17:13).

But while a just penalty will likely have a deterrent effect, that effect must be the byproduct of a just system, not its primary goal. If deterrence becomes the primary goal, it might be appropriate in that system to punish too harshly or to punish an innocent person if those actions would have the greatest deterrent effect. In pursuing deterrence as an end in itself, we are returned to a system where God's image-bearers are treated as objects to be manipulated for the good of others. Deterrence is a byproduct but should not be the chief aim of a just system of punishment.

What about restorative justice?

Restorative justice has become increasingly popular in recent years.[62] As its name indicates, it seeks to bring restoration after a criminal act has been committed. It seeks to restore the relationship between offender and victim and between the offender and society.

Restorative justice seeks to do these things through both "restorative processes" and "restorative outcomes." Restorative processes include mediation and other techniques to bring victims and offenders together (and, at times, other family members or interested parties). Restorative outcomes include such things as restitution, victim support services, and rehabilitation programs for offenders.

Though a thorough analysis of restorative justice is well beyond the scope this chapter, we can say that the motivation for restorative justice is often quite consistent with a biblical approach to justice. The concept that victims should be affirmed and restored is very biblical.

Scripture also promotes restitution, one of the most important outcomes of restorative justice. In the Israelite justice system, for example, offenders regularly were required to make restitution to victims of their actions. A good example is found in Exodus 22:1, 4: "If a man steals an ox or a sheep, and kills it or sells it, he shall repay five oxen for an ox, and four sheep for sheep. ... If the stolen beast is found alive in his possession, whether it is an ox or a donkey or a sheep, he shall pay double."

Restitution plays a central role in redemption as well. One of the ways Scripture describes the atonement of Christ is as a payment of satisfaction to the victim of sin—God. Peter told readers of his first epistle to fear God "knowing that you were ransomed from the futile ways inherited from your forefathers, not with perishable things such as silver or gold, but with the precious blood of Christ, like that of a lamb without blemish or spot" (1 Pet 1:18–19). Jesus suffered punishment as a ransom payment for our sins. His blood also served as restitution to God, the victim of sin.

Restorative justice, then, has much to commend it. One concern, though, is that often the restorative justice movement has had an uneasy relationship with punishment. Some, though not all, supporters oppose punishment as inconsistent with restorative processes and outcomes.

Such an approach is doomed to fail. Without the imposition of a deserved punishment, true justice is not achieved and the moral worth of the victim is not affirmed. Without punishment, we remove the basis for restoration. Professor Stephen Garvey puts it well:

> Restorativism [if separated from punishment]—gentle and inspiring as it may be—is ultimately self-defeating. Restorativism cannot achieve the victim's restoration if it refuses to vindicate the victim's worth through punishment. Nor can it restore the offender, who can only atone for his wrong if he willingly submits to punishment. And if neither the victim nor the wrongdoer is restored, then neither is the community of which they are a part. In short, restorativism longs for atonement without punishment, but punishment—tragically—is for us an inescapable part of atonement.[63]

This means we should embrace restorative justice principles, but only as they fit within an overall retributive system of justice.

IMPLICATIONS FOR THE CHURCH

So far in this chapter I have called for a particular approach to public policy: we should build a criminal justice system built on the foundation of retributive justice, appropriately tying it to restorative principles such as restitution. While I believe that this foundation provides for the just treatment of individuals and makes it possible for restoration and reconciliation to take place, the state is ill equipped to bring about that restoration and reconciliation. For the most part, its efforts to change individual hearts and lives have failed.

It is here, though, where the church must engage. Jesus Christ calls us to care for the hungry, poor, naked, sick, and those in prison. He insists that what we do "to one of the least of these" we do to him (Matt 25:40). The writer of Hebrews also tells us: "Remember those who are in prison, as though in prison with them, and those who are mistreated, since you also are in the body" (Heb 13:3). In addition to commands to care for the "least of these," Christians are also given the ministry of reconciliation. Every Christian knows from personal experience that the gospel of Christ transforms hearts and lives.

This means Christians should be engaged in ministering to those in prison. This includes sharing the gospel and introducing individuals to the one who can truly forgive and bring restoration. But it involves other practical actions as well. We can care for the families of prisoners. We can provide discipleship and life skills training so that prisoners can more quickly and productively transition to post-prison life. We can welcome them wholeheartedly into our churches and hire them to work in our businesses. The latter is particularly important as it is often very difficult for those with a felony on their record to find work.

Thankfully, there are groups that both model and provide opportunities to engage in this important work. One of the best such organizations is Prison Fellowship. Founded by Charles Colson, the group serves prisoners, ex-prisoners, their families, and crime victims in 120 countries around the world. Colson, a former top aide to President Richard Nixon, founded the group after he was released from federal prison after serving time for Watergate-related crimes. After he got out of prison, he wrote, "I found myself increasingly drawn to the idea that God had put me in prison for a purpose and that I should do something for those I had left behind."[64]

CHARLES COLSON

Charles Colson, who served as special counsel to President Richard Nixon, famously described himself as a "hatchet man" who would "walk over my own grandmother" to make sure that Nixon was reelected in 1972.[65] As he faced arrest for crimes relating to the Watergate scandal, Colson became a Christian, and his life was transformed. In 1974, Colson

pleaded guilty to obstruction of justice and served time in prison. Colson
founded Prison Fellowship in 1976 and became a leading evangelical
author, speaker, and statesman. He died in 2012 at the age of 80.

Since its founding, the group has worked with hundreds of thousands of people both in and out of prison. It offers Bible studies and
life skills training to tens of thousands of prisoners on a weekly
basis.[66] It also sponsors many outreaches to prisoners' families.
Perhaps the most well-known is the Angel Tree Christmas program, through which 300,000 kids in 2015 heard the gospel and
received a Christmas gift on behalf of an incarcerated parent.[67]

CONCLUSION

As those who knew her attested, Karla Faye Tucker had become
a new person, and punishment wouldn't truly change her or the
safety of society. Rather than debate the very challenging issue of
whether the death penalty was the appropriate penalty in Tucker's
case—something on which thoughtful Christians will inevitably
disagree—I want to focus here on whether it was right or necessary to punish her at all.

Yes. Central to justice is that just penalties are carried out.
Though this may sound unfeeling toward offenders, especially
those who like Tucker have already been rehabilitated, we must
remember the dangers of a punishment system that has rehabilitation as its ultimate goal, like I noted above. It is a retributive system, based on deserved and proportionate penalties, that
brings order to a society and affirms the worth of both victim and
offender. It is this system that should be embraced by legislatures
constructing penal codes and by judges crafting punishments. And
it should be accompanied by the work of individuals and churches
to help bring about ultimate restoration and reconciliation in the
lives of offenders.

CHAPTER 9:
ENVIRONMENTAL INFLUENCE DEFENSES

To what extent should we hold individuals accountable for their actions?

This is the excellent foppery of the world, that when we are sick in fortune, often the surfeits of our own behavior, we make guilty of our disasters the sun, the moon, and stars; as if we were villains on necessity, fools by heavenly compulsion, knaves, thieves, and treachers, by spherical predominance, drunkards, liars, and adulterers, by enforced obedience of planetary influence; and all that we are evil in, by a divine thrusting on. An admirable evasion of whoremaster man, to lay his goatish disposition on the charge of a star!

–SHAKESPEARE,
King Lear[1]

In 1991, the northwest side of Milwaukee was at times as much battle zone as residential neighborhood. Felicia Morgan would know—it's where she grew up. On October 26, 1991, Morgan, then seventeen, saw Brenda Adams, also seventeen, wearing a trench coat that Morgan wanted. Morgan approached Adams and demanded that she give her the coat. Adams refused. They fought. Then Morgan shot and killed her and took the coat.

Morgan was charged with robbery and first-degree murder and was tried as an adult. Morgan admitted to killing Adams. She pleaded not guilty, however, insisting that the shooting wasn't her fault; it was the product of her environment. Her attorney, Robin Shellow, argued that Morgan was suffering from post-traumatic stress disorder (PTSD) "as a result of overexposure to urban violence."[2] Shellow explained, "Felicia's nerves have been rendered raw by the guns around her. She could no longer distinguish the gunfire that killed her friends and relatives from the gunfire for which she is charged. Like Brenda Adams, she bleeds openly and bears witness to the carnage of the inner city."[3]

We might be tempted to dismiss this defense quickly. Before doing so, however, consider the following evidence about Morgan's upbringing that Shellow sought to introduce into evidence at the trial:

- Kurearte Oliver, a friend of Morgan's who was driving her around on the night of the Adams shooting, had "shot his gun at a liquor bottle in a drug house when Morgan was present three days before";

- "Two weeks before the [Adams] shooting, a man pulled a gun on Morgan, her mother, and a friend, and Morgan stepped in front of the gun before her mother intervened";

- "Gang members shot at Oliver while in Morgan's presence three weeks before" the Adams shooting;

- "Morgan was robbed by a group of girls one month before" the Adams shooting;

- "Morgan's sister's boyfriend, a father-figure to Morgan, was shot and paralyzed in January 1991";

- "Morgan was robbed of her coat at gunpoint, in December 1990";

- "Morgan's cousin was killed in a drive-by shooting in October 1990";

- "Morgan's uncle, a close friend, was shot and killed in September 1990";

- "Morgan was robbed of her jewelry at gunpoint in September 1989";

- Morgan "was tied up and raped by the son of a land-lord in 1988 when she was fourteen years old";

- Another of Morgan's cousins "was shot in a 1988 street fight and subsequently lost the use of her arm";

- Morgan "stepped in front of a man with a gun to pro-tect her aunt" in 1988;

- "Morgan was severely beaten and robbed by a group of girls in June 1987";

- "Morgan's mother shot a man, in front of Morgan, because he was molesting Morgan while giving her a bath";

- "Morgan was regularly beaten by her mother and father";

- "When Morgan was three years old, her father shot at her mother 'because there was too much salt in the gravy'";

- "Morgan, from age four to six years old, witnessed her mother and father 'regularly dine with loaded revolv-ers at their sides during family dinners so that neither one would be unprotected from the violent outbursts of the other.'" [4]

In the end, the trial court refused to admit this evidence during the guilt phase of the trial, admitting it only during the later insanity phase. This decision was upheld on appeal. Morgan was found guilty, though Shellow maintained that the evidence presented during the trial's insanity phase helped lead to an earlier parole date for Morgan.[5]

Morgan's story brings up a difficult—and recurring—issue: the extent to which criminal behavior should be excused as the result of the offender's environment, cultural background, or genetic makeup. Throughout this chapter, I will refer to legal defenses based on these factors collectively as "environmental influence defenses" as I attempt to answer the question, "How should we view such defenses in light of a biblical view of human nature?"

FRAMEWORK FOR CRIMINAL RESPONSIBILITY

In almost all cases, an individual may not be found guilty of a crime unless two elements are present: an unlawful act (the *actus reus*) and a guilty mind (the *mens rea*). The United States Supreme Court described it this way in *Morissette v. U.S.* (1952): To convict a defendant of crime, the government must demonstrate "an evil-meaning mind with an evil-doing hand."[6]

An act alone or even a harmful consequence from that act is not enough for criminal responsibility. Compare defendant A, who shoots his enemy in cold blood, with defendant B, who accidentally shoots his friend while picking up what he thought was an unloaded gun. We naturally—and rightly—view defendant A as more culpable. He not only shot someone, but he did it intentionally. Eighteenth-century common-law judge and legal commentator William Blackstone put it this way: The will "is the only thing that renders human actions either praiseworthy or culpable."[7]

WILLIAM BLACKSTONE

William Blackstone was an eighteenth-century English judge and legal commentator. Blackstone was trained in law at Oxford University and practiced law for a time. He also served as a Member of Parliament and as a judge on the Court of Common Pleas, one of the most important courts in England. He found his greatest success, though, as a legal writer and commentator.

In the eighteenth century, English universities taught the civil law, the form of law that was used on the continent of Europe. Blackstone decided to offer a series of lectures on the common law, the form of law used in England. Although there are many differences between civil law and common law, the most significant is that detailed and comprehensive statutes are the source of most legal rules in civil law countries, while most legal rules in common law countries are developed through judicial decisions over time. In common law countries, statutes supplement the common law; they are not the primary source of law.

Blackstone's lectures on the common law were extremely well received. From 1765 to 1769, Blackstone turned the lectures into a four-volume treatise entitled *Commentaries on the Laws of England*. The *Commentaries* described the complexities of the common law in a clear, organized, and accessible way. The *Commentaries* were influential in England, but they probably had their greatest impact in the United States. There, they served as a key text in legal education and were the main source of knowledge of the common law for American lawyers and judges.

Assessing a defendant's mental state in determining culpability is a biblical notion as well. God established cities of refuge in the Mosaic law in part to protect those who killed unintentionally. One could flee to such a city and be protected if, for example, he was working with an ax and killed someone accidentally when the ax head flew off. The one who "lies in wait" and killed intentionally, by contrast, was afforded no such protection (Deut 19:4–13).

On the other hand, a guilty mind alone is not enough for criminal responsibility either. An act is required. Desiring or even intending to kill my neighbor is morally wrong, but it does not make me guilty under the law. Blackstone again explains:

As no temporal tribunal can search the heart, or fathom the intentions of the mind, otherwise than as they are demonstrated by outward actions, it therefore cannot punish for what it cannot know. For which reason in all temporal jurisdictions an *overt* act, or some open evidence of an intended crime, is necessary, in order to demonstrate the depravity of the will, before the man is liable to punishment.[8]

Joshua Dressler, a professor at The Ohio State University provides an additional explanation for this rule. Under a retributive view of justice, we punish those who "freely choose to harm others; the corollary of this is that society must give each person some breathing space, i.e., the opportunity to choose to desist from planned wrongful activity."[9]

Defenses to criminal prosecution relate to these categories of the guilty mind and the unlawful act. Take self-defense, for example. If I shoot and kill someone who attacks me with a knife, I am not guilty of murder. We consider self-defense a "justification" defense because we have deemed using deadly force to protect oneself from the unlawful use of deadly force to be morally and legally right. While technically both *mens rea* and *actus reus* elements are met in such cases, in a broader sense my act was lawful, not unlawful.

Other successful defenses arise where there is an unlawful act, but not a blameworthy mind. Insanity is a good example. The defendant kills the victim with a baseball bat. He does it acting under the delusion that the victim is not a human but a giant mosquito threatening to infect the community with malaria. If indeed the defendant acted under a mental disease or defect and did not know what he was doing or that it was wrongful, he will likely be found not guilty by reason of insanity.

Why is he not guilty? After all, he committed an unlawful act and the victim is dead, no less than if the defendant had killed with clear-minded intent. And in most cases the law will find both the *mens rea* and *actus reus* elements technically to be met. In a broader sense, however, the defendant has a disease or defect of the mind that absolves him of criminal responsibility.

We call insanity an "excuse" defense as opposed to a justification defense. Dressler explains the difference: "Whereas a justification claim generally focuses upon an *act* (i.e., *D*'s conduct), and seeks to show that the result of the act was not wrongful, an excuse centers upon the *actor* (i.e., *D*), and tries to show that the actor is not morally culpable for his wrongful conduct."[10]

ENVIRONMENTAL INFLUENCE
DEFENSES WITHIN THIS FRAMEWORK

Criminal defendants seek to fit environmental influence defenses within this general criminal law framework. They do so in a number of different ways:

Insanity: Frequently, defendants seek to use environmental factors to support an insanity defense. Most, like Felicia Morgan, are unsuccessful. Some are, however.

One high-profile example of a successful insanity defense is the Andrea Yates case. On June 20, 2001, Houston police received a call from Yates, stating that she had drowned her five children. When police arrived at the home, they found the dead bodies of four children lying side by side on a bed: John, age five; Paul, age three; Luke, age two; and Mary, age six months. Each was wet. They also found Noah, age seven, lying dead in the bathtub.[11] Yates was charged with murder. She mounted an insanity defense, arguing that she suffered from severe postpartum depression and schizophrenia. She was tried and initially found guilty of murder, but that conviction was reversed on appeal. In a second trial, she was found not guilty by reason of insanity.[12] The jury found that Yates suffered from a mental disease and that she did not know that what she was doing when she killed her children was wrong.

The jury foreman stated: "She needs help. ... Although she's being treated, I think she's worse than she was before. I think she'll probably need treatment for the rest for her life."[13]

Another successful—and most unusual—insanity defense was presented in 2009 in *Washington v. Noble*. Washington Superior Court judge David Fray found Daniel Noble not guilty by reason of insanity of vehicular assault and hit-and run driving.[14] Noble had struck two college students with his car and had fled the scene. Noble argued that excessive caffeine consumption had played a role in his actions. He introduced evidence both that he suffered from a bipolar disorder and that he had consumed two sixteen-ounce double shot caffeinated drinks before driving. He was found not guilty by reason of insanity based on a "rare bipolar disorder, with caffeine as the final trigger."[15]

The farther environmental defenses stray from recognized medical diagnoses, the less likely they are to be successful in supporting a finding of legal insanity. The case of *Florida v. Zamora* illustrates this well. In 1977, fifteen-year-old Ronnie Zamora and an accomplice broke into an elderly neighbor's house, intending to steal. When the neighbor returned during the robbery, Zamora shot and killed her. Zamora pleaded not guilty by reason of insanity. The basis for the claimed insanity? Zamora suffered from "television intoxication." Zamora's lawyer sought to introduce evidence that his violent act was the result of watching excessive amounts of violent television. The court refused to allow the evidence, and Zamora was convicted.[16]

Torino Roosevelt Boney was similarly unsuccessful in mounting an insanity defense to a murder charge in 1994. Boney had shot a twenty-year-old man in the head after the two had bumped into each other at a food court in Union Station in Washington, DC. Boney argued that he suffered from "urban survival syndrome," a "defensive mind-set prevalent in tough, inner-city neighborhoods."[17] Boney's attorney insisted that "poor urban areas foster a 'cycle of violence and despair' among young black men, and 'a look, a bump or a glance leads to extreme violence.' [18] The judge rejected the claim and convicted Boney.

Self-Defense: Environmental influence defenses have also been used to support claims of self-defense. One example is found in cases of battered woman syndrome (or, as it is sometimes known, battered spouse syndrome). The term "battered woman syndrome" first appeared in the 1979 book *The Battered Woman* by Dr. Lenore Walker. Walker wrote the book to explain why women often stay in abusive relationships and why some eventually strike back violently against their abusers.

Walker posited that an abused woman experiences "learned helplessness" in which she becomes economically, socially, and psychologically dependent on her abuser and is powerless to leave. Sometimes, though, the woman endures "so much frustration, despair, and isolation that her perceptions of violence are altered. The woman may violently strike back against the batterer in an effort to free herself from the cycle of abuse that she may believe ultimately will lead to her death."[19] Frequently, such violent outbursts take place during a period of relative calm in the aftermath of an abusive episode; for instance, she might strike at her abuser while he is sleeping off his drunkenness.

Testimony that a woman suffers from battered woman syndrome becomes key to a criminal defense when she is charged with murder or aggravated assault. This testimony bolsters a claim that she acted in self-defense to preserve her own life, which is necessary because often a critical element of self-defense is not present: the law has historically required that deadly force be used only in response to the imminent use of force. Battered woman syndrome testimony is frequently offered to explain why a woman chose to kill when the force was not imminent—because of learned helplessness, she could not leave and saw violence as the only way out.

New York v. Sheehan is an example of the successful use of battered woman syndrome. In 2008, Barbara Sheehan shot and killed her husband of twenty-four years, a retired police sergeant, as he was shaving in the bathroom. She testified that she killed him after years of abuse and after he had threatened to kill her. Sheehan's adult children testified that their father was violent and unpredictable. The prosecutor highlighted that Sheehan had shot her husband eleven times using two different weapons. He claimed that Sheehan had killed to collect her husband's life insurance and that it was a "self-serving execution," not self-defense.[20] After three days of difficult deliberations—during which the jury had once declared itself deadlocked—the jury accepted the self-defense claim and found Sheehan not guilty of murder.[21]

It should also be noted that evidence of battered woman syndrome is sometimes used to buttress claims that fit the more traditional model of self-defense. For example, in *New Jersey v. Kelly*,[22] the New Jersey Supreme Court held that Gladys Kelly should be able to present evidence that she suffered from battered woman syndrome when she killed her abusive husband with a pair of scissors. Unlike the *Sheehan* case, Kelly killed her husband when he approached her in a threatening manner in the midst of a violent episode.[23]

Lesser Charges: While many defendants use environmental influence defenses to support a not-guilty claim, others use them to bolster claims that their criminal responsibility should be diminished. In some cases, environmental defenses have been used to reduce charges.

For example, in 1987, Dong Lu Chen killed his wife by repeatedly hitting her in the head with a hammer after she confessed to having an affair. In the case of *New York v. Chen*, Chen, on trial for murder, called on expert testimony to attest that his immense shame over his wife's affair stemmed from his Chinese cultural background, subsequently fueling his violent response.[24]

As judge Edward Pincus of the New York Supreme Court noted, "Chen was the product of his culture. ... The culture was never an excuse, but it is something that made him crack more easily. That was the factor, the cracking factor."[25] In light of the cultural evidence, the jury convicted Chen of second-degree manslaughter rather than murder. Further, Chen was given five years on probation—the minimum sentence for second-degree manslaughter.

An environmental influence defense also led to a reduced level of responsibility in *Wisconsin v. Taylor* (1995). Turhan Taylor was charged with murder after stabbing a sexual partner to death. At trial, Taylor argued that he suffered from PTSD and rape trauma syndrome and sought to present evidence that he had "been abused as a child, sexually assaulted as a youth, and gang-raped in prison."[26] He claimed that he had killed the victim while in a flash-back to the rape. The judge ruled that the evidence was admissible. The prosecution responded by reducing the charge from murder to reckless homicide, to which Taylor pleaded guilty.[27]

Reduced Sentences: Environmental influence defenses can also be used to reduce criminal sentences. The *Morgan* and *Chen* cases are examples of this phenomenon. Like all efforts to use environmental influence defenses, however, efforts to reduce sentences are frequently not successful. For example, the jury rejected a claim by serial killer Bobby Joe Long that he should be spared the death penalty because his 1984 murders were the product of his addiction to violent pornography.[28]

THE FUTURE OF ENVIRONMENTAL INFLUENCE DEFENSES

The use of environmental influence defenses is not new. As early as 1846, William Henry Seward, who later served as secretary of state under Abraham Lincoln, attempted to use a black defendant's cultural background to support an insanity defense against a charge that the defendant had killed four members of a white family. Seward argued, "Such a life, so filled with neglect, injustice, and severity, with anxiety, pain, disappointment, solicitude, and grief, would have its fitting conclusion in a madhouse. If it be true, as the wisest man of inspired writers hast said, 'Verily, oppression maketh a wise man mad,' what may we not expect it to do with a foolish, ignorant, illiterate man!"[29] The jury rejected the claim. On appeal, the defendant was granted a new trial, but he died in prison before that trial could take place.

While it is not new, I believe the use of environmental influence defenses is likely to only increase in the years to come. This is the case for two reasons. First, as described in chapter 4, we continue to see many scientific advances in genetic and brain research. At times, these advances suggest connections between genetic and environmental factors and behavior. Recent headlines drawing these connections include:

- "Life of crime is in the genes, study claims"[30]

- "Two genes linked with violent crime"[31]

- "Genetic link to suicidal behavior confirmed"[32]

- "Media heralds the discovery of 'infidelity gene'"[33]

- "Gene abnormality could be factor behind bad driving"[34]

Increasingly detailed brain scans, too, can show abnormalities that defendants will point to as the cause of their criminal behavior. In 2000, for example, a married schoolteacher in Virginia began to have a sexual interest in children. He collected and viewed child pornography and was convicted of trying to molest his stepdaughter. An MRI revealed that the teacher had a brain tumor in an area of his brain associated with social behavior.[35] In 2012, the ABA Journal reported that one researcher had found 2,000 examples of criminal cases in which lawyers had introduced "neuroscientific evidence" between 2004 and 2012, "with 600 of those cases in 2011 alone."[36] We are likely to see more such claims bolstered by genetic research and the increased use of sophisticated brain imaging.

A second reason we are likely to see the increased use of environmental influence defenses is the number of people returning from military deployments and being diagnosed with PTSD. Studies reveal that a very high percentage of veterans of the Iraq and Afghanistan wars experience PTSD symptoms. As early as 2009, the Department of Veterans Affairs estimated that 11 percent of Afghan War veterans and 20 percent of Iraq War veterans suffered from PTSD.[37] In their article "Last Stand," professors Thomas Hafemeister and Nicole Stockey report that as many as 35 percent—over one-third—of veterans of those wars may ultimately experience such symptoms.[38]

This incidence of PTSD is impacting the criminal justice system. Hafemeister and Stockey note that, by early 2008, 121 Iraq and Afghanistan veterans were known to be involved in homicides.[39] Such veterans are using evidence of PTSD to support insanity defenses. For example, Ricardo Cortez claimed that he was legally insane as a result of PTSD when he shot his wife and their unborn child. The jury rejected that claim and convicted Cortez of murder. In another case, a military jury convicted Archie O'Neil of the murder of his mistress after she threatened to kill several of his family members while he was deployed. O'Neil's attorney argued that O'Neil suffered from PTSD and should be found not guilty by reason of insanity since "the ravages of war" provided the "trigger" for the killing.[40] While the jury found O'Neil guilty, it declined to impose the maximum sentence of life imprisonment.[41]

ENVIRONMENTAL INFLUENCE DEFENSES AND MORAL ACCOUNTABILITY

How do such environmental influence defenses square with the Christian view of human nature we've already discussed? In particular, how do such defenses square with the concept that humans are morally accountable agents?

Some uses of environmental influence defenses fit squarely within existing criminal law doctrines and do not undermine the concept of moral accountability. An example is found in *Tennessee v. Phipps,* where a Gulf War veteran, David Phipps, was charged with murder after killing his wife's lover. Phipps had confronted the lover, who threatened him with a stick. Phipps took the stick, hit the lover repeatedly with it, and killed him. In 1994 the appeals court ruled that it was appropriate for the jury to consider evidence of PTSD, but for the limited question of whether Phipps had the intent—the required *mens rea*—needed to find him guilty of first-degree murder.[42] The question of whether a defendant has the necessary *mens rea* is a fundamental question in any case and is central to a just determination of culpability.

On the other hand, often defendants present environmental influence defenses when evidence shows they satisfy all traditional criminal law requirements for guilt. In such cases a defendant seeks to excuse his behavior because he was unable to restrain himself due to environmental or genetic influence. Such cases can challenge the core notion that humans are morally accountable agents. The case of Felicia Morgan from the beginning of this chapter provides a good example. Morgan took Brenda Adams's coat and killed Adams with the full intent to do so. Her defense was that she had been conditioned by her environment to act violently in such situations.

Such defenses often reflect a determinist view that behavior is caused and not freely chosen. This was the view of one of the early supporters of environmental influence defenses, Judge David Bazelon of the United States Court of Appeals for the District of Columbia Circuit. He urged in a law review article:

> Our best hope of achieving a truly moral social order lies in seeking out the causes of the criminal act. The criminal process—from arrest to sentencing—resembles a post-mortem: A post-mortem cannot revive the dead, and the criminal process cannot undo a heinous act. But in each procedure we can attempt to discover the cause of failure.

ENVIRONMENTAL INFLUENCE DEFENSES

Of course, eliciting the information necessary to understand the forces that drive people to commit crime will not
"cure" the disease. Once we improve our understanding, we
will still need to decide whether the costs of grappling with
the roots of crime are more than we are willing to pay. But
society can never hope to achieve a just and lasting solution to crime without first facing the facts that underlie it.[43]

Bazelon tried to apply this perspective in cases that came
before him. One such case was *U.S. v. Alexander* (1972), in which
Benjamin Murdock, who was black, shot and killed two white men
after one of them had shouted a racial epithet at him. Murdock
pleaded not guilty by reason of insanity and asserted that while
he may have overreacted to the epithet, this was because of his
upbringing, what he called his "rotten social background."[44] His
rotten social background "conditioned him" to react as he did;
"he was denied any meaningful choice."[45] The trial judge rejected
Murdock's insanity defense and convicted Murdock of second-degree murder.

Murdock then appealed the case to Judge Bazelon's court. There
the majority upheld the conviction, but Judge Bazelon dissented:

Murdock was strongly delusional, though not hallucinating
or psychotic; he was greatly preoccupied with the unfair
treatment of Negroes in this country, and the idea that
racial war was inevitable. ... Since his emotional difficul-
ties were closely tied to his sense of racial oppression, it is
probable that when the Marine in the Little Tavern called
him a "black bastard" Murdock had an irresistible impulse
to shoot.[46]

Bazelon's position that Murdock had an "irresistible impulse"
is similar to the sentencing approach of Judge Richard Nygaard
described in the previous chapter:

I suggest that criminals be treated like dreaded diseases and examined just as closely to see what caused them to err. We must "discover" why one commits crimes before we set about in any deliberate fashion to develop appropriate remedies.[47]

JUDGE DAVID BAZELON

Judge David Bazelon served as a judge on the Court of Appeals for the District of Columbia Circuit from 1949 to 1985, serving as chief judge from 1962 to 1978. Born in 1909, Bazelon was the youngest judge in the court's history when he took the bench. Bazelon had a broad view of the court's role and was widely admired by political liberals for using law to fight social injustice. Others opposed his activist approach. In 1978, Supeme Court Justice William Rehnquist, in an opinion overturning a decision of Judge Bazelon's court, accused that court of "judicial intervention run riot."[48]

One of Bazelon's judicial innovations was the creation of the Durham rule for insanity, which states that a person is found not guilty by reason of insanity "if his unlawful act was the product of mental disease or mental defect."[49] The test was first used in the case of *Durham v. United States* (1954), in which Bazelon relied on recent developments in psychological theory to determine the proper rule.[50]

The position articulated by judges Bazelon and Nygaard is embraced by some criminal law scholars as well. For instance, Patricia Falk equates environmental influences on criminal defendants with toxins like acid rain and ozone depletion that impact the physical environment: "Social scientists are beginning to document that our social environment is also becoming increasingly toxic to members of our society. Three of the most pervasive and noxious components of this social toxicity are real-life violence, media violence, and racism."[51] She argues that criminal law must evolve to "accommodate increasing knowledge about the toxicity of the social environment and its psychological sequelae within the context of established criminal law doctrine."[52]

"Conditioned"; "denied meaningful choice"; "social toxins"; "irresistible impulse." All of this is the language of determinism. According to determinism, humans are not morally responsible agents; they are at the mercy of their upbringing, environment, and genes.

The embrace of determinism by some judges and legal scholars reflects the thinking of influential psychologists, such as B. F. Skinner. In his book *Beyond Freedom and Dignity*, Skinner asserted:

> We shall not solve the problems of alcoholism and juvenile delinquency by increasing a sense of responsibility. It is the environment which is "responsible" for the objectional behavior, and it is the environment, not some attribute of the individual, which must be changed. ... The concept of responsibility is particularly weak when behavior is traced to genetic determiners. ... The issue has recently been raised by the possibility that many criminals show an anomaly in their chromosomes. The concept of responsibility offers little help. The issue is controllability.[53]

Environmental influence defenses are rooted in this materialistic and deterministic view of human nature. They proclaim that we are not just influenced by our environment; we are caused to act in certain ways.

Determinism has at times strongly influenced the development of criminal law. Law professor Phillip Johnson gives a great example of the determinist influence on the law of insanity in his essay "Human Nature and Criminal Responsibility: The Biblical View Restored." Johnson's thesis is that by the mid-twentieth century, American criminal law—under the influence of scientific materialism—began to apply a deterministic view of human nature in the realm of insanity. However, by the end of the century, the weaknesses of this view were apparent and the law returned to a position of affirming that humans are morally accountable agents. Johnson puts it this way: "Darwinism at its flood tide certainly did influence our ideas of criminal responsibility, but only temporarily."[54]

PHILLIP JOHNSON

Phillip Johnson is a retired law professor from the Boalt Hall School of Law at the University of California-Berkeley. Johnson is a graduate of Harvard University and the University of Chicago Law School. He is a criminal law expert and the author of one of the casebooks used to teach criminal law to students in American law schools. When Johnson became a Christian, he began exploring the impact evolutionary theory and materialistic philosophy have had on science and the law. He is one of the founders of the Intelligent Design movement and has authored a number of influential books, such as *Darwin on Trial* and *Reason in the Balance.* In the article discussed in the text, Johnson explores the influence that evolutionary theory has had on the development of insanity law.

The dominant standard for determining whether a defendant was legally insane prior to the twentieth century was the M'Naghten rule: A defendant is excused from criminal responsibility only if "at the time of committing the act, the party accused was laboring under such a defect of reason, from disease of the mind, as not to know the nature and quality of the act he was doing, or if he did know it, that he did not know he was doing what was wrong."[55]

The M'Naghten rule is a cognitive test. It focuses on what the defendant knew. A defendant who did not know what he was doing or that what he was doing was wrong is "analogous to small children, who may say 'Bang! Bang!' and point a loaded pistol at a playmate without grasping the consequences of what they are doing."[56] But if the accused knows what he is doing and that it is wrong, he should be convicted. The M'Naghten rule insists that such individuals, knowing what is right, are responsible to choose and act accordingly.

THE M'NAGHTEN RULE

The M'Naghten rule is the influential insanity test that arose out of the 1843 murder acquittal of Daniel M'Naghten. In January of that year, M'Naghten shot and killed Edward Drummond, the secretary of British prime minister Robert Peel, thinking Drummond was Peel. M'Naghten was found not guilty by reason of insanity. After M'Naghten was acquitted, the House of Lords convened a panel of judges to discuss the insanity defense. It then articulated the rule on insanity that was embraced by a majority of courts in England and the United States for the next one hundred years.

While some states abandoned the M'Naghten rule in the second half of the twentieth century, most again embraced it or a modern version of it after John Hinckley was found not guilty by reason of insanity for the 1981 shooting of President Ronald Reagan.

Johnson notes that many jurisdictions abandoned M'Naghten's cognitive test in the first half of the twentieth century as a materialist and deterministic view of human nature grew in influence. For eighteen years, the United States Court of Appeals for the District of Columbia Circuit (Judge Bazelon's court) applied what was known as the Durham rule: an accused is not guilty by reason of insanity if his act was the "product of a mental disease or defect."[57]

More influential was the insanity test proffered by the American Law Institute (ALI) in its Model Penal Code (MPC): "A person is not responsible for criminal conduct if at the time of such conduct as a result of mental disease or defect he lacks substantial capacity either to appreciate the wrongfulness of his conduct or to conform his conduct to the requirements of the law."[58] Many states adopted this ALI-recommended standard. On its face, this standard does not sound dramatically different from the M'Naghten rule. As Johnson notes, however, "The radical difference is in the introduction of a new excuse for a defendant who lacks 'substantial capacity ... to conform his conduct to the requirements of law.' [59] The MPC test adds a volitional element (questioning whether the defendant could control his or her actions) to the traditional cognitive test.

Interestingly, today the federal government and at least half the states have returned to a M'Naghten-like standard focused on cognition. This is largely as a result of the attempted assassination of President Ronald Reagan by John Hinckley Jr. Afterward, Hinckley acknowledged shooting the president, but insisted that he couldn't control his actions as a result of an obsession with actress Jodie Foster. In the words of the MPC standard, he lacked substantial capacity to conform his conduct to the requirements of the law. The jury accepted his claim and returned a verdict of not guilty by reason of insanity.

As Johnson describes the scene, the verdict provoked outrage and swift legislative change. The thought was intolerable that a criminal defendant who intended to kill and knew that what he was doing was wrong should be found not guilty.

> By the end of the twentieth century, the idea of replacing retributive justice with a scientific search for the "root causes" of criminal behavior was virtually dead. ... The failure of the scientific materialists to change the criminal law permanently stems from the inherent shortcomings of the attempt to understand human nature and the human predicament exclusively in scientific categories.[60]

Johnson draws this conclusion from the whole episode: "Man may be born in sin, but he has the capacity to know good from evil and to choose the good."[61] This is the Christian view that humans are morally accountable agents.

ADDRESSING ENVIRONMENTAL INFLUENCE DEFENSES FROM A CHRISTIAN PERSPECTIVE

Cases involving environmental influence defenses are difficult to resolve. Often, there is no question that the defendant has confronted tremendous challenges that seem relevant to their actions. But do those challenges absolve the defendant of all responsibility for his actions? Should he be acquitted? This section examines both Scripture and an insightful decision from a common-law court to answer these questions in light of a biblical view of human nature.

SCRIPTURE ON ENVIRONMENTAL CAUSES OF WRONGDOING

How does Scripture counsel us to address environmental influence defenses? We should begin with compassion for individuals confronting difficult circumstances posed by their environment or genetic makeup. Our environment *can* influence our behavior. This is one of the consequences of living in a fallen world. As 1 Corinthians 15:33 warns, "Do not be deceived: 'Bad company ruins good morals.'" Similarly, Proverbs tells us, "Make no friendship with a man given to anger, nor go with a wrathful man, lest you learn his ways and entangle yourself in a snare" (Prov 22:24–25).

A prayer from Proverbs further highlights the danger that our environment can pose to our behavior, including influencing us to commit crime:

> Two things I ask of you;
>   deny them not to me before I die:

Remove far from me falsehood and lying;
>   give me neither poverty nor riches;
feed me with the food that is needful for me,
>   lest I be full and deny you
>   and say, "Who is the Lord?"
>   or lest I be poor and steal
>   and profane the name of my God. (Prov 30:7–9)

Felicia Morgan and others like her are unquestionably influenced by the violence all around them. Christians should work and pray for change in the environment around us. We should be the first to bring hope, healing, and changed circumstances to those who desperately need them.

That said, while environmental factors *influence* our behavior, we must affirm that such factors do not *cause* it. Sin and criminal behavior are not the inevitable result of our genetic makeup or the environment in which we live. Sin comes from within, from our very nature. Jesus said this to his disciples: "What comes out of a person is what defiles him. For from within, out of the heart of man, come evil thoughts, sexual immorality, theft, murder, adultery, coveting, wickedness, deceit, sensuality, envy, slander, pride, foolishness" (Mark 7:20–22).

Determinism is wrong and incompatible with a biblical view of human nature. Rage, malice, and anger are not inevitable. Scripture warns us to "put away" those things, even though our sinful nature inclines us to do them (Eph 4:31; see also Col 3:5–14). Further, as chapter 2 notes, Scripture describes humans as morally responsible agents. Immediately after Paul tells us that bad company ruins good morals, he urges: "Wake up from your drunken stupor, as is right, and do not go on sinning" (1 Cor 15:34). While we face internal and external pressures to sin, we are held responsible to resist them.

The narrative of the fall in Genesis 3 highlights this dual reality of environmental pressures to do wrong and our moral accountability to resist those pressures. Both Adam and Eve tried to excuse their sin by blaming someone else. Adam blamed Eve and God; Eve blamed the serpent. God held them each responsible for their own choice.

The very next chapter powerfully reflects God's view of human accountability. God confronts an angry Cain, knowing the strong pressure that Cain felt to harm his brother Abel, saying: "Why are you angry, and why has your face fallen? If you do well, will you not be accepted? And if you do not do well, sin is crouching at the door. Its desire is contrary to you, but you must rule over it" (Gen 4:6–7).

Jesus, too, understood that external pressures can make proper decision-making difficult. He acknowledged that it is harder for a camel to go through the eye of a needle than for a rich man to enter the kingdom of heaven. Nonetheless, he held the rich young ruler accountable for his refusal to sell all he had and to follow Jesus (Matt 19:16–26).

Just as God holds humans accountable for their moral choices, despite difficult circumstances and environmental pressures, it is appropriate for civil government to hold humans accountable for their actions despite similar circumstances and pressures (Rom 13:1–7).

QUEEN V. DUDLEY AND STEPHENS: A MODEL FOR APPROACHING ENVIRONMENTAL INFLUENCE DEFENSES

We gain helpful guidance for applying these principles—and a proper view of human nature—to law from the nineteenth-century case of Queen v. Dudley and Stephens (1884).[62] The facts of the case are compelling and chilling. The case involved four men whose yacht sank in the Atlantic Ocean and who were forced to survive for weeks on a lifeboat. They began with only two pounds of turnips for food. On the fourth day on the lifeboat, they were able to catch a small turtle. They ate turnips and the turtle until the twelfth day.

By the twentieth day they had been eight days without food and seven days without substantial water. Two of the men, Thomas Dudley and Edwin Stephens, decided that the only way to survive was to kill one of the crew members and to eat his flesh and drink his blood. They decided that the appropriate victim was eighteen-year-old Richard Parker, who was severely weakened after having drunk seawater. Dudley and Stephens invited a fourth crew member, Ned Brooks, to join them in killing Parker, but he refused. Dudley prayed for forgiveness and then slit Parker's throat with a knife. The three remaining survivors fed upon Parker's flesh and blood for four days, after which they were rescued.[63]

Dudley and Stephens were charged with Parker's murder. They did not deny killing Parker. They claimed, however, that they should not be convicted because they had acted out of necessity. The extreme circumstances they confronted justified killing Parker in order to save the lives of the remaining three.[64]

The Court of Queen's Bench rejected this defense and convicted Dudley and Stephens of murder. Chief Justice Lord Coleridge wrote the opinion and made several key points that are instructive as we evaluate environmental influence defenses today.

First, the court did not ignore or underestimate the terrible temptation that Dudley and Stephens faced while trying to survive in the lifeboat. It acknowledged, "The prisoners were subject to terrible temptation and to sufferings which might break down the bodily power of the strongest man, and try the conscience of the best."[65] Throughout, the opinion used a sympathetic tone that reflected understanding of the very difficult circumstances the defendants faced.

Second, the court canvassed prior precedents and found no legal support for the proposition that it is acceptable to kill an innocent person in order to save one's own life.

Third, the court refused to soften the law of murder in England in light of the trying circumstances of this difficult case. It did so largely based on a full-orbed view of human nature. For one thing, the court treated Dudley and Stevens as morally responsible agents. Yes, they faced a terrible temptation to kill. But they were deemed responsible to overcome that temptation:

> The temptation to the act which existed here was not what the law has ever called necessity. Nor is this to be regretted. Though law and morality are not the same, and though many things may be immoral which are not necessarily illegal, the absolute divorce of law from morality would be of fatal consequence; and such divorce would follow if the temptation to murder in this case were to be held by law an absolute defence of it.[66]

The court continued:

> We are often compelled to set up standards we cannot reach ourselves, and to lay down rules which we could not ourselves satisfy. But a man has no right to declare temptation to be an excuse, though he might himself have yielded to it, nor to allow compassion for the criminal to change or weaken in any manner the legal definition of the crime.[67]

The court cited Jesus, the "Great Example," who sacrificed his life for others, though he had the power to save it.[68]

The court also reflected its biblical understanding of human nature by affirming that all humans are made in the image of God. The court refused to sanction the decision to kill Richard Parker on the basis that he was the weakest survivor. All human life is valuable—even "the weakest, the youngest, the most unresisting."[69]

The court also recognized the fallenness of human nature in two ways. First, it refused to trust Dudley and Stephens—or any other individual—to determine their own necessity. Rejecting the necessity defense, the court asked: "Who is to be the judge of this sort of necessity? By what measure is the comparative value of lives to be measured? Is it to be strength, or intellect, or what? It is plain that the principle leaves to him who is to profit by it to determine the necessity which will justify him in deliberately taking another's life to save his own."[70] Such a determination cannot be trusted to sinful human beings.

The court's understanding of the fallenness of humans did not stop there. Just as fallen individuals cannot be trusted to judge their own necessity, fallen judges cannot be trusted in hard cases to change the law. The court refused to alter the law of murder or the defense of necessity in order to show mercy in this very difficult case. In a powerful example of judicial restraint, the court asserted:

> There is no safe path for judges to tread but to ascertain the law to the best of their ability, and to declare it according to their judgment; and if in any case the law appears to be too severe on individuals, to leave it to the Sovereign to exercise that prerogative of mercy which the Constitution has intrusted to the hands fittest to dispense it.[71]

In the end, the court held Dudley and Stevens to a high standard of accountability. It ruled that they should have resisted the severe temptation that confronted them and respected the value of all human life, even that of the weakest. The court sentenced Dudley and Stevens to death.[72]

Ultimately, as the court had suggested, mercy did come from the queen. Acknowledging the difficult circumstances that they had faced, Queen Victoria commuted their sentence to six months imprisonment without hard labor.[73]

In the end, *Queen v. Dudley and Stephens* articulates a wise, principled approach to environmental influence defenses. It sets a high standard for behavior. It holds individuals—even those facing trying circumstances—to be morally accountable agents. It embraces a biblical view of human nature. And it holds out hope that, in difficult cases, mercy can be shown in sentencing or through executive action.

APPLYING A RIGHT UNDERSTANDING OF HUMAN
NATURE TO ENVIRONMENTAL INFLUENCE DEFENSES

In the end, how should courts respond to environmental influence defenses asserted in insanity, self-defense, or other cases? Here are some suggested guidelines.

First, courts should permit environmental influence defenses to be raised where the environmental or genetic factor caused the defendant to lack the intention required for the crime or a basic understanding of what he or she was doing. The *Phipps* case—of the Gulf War veteran who killed his wife's lover—seems rightly decided, assuming that the evidence truly supports the conclusion that the defendant lacked the *mens rea* for the crime. Individuals should not be held criminally culpable without a guilty mind and a guilty act. Similarly, defendants should be permitted to offer an environmental influence defense if it demonstrates that they suffered from a mental disease or defect and did not know the nature and quality of their action or that what they did was wrong, the traditional test for insanity.

Second, courts should refuse to allow environmental influence defenses to excuse criminal responsibility where defendants knew what they were doing and knew that it was wrong, but claimed lack of control over their actions. In a fallen world, all of us have certain predispositions toward wrongdoing—addiction, alcohol abuse, gluttony, anger, worry, or lust. This does not mean that we are compelled to act on those predispositions.

Accordingly, it was right to turn away from the volition-based insanity test in the late 20th century. It was right of the judge to disallow testimony of Felicia Morgan's difficult upbringing during the guilt phase of her trial. Yes, she was influenced by her environment. But she was not compelled to steal and kill. She knew what she was doing and knew that it was wrong.

In the aftermath of her sister's killing, Brenda Adams's sister Yolanda made an important point about environmental influence and causation:

Although [Morgan] comes from a deprived environment, so did I. So did I, and so did Brenda. Our lives were not a bed of roses, we came from a dysfunctional family, [but] you have a choice. You can either emulate your environment or something better. It's difficult, it's very difficult, but you have a choice. Everyone in society has a choice.[74]

Adams is right. Morgan was not predetermined by environmental factors to kill Brenda Adams. Others from her very difficult and violent neighborhood were exposed to violence and deprivation. But they elected not to make Morgan's violent choice.

The same principle applies to the very difficult circumstance of the teacher with the brain tumor who developed a sexual interest in children. Undoubtedly the tumor had an influence on his decision-making. But that does not excuse his behavior. As law professor Stephen Morse notes: "People want to say his tumor made him do it. *He* made him do it. There is always a reason people do it. We don't give a pass to the other pedophiles. He felt an urge, which he understood and did not resist, but acted on it."[75]

Like Dudley and Stephens, many people face terrible temptation to do wrong. That temptation may come from a difficult background; it may come from a powerful cultural influence; it may reflect a genetic predisposition. But people who know right from wrong are morally accountable to choose to do right.

Third, courts should resist their own temptation to change legal standards to deal with these very difficult cases. The court in *Dudley and Stephens* was exactly right on this point. It is a dangerous game to change the law in order to show mercy in difficult cases.

In particular, we should be wary of decisions that change the legal standard for self-defense (removing the imminence requirement) and excuse willful killing, including in cases involving battered woman syndrome. These cases are difficult. Often they involve women who have suffered severe abuse for many years. There are many reasons why they may feel they cannot leave the home and that killing is their only way out. But the law should encourage them to do the right thing. The law should encourage them to go to the police, seek protection for themselves and their children, and to have their abuser prosecuted. In a fallen world, it is too easy to manipulate a standard like that used in too many battered woman syndrome cases. Who was right, for example, in the *Sheehan* case? Did Sheehan kill because she had no way out? Or did she use the law to carry out a self-serving killing? It is impossible to know the human heart.

This does not mean that evidence of battered woman syndrome should never be used. It is appropriate to introduce such evidence (if supported by the facts and by medical science) in cases like *New Jersey v. Kelly*, where the legal standard is not being changed.

Fourth, the circumstances of the environmental influence defense cases should be considered in the sentencing process. The central function of sentencing is to impose a deserved sanction on defendants based on their level of culpability. It may be appropriate in some of the most difficult environmental defense cases to mitigate punishment to reflect the extreme difficulty the criminal faced when confronted with temptation to do wrong.

It was right for the court to convict Felicia Morgan. She was responsible for her actions. That said, it was also appropriate for the court to take into account Morgan's brutal upbringing when deciding on a just sentence. Her past is relevant when examining desert; the same principle applies to the teacher with the brain tumor.

We must be careful here. It is possible to lower the punishment so far that it actually undermines the defendant's responsibility. The punishment imposed must be within the range of punishments viewed as proportionate to the severity of the offense. But an appropriate lowering of the penalty can reflect society's acknowledgment that we understand the tremendous temptation and difficulty the defendant faced.

There is one other means of showing mercy, too. As in *Dudley and Stephens*, executive clemency can provide another forum for

showing mercy while not changing the criminal law or the legal
bar of responsibility.

CONCLUSION

Cases involving environmental influence defenses are very difficult. In considering them, we must also treat individuals as morally responsible agents. In doing so, we affirm their dignity and
worth as image-bearers of God. They are not patients or cases.
They are not the product of forces beyond their control. And yet
we must demonstrate compassion and understanding for the challenging circumstances individuals face. By appropriately considering such environmental factors in sentencing, we show that we
understand that our world is fallen.

CHAPTER 10:
CHRISTIAN UTOPIANISM

What is the most realistic and effective way to accomplish change?

Of all tyrannies a tyranny sincerely exercised for the good of its victims may be the most oppressive. It may be better to live under robber barons than under omnipotent moral busybodies.

–C. S. LEWIS[1]

Fifteen thousand people gathered in a meeting hall in Norfolk, Virginia, to hear the great evangelist Billy Sunday. The date was January 16, 1920—the day Prohibition took effect across the United States. The event was a mock funeral for John Barleycorn, the fictional personification of liquor. Twenty pallbearers had carried a twenty-foot-long coffin through the streets. Sunday stood to give the eulogy:

> John Barleycorn, we bury you because you destroyed our health; you disfigured our bodies; you ruined our nervous system. You dethroned our reason; you caused idiocy and insanity; you destroyed every principle of manhood and womanhood; you squandered our property; you produced pauperism; you crowded our poor-houses, and jails, and penitentiaries. You corrupted our courts. You defied our laws; you destroyed both soul and body; you darkened our homes; you broke our hearts; you beggared our wives and

children and led men to commit every conceivable crime;
you paralyzed every noble ambition; you dried up the foun-
tains of human affection.[2]

Sunday closed his eulogy in memorable fashion: "Farewell,
you good-for-nothing, God-forsaken, iniquitous, blear-eyed [sic],
bloat-faced, old imp of perdition."[3] He then grabbed an American
flag and climbed on top of the pulpit. He waved the flag back and
forth as the crowd burst forth into the doxology.

BILLY SUNDAY

Billy Sunday (1862–1935) was one of the most popular evangelists in
the late nineteenth and early twentieth centuries. Sunday spent eight
years as a major league baseball player, playing center field for the
Chicago White Stockings, Pittsburgh Pirates, and Philadelphia Athletics.

During his career, he converted to Christianity at Chicago's Pacific
Garden Mission and felt that God was calling him to be an evangelist. He quickly became one of America's leading evangelists and was
known for his plainspoken and animated sermons. One contemporary
newspaper wrote of him: "Sunday was a whirling dervish that pranced
and cavorted and strode and bounded and pounded all over his plat-
form and left them thrilled and bewildered as they have never been
before."[4] During his career he preached to millions and saw an estimated 300,000 people profess faith in Jesus Christ.[5] Sunday addressed
the important social issues of his day, supporting women's suffrage,
child labor laws, and temperance.

It was a day of triumph for those, including many Christian
churches and organizations, who had campaigned tirelessly
against alcohol since the late 1800s. Sitting in the front rows
as Sunday spoke were two hundred members of the Woman's
Christian Temperance Union. Their effort had been rewarded

by ratification of the Eighteenth Amendment to the Constitution, which banned the manufacture, sale, or transportation of alcohol. It was a day of joy and celebration.

But nearby, across the Tidewater region of Virginia—and throughout the country—bootleggers fired up stills and began making and selling whiskey and moonshine. A long and costly battle waged between those seeking to enforce Prohibition and those hoping to evade it. The church engaged in this battle as well. The *Virginian-Pilot* tells the story of one skirmish in 1923, when the Virginia Beach "Purity Squad," made up of volunteers from London Bridge Baptist Church, engaged in a gun battle with bootleggers. Special Officer Allen Gimbert died during the fight.[6]

Three years later, Norfolk police and federal agents "exchanged machine gun fire with bootleggers aboard a 60-foot motorboat named the *Jimmie*":

> When the boat was captured, agents found sealed, 5-gallon bottles of corn liquor neatly stowed in the hold, 2,500 gallons in all, worth about $50,000, or more than half a million of today's dollars. Officers said the boat was responsible for supplying the greater part of the corn liquor consumed in Norfolk.[7]

Norfolk and its environs was not the only location where the enforcement battle raged; it certainly was not the epicenter. In Chicago, lawlessness and violence exploded as crime organizations seeking to control trade in illegal alcohol battled the police and each other. During his violent reign as mob boss, it is estimated that Al Capone's operations generated $100 million in revenue per year.[8] He was able to thrive in large part because he bought the cooperation of those who were supposed to enforce the law. "Everyone from prominent politicians to cops on the street took cuts in the profits made from trafficking alcohol during Prohibition. In Chicago, thousands of police and other officials were on the take, some of them getting over $1,000 a week."[9]

As months and years passed, Americans began questioning the wisdom of Prohibition and the failed efforts to enforce it. State and local governments lost millions of dollars in tax revenues. Crime grew and was increasingly "organized."[10] Billy Sunday had optimistically declared that with Prohibition, "We will turn our prisons into factories and our jails into storehouses and corncribs."[11] Instead, prison populations exploded as both alcohol-related and violent crimes rose.[12] While alcohol consumption dropped at first, it rose steadily throughout the rest of Prohibition.[13] Indeed, while beer drinking dropped during Prohibition, consumption of wine and hard liquor increased.[14] And the hard liquor produced was more dangerous, as home brewers abandoned traditional distilling techniques for quicker and cheaper methods that left dangerous toxins in the final product.[15] Deaths from poisoned liquor rose in the United States from 1,064 in 1920 to 4,154 in 1925.[16]

So it was that on December 5, 1933, less than fourteen years after Billy Sunday's triumphant eulogy, Prohibition itself was dead. On that day, Utah became the thirty-sixth and last state needed to ratify the Twenty-First Amendment to the Constitution, abolishing the ill-fated Eighteenth. The amendment took effect ten days later.

PROHIBITION

Prohibition was mandated by the Eighteenth Amendment to the United States Constitution. The Amendment was ratified on January 16, 1919, and declared that one year after its ratification "the manufacture, sale, or transportation of intoxicating liquors within, the importation thereof into, or the exportation thereof from the United States ... is hereby prohibited."[17] Prohibition ended with the ratification of the Twenty-First Amendment to the Constitution. In a sign of the great unpopularity of Prohibition, the Twenty-First Amendment was passed by Congress on February 20, 1933, and was ratified by the needed three-quarters of states within the year (on December 5, 1933).[18]

What went wrong? Why did the well-intentioned efforts of Sunday, the London Bridge Baptist Church, the Woman's Christian Temperance Union, and many others fail so miserably? These efforts failed to grapple fully with the reality of human nature, particularly the consequences of human sinfulness. They appropriately identified harmful social consequences from the abuse of alcohol, but they had a utopian—and unrealistic—vision that a change in laws would change both hearts and behavior. And they failed to account for unintended consequences that resulted from that legislative vision.

This concluding chapter serves as a cautionary note. Throughout this book, I have explored a number of pressing and controversial issues of law and policy. I have encouraged today's Christians to consider how they might approach these issues faithfully and meaningfully in light of a biblical view of human nature. I have at times suggested legal and policy reforms. The point of this chapter, however, is that we must pursue any legal and policy reforms—including those explored earlier in the book—with humility. Too often, we have our own utopian vision. Particularly for those trained in law or government, we think that if we just have the right laws—or the right party in power—we can make our community everything it should be. The point of this chapter is to say no, we can't, no matter how good our intentions.

When we look for legal and policy solutions to society's problems, good intentions are vital, as is a belief in the dignity and worth of every human being. So, too, however, is a recognition that the human heart is sinful. And reformers must take that heart into account when determining both goals and the means for achieving them.

In this as in every generation, when advocating for legal change we must be careful with our ends and careful with our means. We must fully grasp the implications of human fallenness. If we don't, we will fail, just like the well-intentioned advocates for Prohibition. Like them, we will be left with failed goals and unintended consequences.

HISTORY OF CHRISTIAN UTOPIANISM

Christians have a long history of utopian visions. Poet William Blake famously wrote:

> I will not cease from Mental Fight,
>> Nor shall my Sword sleep in my hand:
> Till we have built Jerusalem,
>> In England's green & pleasant Land.[19]

Few Christians talk so openly about seeing God's kingdom fully established on this earth, but the group that has come the closest in recent years is likely the Christian Reconstructionists, who argue that the Old Testament sets forth God's unchanging laws to be applied to both the church and society as a whole. They believe that through the power of the Holy Spirit and faithful application of the dominion mandate of Genesis 1:28 ("Be fruitful and multiply and fill the earth and subdue it"), God's people will increasingly extend his authority over the earth using his law. While the Christian Reconstructionists gained some prominence in the 1970s and '80s through the works of R. J. Rushdoony, Greg Bahnsen, and Gary North, they have decreased in influence today.[20]

Still, the recent past is replete with slightly more modest—yet still utopian—visions. Some argue that with the right laws, we can Christianize America. Ralph Reed, Christian political strategist and first executive director of the Christian Coalition, declared that the Christian mission must be "to take back this country, one precinct at a time, one neighborhood at a time, one state at a time."[21] Jerry Falwell, the late founder of Liberty University and Thomas Road Baptist Church, similarly asserted: "Modern U.S. Supreme Courts have raped the Constitution ... and raped the churches by misinterpreting what the founders had in mind in the First Amendment. ... We must take back what is rightfully ours."[22] Even more explicitly, Randall Terry, founder of the pro-life organization Operation Rescue, urged: "I want you to let a wave of intolerance wash over you. I want you to let a wave of hatred wash over you. Yes, hate is good. ... We have a biblical duty, we are called by God, to conquer this country."[23]

History reveals more than just utopian visions; it is filled as well with examples of the church attempting to micromanage moral behavior through legislation and government enforcement. Such political overreach was not a temptation for the early church. Politically powerless and often persecuted, the church's key questions were how to submit to governing rulers (see Rom 13:1-7; 1 Pet 2:13-17) and how to confront unjust government mandates (see Acts 5:29; "We must obey God rather than men").

Things changed dramatically, though, when the Roman Emperor Constantine came to faith, setting off events that would transform Christianity from an outlawed religion to the official faith of the Roman Empire. The change brought both freedom and blessing. It also brought temptation: temptation to operate through power rather than service to others; temptation to use power and influence to bring about a utopian earthly vision; temptation to remedy every social—and often spiritual—ill through legislation.

CONSTANTINE

Constantine was a Roman emperor who reigned AD 306-337, first over the western half of the Roman Empire and eventually over the whole empire. He is known to history as Constantine the Great and was an innovative and influential emperor.

Significantly, Constantine converted to Christianity and in AD 313 issued the Edict of Milan, which mandated tolerance of Christianity within the Roman Empire. He also called for the First Council of Nicaea in AD 325, which resulted in the adoption of the Nicene Creed. While

Constantine mandated the tolerance of Christianity throughout the Roman Empire, Christianity did not become the official religion of the empire until the time of Theodosius I, who reigned AD 379–395.

One of the clearest examples of this is the church's use of state power to punish heresy. Especially during the medieval period, most famously through the Inquisition in France, Italy, and Spain, the church tried to keep doctrine and belief pure in part by turning to the state to imprison and even execute heretics. It sometimes resorted to torture to gain evidence in heresy proceedings.[24] For centuries, the church illustrated the truth of biblical scholar F. F. Bruce's claim that "where church leaders were able to exercise political as well as spiritual authority, they did not enjoy any marked immunity from the universally corrupting tendency of power."[25]

John Warwick Montgomery tells the story of how church and state sought to control ideas and belief through witch trials in the fifteenth, sixteenth, and seventeenth centuries. He noted that prosecutions for witchcraft often had nothing to do with the defendant's actions; they were usually solely based on his or her beliefs. Montgomery concluded that "the witch trial courts frequently obliterated the distinction between sin and crime and set themselves to the work of a miniature last judgment—but without benefit of divine omniscience."[26] Montgomery did not view such witch trials as isolated events. He asserted that "evangelicals have a long and sorry history of pushing for the legal enforcement of morals. (Local option campaigns, Sunday closing laws, and the like.)"[27]

Indeed, there are more recent examples of the church seeking to micromanage moral behavior through legislation. A good example is the effort to ban gambling in the United States. Despite gambling's popularity, there is much evidence of the significant social harm it causes: addiction, crime, bankruptcies, domestic violence, child neglect and abuse, and even suicide.[28] Professors Daniel Skeel and William Stuntz tell the story of how Christians, rightly motivated by a desire to address these harms, have opposed gambling and "have treated legal prohibition as the principal tool in the cultural debate on that subject."[29] They give a bleak assessment of the results:

> Judging by the last century of criminal enforcement, gambling's religious opponents may have bet on the wrong horse. At least since the early twentieth century, federal and state criminal codes have banned most forms of gambling. Those criminal prohibitions may have taught some Americans that gambling is wrong, but they seem to have taught millions of others to ignore the law's commands. Far from disappearing in the face of such proscriptions, gambling simply went underground. Bookmakers and numbers rackets took the place of casinos and legal lotteries. Gambling was too ubiquitous for the government to punish across the board, so the line between what was forbidden and what was tolerated was a matter of prosecutors' discretion.[30]

Despite all the efforts of the opposition, gambling has thrived. In 1996, Congress appointed a diverse, bipartisan National Gambling Impact Study Commission to "conduct a comprehensive legal and factual study of the social and economic implications of gambling in the United States."[31] The commission found that the gambling industry had grown tenfold since a previous federal commission had studied gambling in 1975. Total gambling losses (dollars wagered minus payouts) was $50 billion in 1997.[32] That was more than 10 percent of all spending on leisure goods, services, and activities.[33] By 2016, it was estimated that gambling losses totaled $117 billion.[34]

While efforts to micromanage moral behavior through legislation are often associated with political conservatism, this temptation does not just reach people on the Right. It affects the Left, too. A recent example is the effort to reform corporate ethics through increasingly tough and detailed securities laws. Christians again were highly involved in this effort. Skeel and Stuntz note, "The world of corporate finance tends to prompt a moralism of the left, with politically liberal Christians seeking to enforce God's law in corporate boardrooms."[35]

Unquestionably, the first few years of this millennium saw some colossal ethical failures that resulted in tremendous harm to industries and society. Enron, WorldCom, Tyco—the names alone declare a corporate culture of extravagance, deception, and abuse. Congress responded to these scandals by passing the Sarbanes-Oxley Act (2002). In addition to increasing the punishment for a number of existing crimes, the act created several new corporate crimes, essentially prohibiting the things Enron's executives did.[36] Then, 2008 saw the start of the global financial crisis when the collapse of the US real-estate market revealed questionable trading practices and undercapitalized financial institutions. Again, Congress acted to specify appropriate corporate conduct in the Dodd-Frank Act (2010).

Skeel and Stuntz, while understanding the motivation behind such legislation, believe the new laws are doomed to fail:

> The suggestion is that laws can be used as an instrument to teach the next generation of corporate executives how to behave and reshape corporate culture. ... When corporate regulation looks like the tax code, corporate executives respond like taxpayers. Given a list of dos and don'ts, many will find themselves thinking more about what they can get away with and less about what is honorable and right.[37]

ENRON

Enron was a Texas-based energy company that rose to prominence in the late 1990s and collapsed in bankruptcy and disgrace in 2001. From 1995 to 2000, *Fortune* named Enron as the most innovative company in America.[38] In 2001, however, it became clear that Enron's success was built on fraudulent accounting practices in which liabilities were transferred to wholly owned subsidiaries and off of Enron's accounts. After the scandal broke, its share prices fell to $0.67 in January 2002 from their high of $90.75 in August 2000.[39] Enron declared bankruptcy in December 2001. Several Enron officials—including regular church-goer and lay leader Ken Lay—were convicted of fraud and conspiracy.[40] The scandal also resulted in the bankruptcy of Enron's accounting firm, Arthur Andersen. In the wake of the Enron scandal—and similar corporate scandals involving Tyco and Worldcom—Congress passed the Sarbanes-Oxley Act of 2002 in an effort to prohibit fraudulent business practices of the type used by Enron.

FATAL FLAWS OF LEGISLATIVE OVERREACH

Every one of these efforts to enforce moral behavior through detailed legislation has had the right motivations. The harms caused by abuse of alcohol, gambling, and corporate ethical breaches are real and significant. But if this is the case, then why do such efforts so often fail? In short, they fail to take into account human fallenness. Because of this failure to account for fallenness, these efforts to legislate moral behavior amount to legislative over-reach—relying on laws to serve a function they are not capable of serving. Such efforts suffer from four fatal flaws.

FLAW 1: THE FALLENNESS OF LEGISLATORS AND LAW ENFORCERS

First, legislative efforts to micromanage moral behavior fail to acknowledge the fallenness of those who create and enforce the law. We regularly see behavior that we know to be wrong, and we want to stop it. But as fallen human beings ourselves, we often fail utterly in our attempts to regulate or outlaw that behavior.

History and experience show us there are many obstacles when attempting to draft moral legislation. We start with a hermeneutical problem: It is not always simple to know how a principle from God's law should faithfully be applied to modern American culture. Do principles of behavior designed for God's people (whether Israel or the church) apply to a polity with both believers and unbelievers? If so, how? In addition, should the practical application of that principle be different in an industrialized liberal democracy as opposed to an agrarian theocracy?

Further, the legislative process itself poses grave dangers. Our drafting efforts too frequently produce laws that are overly vague or overly prescriptive. The exponential growth of laws and regulations today suggests we frequently succumb to the temptation to over-prescribe behavior. In establishing punishments, we struggle to find a level that is neither too harsh nor too lenient and that produces proper incentives. In any legislative process, there is a danger of decisions that reflect political expediency—or even self-interest—rather than wise application of principle. And there are unintended consequences from any legislative effort. In a fallen world, these things are inevitable; even our best intentions cannot guard against them entirely.

Human fallenness has a huge impact on our ability to appropriately enforce laws as well. The very best law can fail if we lack resources to enforce it or put too much discretion into the hands of prosecutors or the police. Skeel and Stuntz illustrate this point with an example from the effort to ban gambling. They relate that, confronted with limited resources, police and prosecutors chose to focus on gambling that was popular among the lower classes, like numbers games, as opposed to more sophisticated forms of gambling run by bookies and upper-class clients. This selective enforcement "made sense as a way to get the biggest bang for the buck. The bang turned out not to be as big as it seemed: the perception that gambling was a crime if you lived in the wrong neighborhood bred contempt for the laws that did the criminalizing.

In turn, this contempt eroded the very moral principles on which the prohibition was based."[41] In spite of good intentions, unequal enforcement actually promoted greater lawlessness.

The lesson is that any attempt to legislate must take into account human sinfulness. Sin affects legislators, police, and prosecutors. Joel Belz concluded: "Our very fallenness as human beings makes it impossible for us first to adopt, and then to administer, even something so simple as God's good laws."[42]

FLAW 2: THE FALLENNESS OF CITIZENS

Legislative efforts to micromanage moral behavior fail for a second reason: the fallenness of those subject to the law. When passing laws, we have great expectations. We think—or at least hope—that the right laws can shape right behavior, and maybe even right attitudes.[43] Sometimes they do. Some would argue that the laws passed during the civil rights movement changed both behavior and, ultimately, attitudes about race in the United States.

Often, though, legislation has the opposite effect. Prohibition is a good example. People invested incredible amounts of time, energy, and resources into efforts to evade the law. Alcohol use did not disappear; it went underground, and around it sprang up an extensive and powerful criminal industry. This in turn required an extensive—and expensive—law enforcement effort. Driving criminal behavior underground does not change people's hearts; consumption of wine and hard liquor actually increased during Prohibition.

Gambling, too, has grown tremendously, with many more participants and many more states deciding to accept the practice and benefit from the resulting tax revenue. The National Gambling Impact Study Commission, after bluntly identifying numerous harms resulting from gambling, concluded, "It is clear that the American people want legalized gambling, and it has already sunk deep economic roots in many communities. Its form and extent may change, but gambling is here to stay."[44]

A similar phenomenon has occurred with numerous other efforts to regulate behavior through detailed codes of permitted and prohibited conduct. Skeel and Stuntz explain the likely consequences in terms that any parent or child can understand:

> Given a choice between saying "don't hurt your sister" and "here is a list of fifteen ways you might hurt your sister—don't do any of these," wise parents opt for the first approach. Most children, when they are presented with a list of fifteen things not to do, will quickly come up with a sixteenth that is not on the list. Detailed codes that try to define misconduct comprehensively tend to produce the same reaction. Complying with the law becomes an exercise in ticket-punching, following mechanical legal formulae. Regulated actors exercise their creativity by looking for ways to evade legal norms—like taxpayers filling out their tax forms every April 15, trying all the while to hold on to every penny they can.[45]

When they wrote these words in 2006, Skeel and Stuntz projected that the same phenomenon would occur among executives with the new corporate reforms. One might argue that the new and creative risks taken by executives in the financial industry, bringing about the 2007-2008 financial crisis, proved them right.

The goal of seeing changed actions, hearts, and minds is noble. But as Christians, we should know that legislation is often not the best way to accomplish it. Belz notes, "In its best form, it happens by God's Spirit working in people's hearts; it is therefore literally a 'spiritual' work—not accomplished by a heavy-handed state, but by God himself remaking and reshaping the inclination of our desires. It's a profound and magnificent piece of work—something no kingdom or state can ever hope to accomplish with any set of codes."[46] When possible, the church is better off promoting individual and societal change through spiritual, not legislative, means. Often the church will accomplish more through teaching and, especially, example rather than through laws. Though I teach in a law school and know how crucial good legislation and law enforcement are to a just and prosperous society, I recognize that law is usually a better follower than leader. Most often, legal change follows and reinforces cultural change rather than leading the way to it.

FLAW 3: A MISUNDERSTANDING
OF GOVERNMENT'S ROLE

Legislative efforts to micromanage moral behavior, at a deeper level, reflect a misunderstanding of the proper role of government. Recall John Warwick Montgomery's statement that witch trials "obliterated the difference between sin and crime." There is a difference, and it has historically been very important—just because something is a moral wrong does not mean we should outlaw it. God's law and human law are not the same. As Thomas Aquinas famously asserted, "Human laws do not forbid all vices, from which the virtuous abstain, but only the more grievous vices, from which it is possible for the majority to abstain; and chiefly those that are to the hurt of others, without the prohibition of which human society could not be maintained: thus human law prohibits murder, theft and such like."[47]

THOMAS AQUINAS

Thomas Aquinas (1225-1274) was a thirteenth-century theologian and philosopher. He was a prolific thinker and writer whose writings continue to have a profound effect on theology, philosophy, and law. Aquinas's best-known work is his *Summa Theologica*, a summary of Christian doctrine. In it, he laid out a theory of natural law that asserts that God created all human beings with a natural inclination to do good and follow the moral law of God. While he believed that the natural law was imprinted in the hearts of all people, he did not believe that human governments should enforce every aspect of the natural law as part of human law.

We see the difference between sin and crime, for example, in the fact that human law punishes murder, but not anger. This is the case despite Jesus' injunction in the Sermon on the Mount: "You have heard that it was said to those of old, 'You shall not murder; and whoever murders will be liable to judgment.' But I say to you that anyone who is angry with his brother will be liable to judgment" (Matt 5:21–22). Human law punishes theft, but not coveting. This is so even though James says: "What causes quarrels and what causes fights among you? Is it not this, that your passions are at war within you? You desire and do not have, so you murder. You covet and cannot obtain, so you fight and quarrel. You do not have, because you do not ask" (Jas 4:1–2).

Coveting and unrighteous anger are moral wrongs, and humans will be judged for both—but by God, not their fellow humans. Why shouldn't human law punish those offenses, too? In part, human enforcement of sins like this would be very difficult. Humans are particularly bad at assessing thoughts, at least when unaccompanied by actions. At a more fundamental level, God has not delegated to human governments the duty to judge and punish all sin. Government does not have complete power; it is "God's servant" (Rom 13:4). Some things are delegated to Caesar; some are not (Matt 22:21). Despite the urgency we sometimes feel, we are not needed to solve every moral problem. It is not for us to right every wrong. "God is still in His heaven, and the evils we are powerless to correct in accord with His Word He will most assuredly remedy on the last day."[48]

When we disregard this appropriate principle of restraint, we display pride and idolatry.[49] We think we can handle God's role. We can identify and root out sin. We can change attitudes and actions.

We can shape culture into our vision of utopia. "Man wants to carry out God's functions; he wants to build new towers of Babel to reach heaven. Not satisfied with the areas of civil and legal control given to him ('subdue the earth'—Gen. 1:28), man tries also to subdue hell."[50] Further, utopian legislative overreach causes us to look to human beings—and human law—instead of to God for our direction and moral compass. My colleague Louis Hensler puts it well:

> Excessive human law [causes] people to look to their fellow man for good. ... Humans have a natural, sinful tendency to look to each other for authoritative leadership to speak in the place of God and to tell us what is right and wrong. Thus, exalting the authority of mere man is idolatry; it places the state in the place of God. The believer has the Scriptures and the Holy Spirit. These are enough to guide the believer into all Truth. We do not need the fallible state to supplement what God has given us directly.[51]

FLAW 4: DESTRUCTIVENESS TO THE CHURCH

Finally, legislative attempts to micromanage moral behavior can actually be destructive to the church. They can distract and divert the church from its core mission to "go therefore and make disciples of all nations, baptizing them in the name of the Father and of the Son and of the Holy Spirit, teaching them to observe all that I have commanded you" (Matt 28:19-20). It is possible for the church to be so dedicated to legislative and policy efforts that it loses focus on the core mission of making disciples.

This is not a call for Christians to abandon the public sphere. Scripture makes clear that we are called to engage and impact culture. We are described as Christ's ambassadors, salt, and light (2 Cor 5:20; Matt 5:13-14). These can be powerful agents for cultural influence. Indeed, God calls some to be involved in legal and political change. Government officials are God's servants called to bear the sword and do good (Rom 13:1–7). We are told, "Open your mouth for the mute, for the rights of all who are destitute. Open your mouth, judge righteously, defend the rights of the poor and needy" (Prov 31:8–9). We are to "rescue those who are being taken away to death; hold back those who are stumbling to the slaughter" (Prov 24:11).

Scripture and history are filled with examples of God's people influencing law and society for good. God called Joseph, Daniel, Esther, and Nehemiah to serve him in important governmental roles and used them to shape policies and protect lives in their pagan nations. Christians in the Roman Empire promoted the value of life by calling for the end to deadly games in the Colosseum, and in the United States they led the fight to abolish slavery and the discriminatory laws of the Jim Crow South. One of the great heroes of the faith is William Wilberforce, who in the late eighteenth and nineteenth centuries fought tirelessly, and ultimately successfully, to end the slave trade in the British Empire. The previous chapters in this book have explored many areas where Christians can and should seek legal and political change. The next section of this chapter will articulate some principles for wise and appropriate involvement in legal reform efforts.

No, we must not withdraw from cultural engagement. But we must engage with prudence. We must pick battles that are the most strategic, where we can have the greatest impact and best avoid the dangers described in this chapter. We must avoid thinking that we can change the moral fabric of society primarily through legislation. Scripture gives no hope for an earthly utopia. While we are meant to be salt and light, we are also aliens in a strange land. We must not expect perfection in this life. Jesus warned that wheat and tares will grow together until the end of the age (Matt 13:24–30). He resisted the Zealots and others seeking to establish a political kingdom. His kingdom was and is a spiritual kingdom, albeit one with a powerful impact on society.

This realization allows us to pursue our core mission and engage our culture in a holistic way, not focused exclusively on effecting political change. "So long as we act as though all of life revolved on the axis of law and politics, we restrict the arena in which God makes himself known. When we say we'll carry his cause into the fields of education, art, entertainment, music, and everything else, the battle gets interesting indeed."[52] When we focus our efforts on our core mission and avoid the temptation to create a Christian utopia, the church can speak into our culture with moral authority and not just as one more special interest group.

LEGAL AND POLICY IMPLICATIONS

Throughout this book, I have maintained that there are fruitful and appropriate areas for Christian involvement in legislative efforts. As this chapter has shown, however, we must be careful. We have not been called to implement Christ's kingdom legislatively; in fact, legislation is often not the best or even an appropriate tool. There are grave dangers in trying to legislate too much. Thomas Aquinas was right: we should neither proscribe all vices nor prescribe all virtues.

So how do we know when Christians should seek to use the law to prohibit a moral wrong or compel a moral duty? The following thoughts may be useful as guiding principles.

COUNTING THE COST OF LEGISLATING HUMAN ACTION

First, we must be appropriately wary of government's ability to get legislation right and to enforce it properly. No piece of legislation will work like the model we have in our minds. Like the tax code or corporate securities regulation, we may end up with a law that is excessively detailed and overly complicated. It may prompt those subject to it to try to evade it. They may spend more time, energy, and money looking for loopholes than in trying to comply with the law.

Further, before enacting a law, we must carefully consider how it will be enforced. Are there adequate enforcement resources? Is the enforcement likely to be highly selective, leaving too much discretion to police and prosecutors? Prohibition and gambling are good examples of well-intentioned legislative efforts that inevitably resulted in selective enforcement. This is fertile soil for corruption and the fallen nature of government officials to thrive.

When legislating, we must count the cost ahead of time. No law will look exactly as we intend it; no law will work exactly as we hope. We must try to envision likely consequences and know that there will be others that we can't foresee. This should help us decide whether to legislate and, if so, how.

MAKING CONCESSIONS FOR SINFUL HUMAN NATURE

Second, we must acknowledge the sinful human nature of those who will be subject to the proposed law. This may sound odd or even inappropriate, but Jesus gives us a biblical example of this principle in Matthew 19:1–9. In one of their efforts to trap Jesus, the Pharisees asked him, "Is it lawful to divorce one's wife for any cause?" (Matt 19:3). Jesus responded by affirming God's perfect, higher law: marriage should be a perfect uniting of man and woman. "So they are no longer two but one flesh. What therefore God has joined together, let not man separate" (Matt 19:5–6). They should not divorce.

The Pharisees immediately pointed to the difference between Jesus' statement and the law that had been given to Israel through Moses. The Mosaic law allowed divorce in certain circumstances. Jesus' response is telling: "Moses permitted you to divorce your wives because your hearts were hard. But it was not that way from the beginning. I tell you that anyone who divorces his wife, except for sexual immorality, and marries another woman commits adultery" (Matt 19:9 NIV).

God's perfect higher law is that marriage should last. Jesus cites adultery as the one appropriate exception. So why did God not give this perfect standard to his chosen people through the Mosaic law? He knew they could not comply with such a high standard. He made a concession to their sinful natures.

Thomas Aquinas, when considering principles to guide appropriate legislation, similarly noted that human law should only forbid the more grievous vices, "from which it is possible for the majority to abstain."[53] Why should we care if the majority can't comply with a particular law? Because laws that the majority can't reasonably comply with inevitably produce selective and uneven enforcement. Many citizens will quit trying to comply with the law—and perhaps other laws. In the end, the legislative effort may actually cause contempt for law and greater lawlessness.

How might this principle apply to twenty-first-century society? We know that God's law forbids sex outside of marriage. Should our criminal laws forbid fornication? Probably not. In our sex-saturated society, it is unlikely this law would have any meaningful effect in restricting sexual activity to marriage. More likely, it would cause contempt for the law and those seeking to enforce it. Similarly, efforts to ban gambling seem to have failed in either regulating conduct or changing hearts and minds. Despite all efforts to prohibit it, gambling has thrived. This may be an area where Christians must make a concession to human nature and scale back legislative efforts. Skeel and Stuntz, for example, suggest that we should focus our efforts on "more limited efforts that might command widespread support," such as criticizing "state governments' all-out efforts to promote their own lotteries."[54] The National Gambling Impact Study Commission similarly made legislative recommendations that, while more limited, might be more successful than an outright gambling ban.

LEGISLATING MORALITY WHEN ITS ABSENCE CAUSES DIRECT AND SIGNIFICANT HARM

Third, before prohibiting or regulating a moral wrong, we must carefully consider the impact of that wrong on others or on society in general. John Warwick Montgomery argued that government should not regulate beliefs or ideas and should legislate only "where provable harm to the body politic will arise in the absence of law."[55] Skeel and Stuntz suggest the following test:

> Identifying the most destructive wrongs, doing so in terms that allow for fair, accurate adjudication, matching the scope of the criminal code to the resources of the police forces and prosecutors' offices that must enforce it—these are achievable goals. They are also worthy goals: a society whose criminal law meets these objectives is likely to have a criminal justice system that controls crime and does justice.[56]

Legislators should consider the magnitude of harm from a moral wrong, its immediacy, directness, and breadth. Of course, every sin is harmful; it violates God's perfect law and causes harm to the sinner and others. Coveting causes ingratitude and dissatisfaction with God and others, and it may lead to broken relationships and ultimately stealing or even violence. But that does not mean that we should or could ban it. But we can and should ban stealing and violence, which have immediate and significant effects on individuals and on society's ability to function. The pervasive use of profanity and sexual themes on television is unquestionably destructive, but it is not a harm of the magnitude and immediacy of rape or sexual abuse of children, which we must punish.

In another example, in the last decade we have learned much more about the harms from prostitution. What was once seen as a relatively benign trade involving consensual sexual activity, which was even romanticized in film and music, has now proved to be heavily intertwined with human trafficking. As described in chapter 3, many prostitutes are minors, and many of those who are over eighteen were forced into the industry against their will. The evidence we now have of the magnitude of prostitution's harm and its impact on women and children suggests that additional regulation and law enforcement is needed.

We should also be more willing to legislate when a vice causes harm to foundational values or institutions and when the harmful effect is on the poor, the vulnerable, and the oppressed. Thus, we must have an unquestioned commitment to the protection of human life. As described in chapter 4, Christians should support well-planned and well-crafted legislative efforts against genetic engineering that kills human embryos. We should be at the forefront of carefully structured efforts to stop human trafficking, attacking both supply and demand by prosecuting traffickers and buyers.

CONCLUSION

The principles for appropriate legislative efforts are by necessity broad and general. They do not form a test that can be applied with mathematical precision. And they must be applied in light of this key principle: Law cannot become our primary means for seeking societal change. Recognizing our fallenness, we must vigilantly fight the temptation that will always be with us to legislatively micromanage moral behavior.

Essentially, I am urging that we apply the central theme of this book to our legislative efforts. We must embrace a biblical understanding of human nature. We are made in the image of God with dignity and value. Our lives have significance. But as a result of the fall, that image is flawed.

We are morally accountable for our actions, both good and bad. Understanding who we are is critical not just for crafting just legislation, but for meaningfully addressing each of the varied issues discussed in this book—from human trafficking to criminal punishment to the cloning of human beings. Indeed, whether we are legislators, lawyers, teachers, business executives, journalists, pastors, moms, or dads, getting human nature right will help us faithfully address the many challenges we confront in our communities, churches, and families.

ACKNOWLEDGMENTS

My greatest professional joy is spending time with the bright, talented, and dedicated law students whom I have been privileged to teach for the last twenty-three years. These young people are motivated by a strong sense of purpose and calling. It is a privilege to be engaged in their lives and to see them learn, grow, and ultimately fulfill their calling to serve others and their communities through the legal profession. Many of the ideas in this book were first discussed and debated in a Regent Law School classroom with these men and women. I am deeply grateful to them for their inspiration and insights.

I am also deeply grateful to the men and women who offered their time, energy, and creativity to help me write this book. For the past few years I have worked closely with an accomplished and conscientious group of students who have helped with everything from research support to editorial assistance. Thank you Brittany Wrigley, Cortland Bobczynski, Brittany Jones, Art Blanton, Abraham Haven, Jewel Russell, and Cody Goings. This book would not exist without you.

Many friends, family members, and colleagues generously reviewed portions of this book in various stages and offered both editorial suggestions and helpful ways to think about the substantive issues covered. Thank you Scott Alleman; Cynthia, David, and Joanne Brauch; Ann Buwalda; Tessa Dysart; Eric Enlow; Kelly Hollowell; Brad Jacob; Tim and Jo Klenk; Rodney Malouf; Mark Mostert; Eric Patterson; David Prentice; Chris Rehn; Mike Schutt; Craig Stern; and Ernie Walton.

My friend and colleague Kenny Ching deserves particular recognition for investing countless hours in reviewing chapter drafts—sometimes multiple times. He brought not only invaluable legal and editorial expertise, but the eye of a skilled writer. Thank you, Kenny, for your friendship and generosity!

I am especially grateful to my wife Becky and my children Cynthia, Melissa, Christina, and Jeffrey. Becky continually provided encouragement, support, patience, and the time and space needed to complete this project. And my kids offered encouragement and even creativity—the inspiration for the book's title came from my son over a family dinner. Thank you all! I love you more than I can adequately express.

Finally, thank you Brannon Ellis, Abigail Stocker, Justin Marr, Elliot Ritzema, and the dedicated team at Lexham Press. Thank you for seeing the promise in this book and for working with me to bring it to completion.

NOTES

CHAPTER 1: WHY HUMAN NATURE MATTERS

1. PBS Frontline, "Carl Wilkens Interview," *Ghosts of Rwanda,* April 1, 2004, http://www.pbs.org/wgbh/pages/frontline/shows/ghosts/interviews/wilkens.html.
2. Philip Gourevitch, *We Wish to Inform You That Tomorrow We Will be Killed with Our Families: Stories from Rwanda* (New York: Farrar, Straus and Giroux, 1998), 18.
3. Ibid., 18–19.
4. Russell Smith, "The Impact of Hate Media in Rwanda," *BBC News,* December 3, 2002, http://news.bbc.co.uk/2/hi/africa/3257748.stm.
5. Ibid.
6. Ibid., 94.
7. Gourevitch, *We Wish to Inform You,* 134.
8. Ibid., 115.
9. Louis Henkin, Sarah H. Cleveland, Laurence R. Helfer, Gerald Neuman, and Diane F. Orentlicher, *Human Rights,* 2nd ed. (New York: Foundation Press, 2009), 538–39.
10. Ibid., 539.
11. "Bill Clinton: we could have saved 300,000 lives in Rwanda," *CNBC,* March 13, 2013, http://www.cnbc.com/id/100546207.
12. PBS Frontline, "Carl Wilkens Interview."
13. Gourevitch, *We Wish to Inform You,* 28.
14. Tom Howell Jr., "Congress Passes First Budget in 6 Years," *Washington Times,* May 5, 2015, http://www.washingtontimes.com/news/2015/may/5/senate-clears-way-final-passage-congress-budget.
15. "Confidence in Institutions," *Gallup,* http://www.gallup.com/poll/1597/confidence-institutions.aspx.
16. Ibid.
17. "Trends in American Values: 1987 to 2012," *The Pew Research Center,* June 4, 2012, http://www.people-press.org/files/legacy-pdf/06-04-12%20Values%20Release.pdf, 1.
18. Ibid.
19. Ibid., 52.
20. Ibid.
21. Frank Newport, "Role of Gov't Remains Key Source of Party Differences," *Gallup,* October 6, 2015, http://www.gallup.com/poll/186032/role-gov-remains-key-source-party-differences.aspx.
22. Bradley Jones, "Americans' views of immigration marked by widening partisan, generational divides," *Pew Research Center,* April 15, 2016.

23. Joseph P. Willliams, "Ahead of Election, Poll Shows a Nation Divided," *US News and World Report*, October 25, 2016, http://www.usnews.com/news/articles/2016-10-25/ahead-of-election-poll-shows-a-nation-divided.

24. Tim Wallace and Alicia Parlapiano, "Crowd Scientists Say Women's March in Washington Had 3 Times as Many People as Trump's Inauguration," *New York Times*, January 22, 2017, https://www.nytimes.com/interactive/2017/01/22/us/politics/womens-march-trump-crowd-estimates.html.

25. Art Swift, "Birth Control, Divorce Top List of Morally Acceptable Issues," *Gallup*, June 8, 2016, http://www.gallup.com/poll/192404/birth-control-divorce-top-list-morally-acceptable-issues.aspx.

26. Francis Schaeffer, *A Christian Manifesto* (Wheaton: Crossway, 1981), 17.

27. J. Budziszewski, *What We Can't Not Know* (Dallas: Spence Publishing, 2003), 9.

28. C. S. Lewis, *The Abolition of Man* (New York: HarperSanFrancisco, 2001).

29. John Calvin, *Institutes of the Christian Religion*, ed. John T. McNeill (Philadelphia: Westminster, 1960), 273.

CHAPTER 2: CHRISTIANITY ON HUMAN NATURE

1. Charles Sherlock, *The Doctrine of Humanity* (Downers Grove, IL: InterVarsity Press, 1997), 43.

2. Albert W. Alschuler, *Law Without Values: The Life, Work, and Legacy of Justice Holmes* (Chicago: University of Chicago Press, 2000), 42.

3. Ibid., 43.

4. Ibid.

5. Ibid., 44.

6. Ibid., 46.

7. Ibid., 26.

8. Ibid.

9. Ibid., 1.

10. Ibid., 24.

11. Richard A. Posner, "Book Review," *George Washington Law Review* 53 (1985): 870, 872.

12. Alschuler, *Law Without Values*, 23.

13. Ibid.

14. Sheldon M. Novick, *Honorable Justice: The Life of Oliver Wendell Holmes* (New York: Dell, 1990), 469.

15. Supreme Court of the United States, "Members of the Supreme Court of the United States," accessed May 26, 2016, http://www.supremecourt.gov/about/members_text.aspx.

16. 249 U.S. 47

17. Richard Lewontin, "Billions and Billions of Demons," *New York Review of Books*, January 9, 1997, http://www.nybooks.com/articles/1997/01/09/billions-and-billions-of-demons/.

18. Sherlock, *The Doctrine of Humanity*, 34.

19. J. I. Packer, *Knowing Man* (Westchester, IL: Cornerstone, 1979), 22.

20. Ibid., 23.

21. Sherlock, *The Doctrine of Humanity*, 37.

22. Packer, *Knowing Man*, 23–24.

23. *The Westminster Standards*, Westminster Confession of Faith, chapter IV (Suwanee, GA: Great Commission, 1978), 8.

24. *Catechism of the Catholic Church* (Rome: Urbi et Orbi, 1994), 91.

25. Ibid., 13.
26. For example, Aristotle proclaimed: "He who is unable to live in society, or who has no need because he is sufficient for himself, must be either a beast or a god: he is no part of a state. A social instinct is implanted in all men by nature." Aristotle, *Politics*, Book I, section 1253a, in *Great Books of the Western World: 9 Aristotle:II*, edited by Robert Maynard Hutchins (Chicago: Brittanica Great Books, 1952), 446.
27. *Catechism of the Catholic Church*, 91.
28. Ibid., 13.
29. United Nations, *Charter of the United Nations and Statute of the International Court of Justice*, Preamble, 1945, accessed May 26, 2016, https://treaties.un.org/doc/Publication/CTC/uncharter.pdf..
30. United Nations, *Universal Declaration of Human Rights*, Article 1, 1948, http://www.un.org/en/universal-declaration-human-rights/.
31. Ron Highfield, *God, Freedom & Human Dignity* (Downers Grove, IL: InterVarsity Press, 2013), 96.
32. Ibid., 191.
33. Ibid.
34. The operative language from *Casey* that makes clear it is acting under the Fourteenth Amendment: "Constitutional protection of the woman's decision to terminate her pregnancy derives from the Due Process Clause of the Fourteenth Amendment."
35. *Planned Parenthood of Southeastern Pennsylvania v. Casey*, 505 U.S. 833, 851 (1992).
36. *Obergefell v. Hodges*, 135 S.Ct. 2584 (2015). See also chapter 7 of this book for a more in-depth discussion.
37. *Obergefell*, 135 S.Ct. at 2597.
38. Ibid., 2599.
39. Highfield, *God, Freedom & Dignity*, 199.
40. Ibid., 191.
41. Louis Berkhof, *Summary of Christian Doctrine* (Grand Rapids: Eerdmans, 1938), 76.
42. Calvin, *Institutes of the Christian Religion*, 253.
43. Ibid., 267.
44. Sherlock, *The Doctrine of Humanity*, 43.
45. World Council of Churches, *Christian Perspectives on Theological Anthropology*, Faith and Order Paper 199 (Geneva, 2005), 16.
46. *Catechism of the Catholic Church*, 97.
47. J. Gresham Machen, *The Christian View of Man* (Edinburgh: Banner of Truth Trust, 1965), 237.
48. J. I. Packer, *Evangelism and the Sovereignty of God* (Downers Grove, IL: InterVarsity Press, 1961), 25.

CHAPTER 3: HUMAN TRAFFICKING

1. "27 Human Trafficking Quotes to Inspire You & Your Friends," *Destiny Rescue*, August 8, 2014, http://www.destinyrescue.org/us/blog/27-human-trafficking-quotes-inspire-friends/.
2. Yamiche Alcindor, "Sex trafficking in the USA hits close to home," *USA Today*, October 27, 2012, http://usatoday30.usatoday.com/news/nation/story/2012/09/27/human-trafficking-in-the-united-states-finds-a-home-in-the-schoolyard/57846054/1.

3. Ibid.

4. Ibid.

5. Ibid.

6. Jenifer B. McKim, "From Victim to Impassioned Voice: Woman Exploited as a Teen Fights Sexual Trafficking of Children," *Boston Globe,* November 27, 2012, https://www.bostonglobe.com/news/nation/2012/11/27/from-victim-survivor-leader-former-sex-trafficking-victim-speaks-out/mOyhAeptFOioVKZeVZB7NN/story.html.

7. *Trafficking in Persons Report 2014* (Washington, DC: Department of State, 2014), 29.

8. "2016 Global Slavery Index: Findings," *Walk Free Foundation,* accessed June 17, 2017, http://www.globalslaveryindex.org/findings/.

9. "How many people were taken from Africa?" *Port Cities Bristol,* accessed January 31, 2016, http://discoveringbristol.org.uk/slavery/routes/from-africa-to-america/atlantic-crossing/people-taken-from-africa/. Approximately 9–11 million slaves were taken from Africa.

10. *Trafficking in Persons Report 2007* (Washington, DC: Department of State, 2007), 8.

11. "21 million people are now victims of forced labour, ILO says," *International Labour Organization,* June 1, 2012, http://www.ilo.org/global/about-the-ilo/newsroom/news/WCMS_181961/lang--en/index.htm.

12. "Factsheet on Commercial Sexual Exploitation and Trafficking of Children," *UNICEF,* accessed February 3, 2016, http://www.unicef.org/indonesia/Factsheet_CSEC_trafficking_Indonesia.pdf.

13. Ricard J. Estes and Neil Alan Weiner, "The Commercial Sexual Exploitation of Children in the US, Canada and Mexico," *University of Pennsylvania, School of Social Work, Center for the Study of Youth Policy,* September 18, 2001.

14. Ibid.

15. "Profits and Poverty: The Economics of Forced Labour," *International Labour Organization,* 2014, accessed February 3, 2016, http://www.ilo.org/wcmsp5/groups/public/---ed_norm/---declaration/documents/publication/wcms_243391.pdf.

16. "Human Trafficking – Questions & Answers," *UNGIFT,* accessed February 3, 2014, http://www.unglobalcompact.org/docs/issues_doc/labour/Forced_labour/HUMAN_TRAFFICKING_-_BACKGROUND_BRIEFING_NOTE_-_final.pdf.

17. "2016 Global Slavery Index: Findings."

18. Ibid.

19. Ibid.

20. Estes and Weiner, "Commercial Sexual Exploitation."

21. Alcindor, "Sex trafficking."

22. *Trafficking in Persons Report 2014,* 21.

23. Ibid.

24. *Trafficking in Persons Report 2009* (Washington, DC: Department of State, 2009), 17.

25. Ibid.

26. "Trafficking in Persons for the Purpose of Organ Removal," *United Nations Office on Drugs and Crime,* 2015, https://www.unodc.org/documents/human-trafficking/2015/UNODC_Assessment_Toolkit_TIP_for_the_Purpose_of_Organ_Removal.pdf.

27. Yosuke Shimazono, "The state of the international organ trade: a provisional picture based on integration of available information," *World Health Organization*, accessed February 3, 2016, http://www.who.int/bulletin/volumes/85/12/06-039370/en/.

28. Ibid.

29. Ibid.

30. Will Storr, "Kony's child soldiers: 'When you kill for the first time, you change,' " *The Telegraph*, February 2, 2014, http://www.telegraph.co.uk/news/worldnews/africaandindianocean/uganda/10621792/Konys-child-soldiers-When-you-kill-for-the-first-time-you-change.html.

31. Ibid.

32. Ibid.

33. "Factsheet: Child Labour," *UNICEF*, 2015, http://www.unicef.org/protection/files/child_labour.pdf.

34. "Questions and Answers, Appeals Judgment on Reparations in the Lubanga case," *International Criminal Court*, March 3, 2015, http://www.icc-cpi.int/en_menus/icc/situations%20and%20cases/situations/situation%20icc%200104/related%20cases/icc%200104%200106/Pages/democratic%20republic%20of%20the%20congo.aspx.

35. Storr, "Kony's child soldiers."

36. "Case Information Sheet: The Prosecutor v. Joseph Kony and Vincent Otti," *International Criminal Court*, September 10, 2015, https://www.icc-cpi.int/iccdocs/PIDS/publications/KonyEtAlEng.pdf.

37. "Factsheet: Child Labour."

38. Nicholas D. Kristof and Sheryl WuDunn, *Half the Sky: Turning Oppression into Opportunity for Women Worldwide* (New York: Alfred A. Knopf, 2009), 3.

39. Ibid, 4.

40. Ibid.

41. Ibid., 5.

42. Ibid.

43. *Trafficking in Persons Report 2014*, 29.

44. Ibid.

45. Alcindor, "Sex trafficking."

46. Ibid.

47. "Leader of Crips Gang Pleads Guilty in Virginia to Prostituting Eight Juveniles," *Federal Bureau of Investigation*, June 26, 2012, https://www.fbi.gov/washingtondc/press-releases/2012/leader-of-crips-gang-pleads-guilty-in-virginia-to-prostituting-eight-juveniles.

48. Ibid.

49. Ibid.

50. Alcindor, "Sex trafficking."

51. Justin Jouvenal, "Fairfax-based Crips members charged with recruiting girls for prostitution," *Washington Post*, March 29, 2012, https://www.washingtonpost.com/local/crime/fairfax-based-crips-members-charged-with-recruiting-girls-for-prostitution/2012/03/29/gIQAJRx6iS_story.html.

52. Alcindor, "Sex trafficking."

53. Ibid.

54. "Report of the APA Task Force on the Sexualization of Girls," *American Psychological Association*, 2010, http://www.apa.org/pi/women/programs/girls/report-full.pdf.

55. Bridget Anderson and Julia O'Connell Davidson, "Is Trafficking in Human Beings Demand Driven? A Multi-Country Pilot Study," *International Organization for Migration*, Migration Research Series, 2003, https://www.compas.ox.ac.uk/media/ER-2004-Trafficking_Demand_Driven_IOM.pdf.

56. Ibid.

57. "Violence against women and HIV/AIDS: Critical Intersections," *World Health Organization*, 2005, http://www.who.int/gender/documents/sexworkers.pdf.

58. Ibid.

59. Ibid.

60. Anderson and O'Connell Davidson, "Trafficking in Human Beings."

61. Ibid.

62. United Nations Office of the High Commissioner, *Protocol to Prevent, Suppress and Punish Trafficking in Persons, especially Women and Children, supplementing the United Nations Convention against Transnational Organized Crime*, November 2000, http://www.ohchr.org/EN/ProfessionalInterest/Pages/ProtocolTraffickingInPersons.aspx.

63. Janice G. Raymond, "Guide to the New UN Trafficking Protocol," *Coalition Against Trafficking in Women*, 2001, http://www.no-trafficking.org/content/pdf/guide_to_the_new_un_trafficking_protocol.pdf,

64. Ibid.

65. H.R. 3244, *Victims of Trafficking and Violence Protection Act of 2000*, 106th Cong., 2nd sess., 2000, http://www.state.gov/j/tip/laws/61124.htm.

66. Ibid.

67. Ibid.

68. H.R. 2620, *Trafficking Victims Protection Reauthorization Act of 2003*, 108th Cong., 1st sess., 2003, http://www.state.gov/j/tip/laws/61130.htm.

69. H.R. 898, *Trafficking Victims Protection Reauthorization Act of 2013*, 113th Cong., 1st sess., 2013, https://www.congress.gov/bill/113th-congress/house-bill/898.

70. S.B. 151, *Prosecutorial Remedies and Other Tools to End the Exploitation of Children Today Act of 2003 (PROTECT Act)*, 108th Cong., 1st sess., 2003, https://www.gpo.gov/fdsys/pkg/BILLS-108s151enr/pdf/BILLS-108s151enr.pdf.

71. Ibid.

72. *United States v. Clark*, 435 F.3d 1100 (9th Cir. 2006).

73. Gary A. Haugen and Victor Boutros, *The Locust Effect: Why the End of Poverty Requires the End of Violence* (Oxford: Oxford University Press, 2014), 16.

74. Ibid., 17.

75. Ellen Wright Clayton, Richard D. Krugman, and Patti Simon, eds., *Commercial Sexual Exploitation and Sex Trafficking of Minors in the United States* (Washington, DC: National Academies Press, 2013), 8.

76. "What is the Nordic Model?" *Equality Now*, accessed February 5, 2016, http://www.equalitynow.org/sites/default/files/Nordic_Model_EN.pdf.

77. Michelle Goldberg, "Swedish prostitution law is spreading worldwide—here's how to improve it," *The Guardian*, August 8, 2014, http://www.theguardian.com/commentisfree/2014/aug/08/criminsalise-buying-not-selling-sex.

78. "Selected Extracts of the Swedish Government report SOU 2010:49: 'The Ban against the Purchase of Sexual Services. An Evaluation 1999–2008," *Swedish Institute*, November 2010, https://ec.europa.eu/anti-trafficking/sites/antitrafficking/

files/the_ban_against_the_purchase_of_sexual_services._an_
evaluation_1999-2008_1.pdf.
79. Ibid.
80. Ibid., 7.
81. Ibid.
82. Ibid., 8–9.
83. Ibid., 9.
84. Ibid., 8.
85. "Norway's closely watched prostitution ban works, study
finds," *Reuters*, August 11, 2014, http://www.reuters.com/article/
us-norway-prostitution-idUSKBN0GB1BL20140811.
86. Ibid.
87. Elizabeth Nolan Brown, "What the Swedish Model Gets Wrong
About Prostitution" *Time*, July 19, 2004, http://time.com/3005687/
what-the-swedish-model-gets-wrong-about-prostitution/.
88. Ibid.
89. Ibid.
90. "Draft Policy on State Obligations to Respect, Protect and Fulfill the Human
Rights of Sex Workers," *Amnesty International*, accessed February 5, 2016,
https://amnestysgprdasset.blob.core.windows.net/media/10243/draft-sw-
policy-for-external-publication.pdf.
91. Scott Alleman, "Panel Two: Sex as a Business," Human Rights and the
Sexualization of Culture: 4th Annual Symposium, *Journal of Global
Justice and Public Policy*, 204–8, 2015, http://media.wix.com/ugd/
d74082_920bde49bc464eca99f78ecc37af9880.pdf.
92. Ibid., 206.
93. Barbara G. Brents & Kathryn Hausbeck, "State-Sanctioned Sex: Negotiating
Formal and Informal Regulatory Practices in Nevada Brothels," *Social
Perspective* 44 (2009): 308.
94. Bureau of Public Affairs, "The Link Between Prostitution and Sex
Trafficking," *U.S. Department of State*, November 24, 2004, http://2001-2009.
state.gov/r/pa/ei/rls/38790.htm.
95. Franklin County Municipal Court, "Press Release: Franklin County
Municipal Court Receives State Certification of its Changing Actions to
Change Habits (CATCH) Specialized Docket," June 16, 2014, http://www.
fcmcclerk.com/documents/media/Certification%20Press%20Release_v_3.
pdf.
96. Amy L. Sherman, "Oldest Profession, or Oldest Oppression? Ohio Judge
Creates Court for Abused Prostitutes," *Christianity Today*, June 1, 2012,
http://www.christianitytoday.com/thisisourcity/7thcity/oldestprofession.
html.
97. Christopher D. Hancock, "The 'Shrimp' Who Stopped Slavery," *Christian
History* 53 (1997), http://www.christianitytoday.com/history/issues/issue-
53/shrimp-who-stopped-slavery.html
98. "Freedom Strategy—Engage Together," *Alliance for Freedom, Restoration, and
Justice*, http://engagetogether.com/freedomstrategy.
99. "Truckers Against Trafficking," http://www.truckersagainsttrafficking.org/.
100. "Our Story," *iEmphathize*, http://iempathize.org/about/our-story/.

101. "U.S. Attorney Neil H. MacBride Announces Departure From Eastern District Of Virginia," *Department of Justice*, August 22, 2013, http://www.justice.gov/usao-edva/pr/us-attorney-neil-h-macbride-announces-departure-eastern-district-virginia.

102. Chris Morris, "Porn Industry Feeling Upbeat about 2014," *NBC News*, January 14, 2014, http://www.nbcnews.com/business/business-news/porn-industry-feeling-upbeat-about-2014-n9076.

103. Ibid.

104. "Porn Sites Get More Visitors Each Month Than Netflix, Amazon and Twitter Combined" *HuffPost Tech*, May, 4, 2013, http://www.huffingtonpost.com/2013/05/03/internet-porn-stats_n_3187682.html.

105. Ibid.

106. "Key Facts," *National Center for Missing & Exploited Children*, accessed February 6, 2016, http://www.missingkids.com/KeyFacts.

107. "2014 Pornography Survey of Christian Men: Shocking New National Survey Reveals High Levels of Pornography Use and Rampant Extramarital Affairs among Christian Men," *Proven Men*, October 24, 2014, http://www.provenmen.org/press-releases/2014-pornography-survey-of-christian-men-shocking-new-national-survey-reveals-high-levels-of-pornography-use-and-rampant-extramarital-affairs-among-christian-men/.

108. "Pornography Use and Addiction," *Proven Men*, 2014, http://www.provenmen.org/2014pornsurvey/pornography-use-and-addiction/#copyright.

109. Ibid.

110. Ibid.

111. "ChristiaNet Poll Finds that Evangelicals Are Addicted to Porn," *MarketWire* August 7, 2006, http://www.marketwired.com/press-release/christianet-poll-finds-that-evangelicals-are-addicted-to-porn-703951.htm.

112. *Pornography Statistics: 250+ Facts, Quotes, and Statistics About Pornography Use*, 2015 ed. (Owosso, MI: Covenant Eyes, 2015), 21.

113. Michael Flood, "The Harms of Pornography Exposure among Children and Young People," *Child Abuse Review* 18 (2009): 391. http://pornharmsresearch.com/wpcontent/uploads/Flood__The_harms_of_pornography_exposure_09.pdf.

114. Ibid., 393.

115. Ibid.

116. M. Farley, A. Cotton, J. Lynne, S. Zumbeck, F. Spiwak, M. E. Reyes, D. Alvarez, U. Sezgin, "Prostitution and Trafficking in Nine Countries: An Update on Violence and Posttraumatic Stress Disorder," *Journal of Trauma Practice* 2 (2004): 33–74.

CHAPTER 4: BIOTECHNOLOGY

1. Leon R. Kass, "A Way Forward on Stem Cells," *Washington Post Online*, July 7, 2015, http://www.washingtonpost.com/wp-dyn/content/article/2005/07/11/AR2005071101415.html.

2. David Cyranoski and Sara Reardon, "Chinese scientists genetically modify human embryos," *Nature*, April 22, 2015, http://www.nature.com/news/chinese-scientists-genetically-modify-human-embryos-1.17378.

3. "Editing Humanity," *The Economist*, August 22, 2015, http://www.economist.com/news/

leaders/21661651-new-technique-manipulating-genes-holds-great-promisebut-rules-are-needed-govern-its.

4. Cyranoski and Reardon, "Chinese scientists genetically modify human embryos."

5. Ibid.

6. Ibid.

7. Ibid.

8. Ibid.

9. Ibid. Another Chinese research team published results from gene editing of human embryos in May 2016. This team, similar to Huang's, reported "significant technical issues," including "wild type or contained indel mutations." Xiangjin Kang, Wenyin He, Yuling Huang, Qian Yu, Yaoyong Chen, Xingcheng Gao, Xiaofang Sun, and Yong Fan, "Introducing precise genetic modifications into human 3PN embryos by CRISPR/Cas-mediated genome editing," *Journal of Assisted Reproduction and Genetics* 33 (May 2016): 581.

10. Merrit Kennedy, "UK Regulator Gives Go-Ahead for Scientists to Edit Genes in Human Embryos," *National Public Radio*, February 1, 2016, http://www.npr.org/sections/thetwo-way/2016/02/01/465131900/u-k-regulator-gives-go-ahead-for-scientists-to-edit-genes-in-human-embryos.

11. Ewen Callaway, "Gene-editing research in human embryos gains momentum," *Nature*, April 19, 2016, accessed June 17, 2017, http://www.nature.com/news/gene-editing-research-in-human-embryos-gains-momentum-1.19767.

12. Francie Diep, "The Process that Created Dolly the Sheep in 1996 Has Now Been Proven Successful in Humans," *Popular Science*, May 15, 2013, http://www.popsci.com/science/article/2013-05/scientists-create-human-clone-embryo-stem-cell-harvesting.

13. "Overview of the Human Genome Project," *Human Genome Research Institute*, accessed May 16, 2016, www.genome.gov/12011238.

14. Daniel Allott and George Neumayr, "Eugenic Abortion 2.0," *The American Spectator*, May 23, 2013, http://spectator.org/55745_eugenic-abortion-20/.

15. Megan Allyse et al., "Non-invasive prenatal testing: a review of international implementation and challenges," *International Journal of Women's Health* 7 (2015): 113–26, https://www.ncbi.nlm.nih.gov/pmc/articles/PMC4303457/.

16. Ibid.

17. Ibid.

18. Ibid.

19. Allott and Neumayr, "Eugenic Abortion 2.0."

20. Mark Bradford, "New Study: Abortion after Prenatal Diagnosis of Down Syndrome Reduces Down Syndrome Community by Thirty Percent," *Charlotte Lozier Institute*, April 21, 2015, https://lozierinstitute.org/new-study-abortion-after-prenatal-diagnosis-of-down-syndrome-reduces-down-syndrome-community-by-thirty-percent/.

21. Ibid.

22. Clare Godwin and Sadie Nicholas, "Doctors wanted to abort these children. So how did their mothers find the strength to defy them?" *Dailymail.com*, June 5, 2013, http://www.dailymail.co.uk/femail/article-2336613/Doctors-wanted-abort-children-So-did-mothers-strength-defy-them.html.

23. Ibid.

24. Ibid. Women across the world have experienced similar situations, such as Canadian mother Myrah Walker, who was pressured to abort her baby, Celine. She now operates a website to encourage other mothers facing pressure to abort: www.mychildmygift.com. She writes, "Women in many cases have to fight to continue their pregnancy. There is a severe disability, the medical protocol is to terminate. They think it's better for that child to be dead." Julia Duin, "Choosing not to abort babies with disabilities," *The Washington Times*, May 10, 2009, http://www.washingtontimes.com/news/2009/may/10/mothers-choosing-not-abort-children-disabilities.

25. Allott and Neumayr, "Eugenic Abortion 2.0."

26. Ibid.

27. Paul Diehl, "CRISPR: What's All the Excitement About?" *About Money*, February 23, 2016, http://biotech.about.com/od/technicaltheory/a/Crispr-Whats-All-The-Excitement-About.htm.

28. Jill A. Adams, "Manipulating the Human Genome," *CQ Researcher*, accessed May 24, 2016, http://library.cqpress.com/cqresearcher/document.php?id=cqresrre2015061900.

29. Ibid; Michael McKenzie, "The Christian and Genetic Engineering," *Christian Research Institute*, accessed May 21, 2016, http://www.equip.org/article/the-christian-and-genetic-engineering/.

30. Sources just use the phrase "approved" use or "approved" without describing the approval process. It appears, though, that it was the National Institutes of Health who have the approval; their researchers did the procedure.

31. Jeffrey Laurence and Michael Franklin, eds., *Translating Gene Therapy to the Clinic: Techniques and Approaches* (London: Academic Press, 2015), xi.

32. Lisa Yount, *Modern Genetics: Engineering Life* (New York: Chelsea House, 2006), 63–67.

33. Genetic Science Learning Center, "Gene Therapy Successes," *Learn Genetics*, accessed May 16, 2016, http://learn.genetics.utah.edu/content/genetherapy/gtsuccess/.

34. "'Suicide' gene therapy kills prostate cancer cells," *BBC*, December 12, 2015, http://www.bbc.com/news/health-35072747.

35. Antonio Regalado, "Engineering the Perfect Baby," *MIT Technology Review*, March 5, 2015, https://www.technologyreview.com/s/535661/engineering-the-perfect-baby/; Kennedy, "UK Regulator Gives Go-Ahead."

36. Norell Hadzimichalis, "Genetic Engineering: The Past, Present, and Future," *The Future of Human Evolution*, accessed May 17, 2016, http://futurehumanevolution.com/genetic-engineering-the-past-present-and-future.

37. Regalado, "Engineering the Perfect Baby."

38. Ibid.

39. Ibid.

40. Edward Lanphier, Fyodor Urnov, Sarah Ehlen Haecker, Michael Werner, and Joanna Smolenski, "Don't edit the human germ line," *Nature*, March 12, 2015, accessed June 17, 2017, http://www.nature.com/news/don-t-edit-the-human-germ-line-1.17111.

41. Cyranoski and Reardon, "Chinese scientists genetically modify human embryos."

42. Council of Europe, *Convention for the Protection of Human Rights and Dignity of the Human Being with regard to the Application of Biology and Medicine:*

Convention on Human Rights and Biomedicine, April 4, 1997, accessed June 17, 2017, https://rm.coe.int/168007cf98.

43. Dara Dovey, "The Science Of Human Cloning: How Far We've Come And How Far We're Capable Of Going," *Medical Daily,* June 26, 2015, http://www.medicaldaily.com/science-human-cloning-how-far-weve-come-and-how-far-were-capable-going-340006; "Issue Analysis: Human cloning," *Ethics and Religious Liberty Commission,* April 24, 2014, http://erlc.com/resource-library/articles/issue-analysis-human-cloning.

44. Leon R. Kass, "The Wisdom of Repugnance: Why We Should Ban the Cloning of Humans," *Valparaiso University Law Review* 32 (1998): 694.

45. Marion Hilligan, Nelson P. Miller, Don Petersen, and Chris Hastings, "Superhuman—Biotechnology's Emerging Impact on the Law," *Thomas M. Cooley Law Review* 24 (2007): 20.

46. Ibid.

47. "National Legislation Concerning Human Reproductive and Therapeutic Cloning," *UNESCO,* July 2004, http://unesdoc.unesco.org/images/0013/001342/134277e.pdf.

48. "Cloning: Frequently Asked Questions," *National Public Radio,* accessed June 5, 2017, http://www.npr.org/news/specials/cloning/faq_blanknav.html.

49. Hilligan, Miller, Petersen, and Hastings, "Superman," 20.

50. Diep, "The Process that Created Dolly the Sheep."

51. Ibid; "What are Embryonic Stem Cells?" *National Institutes of Health,* accessed May 17, 2016, http://stemcells.nih.gov/info/basics/pages/basics3.aspx.

52. "CGS Summary of Public Opinion Polls," *Center for Genetics and Society,* https://www.geneticsandsociety.org/internal-content/cgs-summary-public-opinion-polls.

53. "Cloning: Frequently Asked Questions."

54. Ibid.

55. In therapeutic cloning, researchers create an embryonic clone of a patient and then destroy the embryo to harvest its stem cells. In gene therapy, stem cells are one of the ways to transmit genetic modifications to a patient. Ian Murnaghan, "Stem Cells and Gene Therapy," *Explore Stem Cells,* accessed May 19, 2016,
http://www.explorestemcells.co.uk/stemcellsandgenetherapy.html.

56. "Stem Cell Basics I: What are stem cells, and why are they important?" *National Institutes of Health,* accessed May 19, 2016, http://stemcells.nih.gov/info/basics/pages/basics1.aspx.

57. Ibid.

58. "Stem Cell Basics II: What are the unique properties of all stem cells?" *National Institutes of Health,* accessed May 19, 2016, http://stemcells.nih.gov/info/basics/pages/basics2.aspx.

59. "Stem Cell Basics I," *National Institutes of Health.*

60. "About Stem Cells," *StemCellsAustralia,* accessed May 19, 2016, http://www.stemcellsaustralia.edu.au/About-Stem-Cells.aspx.

61. "Stem Cell Basics II," *National Institutes of Health.*

62. "Stem Cell Basics IV: What are the similarities and differences between embryonic and adult stem cells?" *National Institutes of Health,* accessed May 19, 2016, http://stemcells.nih.gov/info/basics/pages/basics5.aspx.

63. "'Support cells' in brain play important role in Down syndrome," *UCDavis Health System,* July 18, 2014, http://www.ucdmc.ucdavis.edu/publish/news/

newsroom/9116; "Non-Embryonic Stem Cell 'Alternatives' Again Taking
the Lead," *Coalition of Americans for Research Ethics*, October 10, 2014, http://
stemcellsthatwork.blogspot.com/2014/10/non-embryonic-stem-cell-
alternatives.html.
64. Ibid.
65. *Sherley v. Sebelius*, 644 F.3d 388, 390 (D.C. Cir. 2011).
66. Ibid., 399.
67. Joe Carter, "Issue Analysis: Embryonic Stem Cell Research," *Ethics and
Religious Liberty Commission*, accessed May 19, 2016, http://d1nwfrzxhi18dp.
cloudfront.net/uploads/resource_library/attachment/file/17/20140428_IA_
Stem_Cell.pdf.
68. "Darwinism: Science or Naturalistic Philosophy? A debate between William
B. Provine and Phillip E. Johnson at Stanford University, April 30, 1994,"
Access Research Network, http://www.arn.org/docs/orpages/or161/161main.
htm.
69. Carole Cadwalladr, "Richard Dawkins Interview," *The Guardian*,
September 11, 2015, https://www.theguardian.com/science/2015/sep/11/
richard-dawkins-interview-twitter-controversy-genetics-god.
70. Gregory Stock, *Redesigning Humans: Our Inevitable Genetic Future* (New York:
Houghton Mifflin, 2003), 2.
71. Ibid., 197.
72. Carolyn Williams, "Human Cloning, Genetic Engineering and Privacy," *Yale-
New Haven Teachers Institute*, accessed May 20, 2016, http://www.yale.edu/
ynhti/curriculum/units/2000/3/00.03.07.x.html.
73. Regalado, "Engineering the Perfect Baby."
74. Hilligan, Miller, Petersen, and Hastings, "Superman," 42.
75. Ibid.
76. Karin Frick, Peter Gloor, and Detlef Gürtler, "Global Thought Leaders 2013,"
Gottlieb Duttweiler Institute, accessed June 7, 2016, http://www.gdi.ch/de/
Think-Tank/Global-Thought-Leaders-2013.
77. Peter Singer, "Speciesism and Moral Status," *Metaphilosophy* 40 (2009): 573.
78. Ibid., 572–73.
79. Ibid., 573.
80. Ibid., 575.
81. Ibid., 576.
82. Hilligan, Miller, Petersen, and Hastings, "Superman," 43.
83. Ibid., 58.
84. Jeremy Rifkin, *The Biotech Century* (New York: Putnam, 1998), 32.
85. Ibid.
86. Michael Spector, "The Gene Hackers," *The New Yorker*, November 16, 2015,
http://www.newyorker.com/magazine/2015/11/16/the-gene-hackers.
87. Patrick Dixon, "Genetic Engineering: What Is Genetic Engineering?"
GlobalChange.com, accessed May 20, 2016, http://www.globalchange.com/
geneticengin.htm.
88. Ibid.
89. Susan Brown, "International Group Proposes Guidelines for Embryonic-
Stem-Cell Research," *The Chronicle of Higher Education* 53 (2007): A21.
90. Press Release, "Guidelines Released for Embryonic Stem Cell Research," *The
National Academies*, April 26, 2005, http://www8.nationalacademies.org/
onpinews/newsitem.aspx?RecordID=11278.
91. Mark Mostert, "Useless Eaters," *Journal of Special Education* 36 (2002): 158.

92. Allott and Neumayr, "Eugenic Abortion 2.0."
93. Ibid.
94. Hilligan, Miller, Petersen, and Hastings, "Superman," 54.
95. David Gems, "Politically Correct Eugenics," *Theoretical Medicine and Bioethics* 20 (1999): 200.
96. *Buck v. Bell*, 274 U.S. 200, 205 (1927).
97. Virginia House Joint Resolution No. 607, "Expressing the General Assembly's regret for Virginia's experience with eugenics," agreed to by the House of Delegates, February 2, 2001, and agreed to by the Senate, February 14, 2001, http://lis.virginia.gov/cgi-bin/legp604.exe?011+ful+HJ607ER.
98. *Buck v. Bell*, 274 U.S. 200, 207 (1927).
99. Ibid.
100. Mark Mostert, "Useless Eaters," 159.
101. Ibid., 161.
102. Maurice Berube, "A Spiritual Pilgrimage," *Virginian-Pilot*, April 12, 2015, 23.
103. Mostert, "Useless Eaters," 157.
104. Peter Schworm, "Court strikes decision for mentally ill woman's abortion," *Boston Globe*, January 17, 2012.
105. Ibid.
106. Emily Bazelon, "The Place of Women on the Court," *The New York Times Magazine*, July 7, 2009, http://www.nytimes.com/2009/07/12/magazine/12ginsburg-t.html.
107. Allott and Neumayr, "Eugenic Abortion 2.0."
108. Leon R. Kass, *Life, Liberty and the Defense of Dignity: The Challenge for Bioethics* (San Francisco: Encounter Books, 2002), 689.
109. Nigel M. de S. Cameron, "The Ethics of Human Cloning," *Discernment* 6 (1999): 9.
110. McKenzie, "The Christian and Genetic Engineering."
111. Cameron, "The Ethics of Human Cloning," 9–10.
112. Robert P. George, "Embryo Ethics: Justice and Nascent Human Life," *Regent University Law Review* 17 (2005): 3–4.
113. "Fetal Development: Stages of Growth," *Cleveland Clinic*, accessed April 21, 2017, https://my.clevelandclinic.org/health/articles/fetal-development-stages-of-growth.
114. Michael McKenzie, "The Christian and Genetic Engineering."
115. Leon R. Kass, "A Way Forward on Stem Cells."
116. Kass, *The Wisdom of Repugnance*, 694.
117. Cameron, "The Ethics of Human Cloning," 11.
118. Ibid.
119. Kass, *The Wisdom of Repugnance*, 698.
120. Ibid.
121. Michael J. Sandel, "The Case Against Perfection," *The Atlantic*, April 2004, http://www.theatlantic.com/magazine/archive/2004/04/the-case-against-perfection/302927/.

CHAPTER 5: GENOCIDE

1. "The Doctors Trial: The Medical Case of the Subsequent Nuremberg Proceedings," *The United States Holocaust Memorial Museum*, accessed May 18, 2016, https://www.ushmm.org/wlc/en/article.php?ModuleId=10007035.
2. Emily Wax, "We Want to Make a Light Baby," *The Washington Post*, June 30, 2004, www.washingtonpost.com/wp-dyn/articles/A16001-2004Jun29.html.

3. Ibid.

4. Ibid.

5. Ibid.

6. Ibid.

7. Justin Wagner, "The Systematic Use of Rape as a Tool of War in Darfur: A Blueprint for International War Crimes Prosecutions, *Georgetown Journal of International Law* 37 (2005): 204-7.

8. "Convention on the Prevention and Punishment of the Crime of Genocide," December 9, 1948, 78 U.N.T.S. 277.

9. David Luban, Julie R. O'Sullivan, and David P. Stewart, *International and Transnational Criminal Law* (New York: Wolters Kluwer, 2010), 985.

10. Gerard Mulligan, "Genocide in the Ancient World," *Ancient History Encyclopedia*, last modified January 27, 2013, http://www.ancient.eu/article/485.

11. Ibid.

12. Ibid.

13. Ibid.

14. David Weissbrodt, Fionnuala Ní Aoláin, Joan Fitzpatrick, and Frank Newman, *International Human Rights: Law, Policy, and Process*, 4th ed. (Dayton, OH: LexisNexis, 2009), 6.

15. Arnold Krammer, *War Crimes, Genocide, and the Law: A Guide to the Issues* (Santa Barbara, CA: Praeger, 2010), 61.

16. Weissbrodt, Aoláin, Fitzpatrick, and Newman, *International Human Rights*, 5-6.

17. "Bosnia-Herzegovina," *The United States Holocaust Memorial Museum*, accessed March 1, 2016, https://www.ushmm.org/confront-genocide/cases/bosnia-herzegovina.

18. Ibid.

19. Luban, O'Sullivan, and Stewart, *International and Transnational Criminal Law*, 1002, 1007.

20. Lisa Sharlach, "Rape as Genocide: Bangladesh, the Former Yugoslavia, and Rwanda," *New Political Science* 22 (2000): 96.

21. Ibid.

22. Siobhan K. Fisher, "Occupation of the Womb: Forced Impregnation as Genocide," *Duke Law Journal* 46 (1996): 108.

23. Ibid., 106-7.

24. Ibid., 111.

25. Ibid., 113.

26. Sharlach, "Rape as Genocide," 98.

27. Ibid.

28. Ibid., 99.

29. The introduction to this chapter tells the stories of Sawela Suliman and Aisha Adam, two of hundreds of thousands of victims of genocide in Darfur.

30. Jennifer Trahan, "Why the Killing in Darfur is Genocide," *Fordham International Law Journal* 31 (2008): 995.

31. Ibid., 1027.

32. Ibid.

33. Matthew D. Hockenos, "The Church Struggle and the Confessing Church: An Introduction to Bonhoeffer's Context," *Studies in Christian-Jewish Relations* 2 (2007): 2.

34. Timothy Longman, "Christian Churches and Genocide in Rwanda: Revision of a paper originally prepared for Conference on Genocide, Religion, and Modernity," *The United States Holocaust Memorial Museum*, May 11–13, 1997, http://faculty.vassar.edu/tilongma/Church&Genocide.html.

35. Eric Metaxas, *Bonhoeffer: Pastor, Martyr, Prophet, Spy* (Nashville: Thomas Nelson, 2010), 151.

36. Hockenos, "The Church Struggle," 5.

37. Metaxas, *Bonhoeffer*, 172.

38. Hockenos, "The Church Struggle," 19.

39. Ibid.

40. Doug Schlegel, "The Barmen Confession," *Leben: A Journal of Reformation Life* 7 (April–June 2011): 5.

41. *The Constitution of the Presbyterian Church (U.S.A.) Part I Book of Confessions* (Louisville, KY: Office of the General Assembly, 2005), 250.

42. Tim Judah, *The Serbs: History, Myth, and the Destruction of Yugoslavia* (New Haven: Yale University Press, 2000), 36.

43. Gourevitch, *We Wish to Inform You*, 55–56.

44. Mikaela Colleen, "The International Criminal Tribunal and the Rwandan National Courts," *Dartmouth College Undergraduate Journal of Law* 3 (Fall 2005): 41.

45. Samantha Power, "Bystanders to Genocide," *The Atlantic*, September 2001, http://www.theatlantic.com/magazine/archive/2001/09/bystanders-to-genocide/304571/.

46. Longman, "Christian Churches and Genocide in Rwanda"; Colleen, "The International Criminal Tribunal," 42.

47. Longman, "Christian Churches and Genocide in Rwanda," 11.

48. Colleen, "The International Criminal Tribunal," 42.

49. Ibid., 80.

50. Ibid.

51. Luban, O'Sullivan, and Stewart, *International and Transnational Criminal Law*, 882.

52. Ibid.

53. Colleen, "The International Criminal Court," 46.

54. Metaxas, *Bonhoeffer*, 174–75.

55. "Rwandan Genocide Survivor Recalls Horror," *CBS News*, November 30, 2006, http://www.cbsnews.com/news/rwandan-genocide-survivor-recalls-horror/2/.

56. Ibid.

57. Gourevitch, *We Wish to Inform You*, 115.

58. PBS Frontline, "Transcript," *Ghosts of Rwanda*, April 1, 2004, http://www.pbs.org/wgbh/pages/frontline/shows/ghosts/etc/script.html.

59. Peter Tyson, "Holocaust on Trial: The Experiments," *NOVA Online*, October 2000, http://www.pbs.org/wgbh/nova/holocaust/experiside.html.

60. Ibid.

61. Hockenos, "The Church Struggle," 9.

62. David L. Smith, *Less Than Human: Why We Demean, Enslave, and Exterminate Others* (New York: St. Martin's Press, 2011), 5.

63. Ibid.

64. Ibid.

65. Robert J. Lifton, "German Doctors and the Final Solution," *New York Times*, September 21, 1986, http://www.nytimes.com/1986/09/21/magazine/german-doctors-and-the-final-solution.html?pagewanted=all.

66. Mark Mostert, "Useless Eaters," *Journal of Special Education* 36 (2002): 157.

67. Ibid.

68. Karl Binding and Alfred Hoche, *Permission for the Destruction of Life Unworthy of Life*, quoted in Mostert, "Useless Eaters," 157.

69. "The Biological State: Nazi Racial Hygiene, 1933–1939," *The United States Holocaust Memorial Museum*, accessed May 25, 2016, https://www.ushmm.org/wlc/en/article.php?ModuleId=10007057.

70. David Bruce Macdonald, *Balkan Holocausts? Serbian and Croatian Victim-Centred Propaganda and the War in Yugoslavia* (Manchester: Manchester University Press, 2002), 233.

71. Krammer, *War Crimes, Genocide, and the Law*, 73.

72. Gourevitch, *We Wish to Inform You*, 96.

73. Ibid., 94.

74. Russell Smith, "The Impact of Hate Media in Rwanda," *BBC News*, December 3, 2002, http://news.bbc.co.uk/2/hi/africa/3257748.stm.

75. Gourevitch, *We Wish to Inform You*, 134.

76. Justin Wagner, "The Systematic Use of Rape as a Tool," 206.

77. United Nations Office of the High Commissioner on Human Rights, *Convention on the Prevention and Punishment of the Crime of Genocide* (1948), accessed May 19, 2016, http://www.ohchr.org/EN/ProfessionalInterest/Pages/CrimeOfGenocide.aspx

78. "Convention on Rights and Duties of States (Montevideo Convention)," December 26, 1933, http://avalon.law.yale.edu/20th_century/intam03.asp.

79. Power, "Bystanders to Genocide."

80. R. Charli Carpenter, *Innocent Women and Children: Gender, Norms and the Protection of Civilians* (Wiltshire, UK: Ashgate, 2006), 77.

81. PBS Frontline, "Transcript," *Ghosts of Rwanda*.

82. Henkin et al., *Human Rights*, 564.

83. Ibid., 563–67; "China, Russia Bar Sudan Sanctions," *BBC News*, April 18, 2006, http://news.bbc.co.uk/2/hi/africa/4917970.stm.

84. Department of the Treasury, Office of Foreign Assets Control, "Sudan Sanctions Program," July 25, 2008, www.treasury.gov/resource-center/sanctions/documents/sudan.pdf.

85. United Nations, *Charter of the United Nations and Statute of the International Court of Justice*, Arts.2, 24, and 51,1945, accessed February 17, 2016, https://treaties.un.org/doc/Publication/CTC/uncharter.pdf.

86. Jean Bethke Elshtain, *Just War Against Terror: The Burden of American Power in a Violent World* (New York: Basic Books, 2003), 51.

87. Ibid., 57.

88. Ibid.

89. John F. Coverdale, "An Introduction to the Just War Tradition," *Pace International Law Review* 16 (2004): 229.

90. Henkin et al., *Human Rights*, 547.

91. Fernando R. Tesón, "Kosovo: A Powerful Precedent for the Doctrine of Humanitarian Intervention," *Amsterdam Law Forum* 1, no. 2 (2009), http://amsterdamlawforum.org/article/view/62/119.

92. United Nations Security Council, Resolution 1160, March 31, 1998, https://documents-dds-ny.un.org/doc/UNDOC/GEN/N98/090/23/PDF/N9809023.pdf?OpenElement.

93. Tesón, "Kosovo: A Powerful Precedent for the Doctrine of Humanitarian Intervention."

94. Henkin et al., *Human Rights*, 547.

95. Ibid., 548.

96. Ibid.

97. PBS Frontline, "A Kosovo Chronology," *War in Europe: NATO's 1999 War Against Serbia Over Kosovo*, February 2000, http://www.pbs.org/wgbh/pages/frontline/shows/kosovo/etc/cron.html.

98. Henkin et al., *Human Rights*, 547.

99. Tesón, "Kosovo: A Powerful Precedent for the Doctrine of Humanitarian Intervention."

100. Henkin et al., *Human Rights*, 552.

101. Gareth Evans, "From Humanitarian Intervention to the Responsibility to Protect, *Wis. International Law Journal* 24 (2006): 710–11.

102. Henkin et al., *Human Rights*, 556–57.

103. Ibid., 557.

104. Anne-Marie Slaughter, "A New U.N. for a New Century," *Fordham Law Review* 74 (2006): 2964.

105. Albrecht Schnabel, "The Responsibility to Rebuild," in *The Routledge Handbook of the Responsibility to Protect*, ed. W. Andy Knight and Frazier Egerton (New York: Routledge, 2012), 54.

106. Ibid.

107. Roland Paris, "Is It Possible to Meet the Responsibility to Protect," *The Washington Post*, December 9, 2014, http://www.washingtonpost.com/blogs/monkey-cage/wp/2014/12/09/is-it-possible-to-meet-the-responsibility-to-protect/.

108. Eric D. Patterson, *Ending Wars Well* (London: Yale University Press, 2012), 171.

109. Michael Lipka, "Many U.S. congregations are still racially segregated, but things are changing," *Pew Research Center*, December 8, 2014, http://www.pewresearch.org/fact-tank/2014/12/08/many-u-s-congregations-are-still-racially-segregated-but-things-are-changing-2/.

110. Ibid.

111. Martin Luther King Jr., "Letter from Birmingham City Jail," May 1, 1963, http://www.thekingcenter.org/archive/document/letter-birmingham-city-jail-0.

Chapter 6: Human Rights

1. Habib C. Malik, ed., *The Challenge of Human Rights: Charles Malik and the Universal Declaration* (Oxford: Charles Malik Foundation, 2000), 4.

2. "ECHR Upholds Religious Freedom in Landmark Case, *The Salvation Army v. Russia*," *Slavic Center for Law and Justice*, October 9, 2006, http://sclj.org/press_releases/06-1009-Religious_Freedom_Protected.htm.

3. *Moscow Branch of the Salvation Army v. Russia*, App. No. 72881/01, § 8 (ECtHR 2006).

4. Ibid., ¶ 16 & 91.

5. Ibid., ¶ 31–33.

6. Council of Europe, *European Convention on Human Rights*, Art. 34, accessed May 16, 2016, http://www.echr.coe.int/Documents/Convention_ENG.pdf.

7. *Moscow Branch of the Salvation Army v. Russia*, App. No. 72881/01, ¶ 98 (ECtHR 2006).

8. Ibid., ¶ 105

9. "The Salvation Army," *The Salvation Army*, accessed February 16, 2016, http://www1.salvationarmy.org/eec%5Cwww_eec.nsf/vw-news/1B84D17727042260C32575A800224176?opendocument.

10. United Nations, *Universal Declaration of Human Rights: Preamble*, 1948, accessed February 17, 2016, http://www.un.org/en/universal-declaration-human-rights/.

11. United Nations, *Charter of the United Nations and Statute of the International Court of Justice*, 1945, accessed February 17, 2016, https://treaties.un.org/doc/Publication/CTC/uncharter.pdf.

12. United Nations, *Universal Declaration of Human Rights*.

13. Ibid.

14. Ibid.

15. John F. Sears, "Eleanor Roosevelt and the Universal Declaration of Human Rights," https://fdrlibrary.org/documents/356632/390886/sears.pdf/c300e130-b6e6-4580-8bf1-07b72195b370. The nations that abstained were Byelorussia, Czechoslovakia, Poland, Saudi Arabia, South Africa, the Soviet Union, Ukraine, and Yugoslavia.

16. Mary Ann Glendon, "Propter Honris Respectum: Knowing the Universal Declaration of Human Rights," *Notre Dame Law Review* 73 (1998): 1153.

17. President Carter signed this treaty, but the United States has never ratified it.

18. "Human Rights Bodies," *United Nations Human Rights Office of the High Commissioner*, accessed February 17, 2016, http://www.ohchr.org/EN/HRBodies/Pages/HumanRightsBodies.aspx.

19. "Drafting of the Universal Declaration of Human Rights," *United Nations*, accessed February 18, 2016, http://research.un.org/en/undhr/draftingcommittee.

20. Malik, *The Challenge of Human Rights*, 4.

21. United Nations Human Rights Office of the High Commissioner, *International Covenant on Civil and Political Rights: Preamble*, December 16, 1966, accessed February 19, 2016, http://www.ohchr.org/en/professionalinterest/pages/ccpr.aspx; United Nations Human Rights Office of the High Commissioner, *International Covenant on Economic, Social and Cultural Rights: Preamble*, December 16, 1966, accessed February 19, 2016, http://www.ohchr.org/EN/ProfessionalInterest/Pages/CESCR.aspx.

22. Organization of American States, *American Convention on Human Rights 'Pact of San Jose, Costa Rica: Preamble,'* accessed February 20, 2016, http://www.oas.org/dil/treaties_B-32_American_Convention_on_Human_Rights.pdf.

23. Louis Henkin, Sarah H. Cleveland, Laurence R. Helfer, Gerald Neuman, and Diane F. Orentlicher, *Human Rights*, 2nd. ed. (New York: Foundation Press, 2009), 141.

24. H. L. A. Hart, "Positivism and the Separation of Law and Morals," *Harvard Law Review* 71 (1958): 616.

25. Hans Kelsen, "The Pure Theory of Law Part I," *Law Quarterly Review* 50 (1934): section 1.

26. "European Neighborhood Policy and Enlargement Negotiations," *European Commission*, accessed June 16, 2016, http://ec.europa.eu/enlargement/policy/conditions-membership/index_en.htm.

27. Edwin Rekosh, "Constructing Public Interest Law: Transnational Collaboration and Exchange in Central and Eastern Europe," *UCLA J. of Int'l Law and Foreign Affairs* 13 (2008), 55, 63.

28. "Enforced Disappearances: Progress and Challenges in South America," *United Nations Office of the High Commissioner*, accessed March 5, 2016, http://www.ohchr.org/EN/NewsEvents/Pages/EnforcedDisappearancesprogressandchallengesinSouthAmerica.aspx.

29. Global Legal Monitor, "European Union: Implementation of Judgments Issued by European Court of Human Rights," *Library of Congress*, accessed February 27, 2016, http://www.loc.gov/lawweb/servlet/lloc_news?disp3_l205402772_text.

30. David W. Kennedy, "The International Human Rights Regime: Still Part of the Problem?" in *Examining Critical Perspectives on Human Rights*, ed. Rob Dickinson, Elena Katselli, Colin Murray, and Ole W. Pedersen (Cambridge: Cambridge University Press, 2012), 19.

31. Charles Malik, "The Two Tasks," *Journal of the Evangelical Theological Society* 23 (1980): 289.

32. Malik, *The Challenge of Human Rights*, 5.

33. Henkin, Cleveland, Helfer, Neuman, and Orentlicher, *Human Rights 2d ed.*, 155.

34. United Nations, *Universal Declaration of Human Rights*.

35. Ibid.

36. Ibid.

37. United Nations Human Rights Council, "Combating Defamation of Religions," HRC 13/16, 2010. Again it urged "all States to provide, within their respective legal and constitutional systems, adequate protection against acts of hatred, discrimination, intimidation and coercion resulting from defamation of religions and incitement to religious hatred in general, and to take all possible measures to promote tolerance and respect for all religions and beliefs." Ibid., ¶ 14.

38. Organization of American States, *American Convention on Human Rights*, Art. 4, accessed April 9, 2016, http://www.oas.org/dil/treaties_B-32_American_Convention_on_Human_Rights.htm.

39. Case 2141, Resolution 23/81, March 6, 1981, accessed March 7, 2016 https://www.wcl.american.edu/humright/digest/1980/res2381.cfm.

40. *Goodwin v. UK*, ¶ 74, App. No. 28957/95 (ECtHR, 11 July 2002).

41. *Rees v. United Kingdom*, ¶ 37, App. No. 9532/81 (ECtHR, 28 October 1986); *Cossey v. United Kingdom*, ¶ 40, App. No. 10834/84 (ECtHR, 29 August 1990); *Sheffield and Horsham v. United Kingdom*, ¶¶ 57–58, App. No. 22985/93 and 23390/94 (ECtHR 30 July 1998).

42. *Goodwin v. UK*, ¶ 74, App. No. 28957/95 (ECtHR, 11 July 2002).

43. Ibid.

44. Louis Henkin, *The Age of Rights* (New York: Columbia University Press, 1990), 2–3.

45. *Klass v. Germany*, 5029/71 (ECtHR, 6 September 1978).

46. Jacob Mchangama and Guglielmo Verdirame, "The Danger of Human Rights Proliferation: When Defending Liberty, Less is More," *Foreign Affairs*, July

24, 2013, https://www.foreignaffairs.com/articles/europe/2013-07-24/
danger-human-rights-proliferation.

47. David M. Smolin, "Church, State, and International Human Rights: A
Theological Appraisal," *Notre Dame Law Review* 73 (2014): 1540.

48. United Nations Human Rights Office of the High Commissioner,
International Covenant on Economic, Social and Cultural Rights, Arts. 7, 9,
December 16, 1966, http://www.ohchr.org/EN/ProfessionalInterest/
Pages/CESCR.aspx; African Charter on Human and Peoples' Rights, Art
24, accessed March 8, 2016, http://www.hrcr.org/docs/Banjul/afrhr4.
html; United Nations General Assembly, *Declaration on the Right to Peace*,
December 19, 2016, accessed June 17, 2017, http://www.un.org/ga/search/
view_doc.asp?symbol=A/C.3/71/L.29.

49. United Nations, *Convention on the Elimination of All Forms of Discrimination
against Women*, Art 5(a), accessed March 8, 2016, http://www.un.org/
womenwatch/daw/cedaw/text/econvention.htm.

50. Eric Posner, "The Case against Human Rights," *The Guardian*,
December 4, 2014, http://www.theguardian.com/news/2014/
dec/04/-sp-case-against-human-rights.

51. Mchangama and Verdirame, "The Danger of Human Rights Proliferation."

52. Posner, "The Case against Human Rights."

53. Samuel Moyn, *The Last Utopia* (Cambridge, MA: Belknap, 2010), 1.

54. Smolin, "Church, State, and International Human Rights," 1535.

55. Ibid., 1540.

56. Posner, "The Case against Human Rights."

57. Smolin, "Church, State, and International Human Rights," 1545.

58. United Nations, *Charter of the United Nations and Statute of the International
Court of Justice*, Arts.2, 24, and 51,1945, accessed May 19, 2016, https://treaties.
un.org/doc/Publication/CTC/uncharter.pdf.

59. Brett D. Schaefer, "A Progress Report on U.N. Reform," *Heritage
Foundation*, May 19, 2006, http://www.heritage.org/research/
reports/2006/05/a-progress-report-on-un-reform.

60. Thalif Deen, "Politics: US Ouster from Rights Body Reflects Third World
Anger," *Inter Press Service*, May 4, 2001, http://www.ipsnews.net/2001/05/
politics-us-ouster-from-rights-body-reflects-third-world-anger/.

61. Libya takes human rights role," *BBC News*, January 20, 2003, http://news.bbc.
co.uk/2/hi/africa/2672029.stm.

62. Joseph Loconte and Nile Gardiner, "Another Charade at the United
Nations," *The Heritage Foundation*, 2006, http://www.heritage.org/research/
commentary/2006/03/another-charade-at-the-united-nations.

63. Brett D. Schaefer, "The United Nations Human Rights Council:
Repeating Past Mistakes," *Heritage Foundation*, September
6, 2006, http://www.heritage.org/research/lecture/
the-united-nations-human-rights-council-repeating-past-mistakes.

64. Ibid.

65. Brett D. Schaefer, "U.N. Human Rights Council: A Flawed
Body That Should Be Replaced," *Heritage Foundation*, 2013,
http://www.heritage.org/research/reports/2013/11/
un-human-rights-council-a-flawed-body-that-should-be-replaced.

66. Joseph Klein, "The UN's Failure to Live Up to Its Charter's Ideals," *Frontpage
Mag*, June 29, 2015, http://www.frontpagemag.com/fpm/259237/
uns-failure-live-its-charters-ideals-joseph-klein.

67. Malik, *The Challenge of Human Rights*, 4.
68. Ibid., 3.
69. John Witte, "Between Sanctity and Depravity: Human Dignity and Human Rights in Classical Lutheran Perspective," in *Human Rights and the Impact of Religion*, ed. by Johannes A. van der Ven et al. (Leiden: Koninklijke Brill NV, 2013), 12.
70. Smolin, "Church, State, and International Human Rights," 1533.
71. Jacob Katz Cogan, "Competition and Control in International Adjudication," *Virginia J. of Int'l Law* 41 (2008): 413.
72. See Gary Haugen and Victor Boutros, *The Locust Effect* (Oxford: Oxford University Press, 2014), 16.
73. Ibid., 39.
74. Ibid., 17.
75. Ibid., 83.
76. Ibid., 167.
77. "Who We Are," *International Justice Mission*, accessed March 19, 2016, https://www.ijm.org/who-we-are.
78. "Gary Haugen," *International Justice Mission*, accessed March 19, 2016, https://www.ijm.org/bios/gary-haugen.
79. "Justice Review: A Journal on Protection and Justice for the Poor, 2014–2015," *International Justice Mission*, accessed April 22, 2016, https://www.ijm.org/sites/default/files/download/IJM-Justice-Review-2014-2015.pdf.
80. "2014 Annual Report," *International Justice Mission*, accessed March 19, 2016 https://www.ijm.org/content/2014-annual-report.
81. "Yousef Nadarkhani FREED," *Jubilee Campaign*, accessed March 21, 2016, http://jubileecampaign.org/campaigns/free-yousef-nadarkhani/.

CHAPTER 7: RULE OF LAW

1. Lord John Emerich Edward Dalberg Acton to Archbishop Mandell Creighton, Letter I: April 5, 1887, in *Online Library of Liberty*, http://oll.libertyfund.org/titles/acton-acton-creighton-correspondence#lf1524_label_010.
2. "Robert Mugabe," *Biography.com*, accessed June 16, 2016, http://www.biography.com/people/robert-mugabe-9417391#2013-election.
3. "Robert Mugabe," *History*, accessed June 16, 2016, http://www.history.co.uk/biographies/robert-mugabe.
4. David Blair, "Court rules Mugabe's land grab is illegal," *Telegraph*, November 11, 2000, http://www.telegraph.co.uk/news/worldnews/europe/1374082/Court-rules-Mugabes-land-grab-is-illegal.html.
5. "Backs to the wall," *The Economist*, October 3, 2015, http://www.economist.com/news/middle-east-and-africa/21669966-drought-and-weak-rand-may-do-more-decade-sanctions-spur.
6. Mindy Belz, "Out to Dry," *World*, December 4, 2010, https://world.wng.org/2010/11/out_to_dry.
7. Ibid.
8. Ibid.
9. *The Economist*, "Backs to the wall"; Conor Gaffey, "Zimbabwe's New 'Currency': What You Should Know About Bond Notes," *Newsweek*, November 28, 2016, http://www.newsweek.com/what-you-should-know-about-bond-notes-zimbabwes-new-currency-526003.

10. Belz, "Out to Dry," 37; "Zim unemployment skyrockets," *Mail & Guardian*, January 29, 2009, accessed June 21, 2017, https://mg.co.za/article/2009-01-29-zim-unemployment-skyrockets.

11. Christian Nordquist, "Zimbabwe Life Expectancy Lowest in the World," *Medical News Today*, April 10, 2006, http://www.medicalnewstoday.com/articles/41339.php.

12. Monte Reel and J.Y. Smith, "A Chilean Dictator's Dark Legacy," *Washington Post*, December 11, 2006, http://www.washingtonpost.com/wp-dyn/content/article/2006/12/10/AR2006121000302.html.

13. Ibid.

14. United Nations Human Rights Council, "Report of the detailed findings of the commission of inquiry on human rights in the Democratic People's Republic of Korea," A/HRC/25/63, February 17, 2014, 6.

15. Ibid., 7.

16. Ibid., 15.

17. "A Century of Decline," *The Economist* (February 15, 2014), 20.

18. "The Parable of Argentina," *The Economist* (February 15, 2014), 9.

19. Ibid.

20. Ibid.; "A Century of Decline," 22.

21. "The Parable of Argentina," 9.

22. Henrici de Bracton, *De Legibus et Consuetudinibus Angliae, Vol. 1*, ed. Sir Travers Twiss (Buffalo: Hein, 1990), 39.

23. W. L. Warren, *King John* (Berkeley: University of California Press, 1961), 181–85.

24. Ibid., 181–83; Sidney Painter, *The Reign of King John* (Baltimore: Johns Hopkins Press, 1949), 236–37.

25. John M. Riddle, *A History of the Middle Ages, 300–1500* (Lanham, MD: Rowman & Littlefield, 2008), 383.

26. *Magna Carta*, Art. 39, reprinted in J. C. Holt, *Magna Carta* (Cambridge: Cambridge University Press, 1965), 327.

27. Louis Henkin, Gerard L. Neuman, Diane F. Orentlicher, David W. Leebron, *Human Rights* (New York: Foundation Press, 1999), 28.

28. Lacey Baldwin Smith, *This Realm of England: 1399–1688*, 4th ed. (Lexington: D.C. Heath, 1983), 221.

29. Ibid., 222, 230.

30. Ibid., 258.

31. *English Bill of Rights 1689*, The Avalon Project, Yale Law School, accessed June 15, 2016, http://avalon.law.yale.edu/17th_century/england.asp.

32. Lacey Baldwin Smith, *This Realm of England: 1399 to 1688* (Lexington, MA: D. C. Heath and Co., 2000), 305.

33. U.S. Const. amends. I, V, VIII.

34. Ibid., 258.

35. Kevin Mooney, "Supreme Court Justice Scalia: Constitution, Not Bill of Rights, Makes Us Free," *The Daily Signal*, May 11, 2015, http://dailysignal.com/2015/05/11/supreme-court-justice-scalia-constitution-not-bill-of-rights-makes-us-free/.

36. U.S. Const., art. I. sec. 1.

37. Mooney, "Supreme Court Justice Scalia."

38. Note that some might inquire whether the progress made on the issues noted here was through the application of substantive due process, a use of the Fourteenth Amendment that I criticize later in the chapter. It was not.

I believe most of the progress made in the treatment of racial and ethnic minorities was made by properly applying the equal protection clause of the Fourteenth Amendment, as well as through important pieces of Congressional legislation.

39. Craig Stern, "The Common Law and the Religious Foundations of the Rule of Law before Casey," *University of San Francisco Law Review* 38 (2004): 514.

40. Lord Acton to Archbishop Creighton.

41. Abraham Kuyper, "Calvinism and Politics," in *Lectures on Calvinism* (Grand Rapids: Eerdmans, 1999), 81.

42. James Madison, *Federalist*, No. 55, in *The Federalist Papers* (New York: Bantam Books, 1982), 284.

43. Madison, *Federalist*, No. 48, 250.

44. Madison, *Federalist*, No. 51, 262.

45. Alexander Hamilton, *Federalist*, No. 15, 72.

46. Hamilton, *Federalist*, No. 76, 387.

47. Hamilton, *Federalist*, No. 71, 365.

48. James Madison, in *The American Presidents, Washington to Tyler*, ed. Robert A. Nowlan (Jefferson: McFarland & Company, 2012), 171. George Washington is said to have told Thomas Jefferson that the Senate was designed to "cool" House legislation just as a saucer was used to cool hot tea. "Senate History: 1787–1800," *United States Senate*, accessed June 6, 2016, http://www.senate.gov/artandhistory/history/minute/Senate_Created.htm.

49. Jean-Jacques Rousseau, *The Social Contract* (London: Penguin, 1968), 49.

50. J. Bronowski and Bruce Mazlish, *The Western Intellectual Tradition* (New York: Barnes & Noble, 1960), 297–98.

51. Ibid., 300.

52. Susan Dunn, *Sister Revolutions* (New York: Faber and Faber, 1999) 11–12.

53. Robert E. Lerner, Standish Meacham, and Edward McNall Burns, *Western Civilizations*, Vol. 2 (New York: W. W. Norton & Co., 1988), 704.

54. Ibid.

55. Bronowski and Mazlish, *The Western Intellectual Tradition*, 300.

56. During the Revolution's first phase, a single legislative body, the National Assembly, largely reigned supreme while retaining a form of limited monarchy. Observing this from England in 1790, Edmund Burke wrote: "That Assembly, since the destruction of the orders, has no fundamental law, no strict convention, no respected usage to restrain it. Instead of finding themselves obliged to conform to a fixed constitution, they have a power to make a constitution which conforms to their designs. Nothing in heaven or upon earth can serve as a control on them." Edmund Burke, *Reflections on the Revolution in France* (New York: Anchor, 1973), 57.

57. Elizabeth Becker, *When the War Was Over* (New York: Touchstone, 1986), 195–96, 203–4.

58. Ibid., 196.

59. Ibid., 197.

60. Adam Taylor, "Why the world should not forget Khmer Rouge and the killing fields of Cambodia," *Washington Post*, August 7, 2014, https://www.washingtonpost.com/news/worldviews/wp/2014/08/07/why-the-world-should-not-forget-khmer-rouge-and-the-killing-fields-of-cambodia/.

61. Seth Mydans, "11 Years, $300 Million and 3 Convictions. Was the Khmer Rouge Tribunal Worth It?" *The New York Times*, April 10, 2017, https://www.

nytimes.com/2017/04/10/world/asia/cambodia-khmer-rouge-united-nations-tribunal.html.

62. Ibid.
63. Jonathan Turley, "The President's Power Grab," *Los Angeles Times*, March 9, 2014, http://articles.latimes.com/2014/mar/09/opinion/la-oe-turley-obama-separation-of-powers-20140309.
64. U.S. Const. art. I. sec. 1.
65. Erwin Chemerinsky, "The Assault on the Constitution: Executive Power and the War on Terror," *U.C. Davis Law Review* 40 (2006): 16–17.
66. Tara L. Branum, "President or King—The Use and Abuse of Executive Orders in Modern-Day America," *Journal of Legislation* 28 (2002): 28.
67. Ibid., 30.
68. U.S. President, Proclamation, "Protection of Children from Environmental Health Risks and Safety Risks," *Federal Register*, 82, no. 78, April 21, 1997, 19885, https://www.gpo.gov/fdsys/pkg/FR-1997-04-23/pdf/97-10695.pdf.
69. Branum, "President or King," 36.
70. "Text of Bush's Order on Abortion," *ABC News*, January 22, 2001, http://abcnews.go.com/Politics/story?id=121989&page=1.
71. Sam Dillon, "Obama turns some powers of education back to the states," *New York Times*, September 23, 2011, http://www.nytimes.com/2011/09/24/education/24educ.html?_r=0.
72. Turley, "The President's Power Grab."
73. White House, Office of the Press Secretary, "Presidential Executive Order Promoting Free Speech and Religious Liberty" (May 4, 2017), https://www.whitehouse.gov/the-press-office/2017/05/04/presidential-executive-order-promoting-free-speech-and-religious-liberty.
74. Tom Gjelten, "The Johnson Amendment in 5 Questions and Answers," *NPR*, February 3, 2017, http://www.npr.org/2017/02/03/513187940/the-johnson-amendment-in-five-questions-and-answers.
75. Ibid.
76. James Bennet, "True to Form, Clinton Shifts Energies Back to US Focus," *New York Times*, July 5, 1998, http://www.nytimes.com/1998/07/05/us/true-to-form-clinton-shifts-energies-back-to-us-focus.html.
77. The White House Office of the Press Secretary, "President Barack Obama's State of the Union Address," January 28, 2014, https://www.whitehouse.gov/the-press-office/2014/01/28/president-barack-obamas-state-union-address.
78. Jonathan Turley, U.S. Congress, Committee on the Judiciary, *Enforcing the President's Constitutional Duty to Faithfully Execute The Laws: Hearing Before the House Committee on the Judiciary*, 113th Cong. 2nd sess., 2014, 32–33.
79. Madison, *Federalist*, No. 48, 250.
80. Hamilton, *Federalist*, No. 78, 393–94.
81. Craig Stern, "The Common Law and the Religious Foundations of the Rule of Law before Casey," 516.
82. U.S. Const., amend. IXIV.
83. *Roe v. Wade*, 410 U.S. 113, 164 (1973).
84. *Planned Parenthood v. Casey*, 505 U.S. 833, 849 (1992).
85. Ibid., 850.
86. Ibid., 851.
87. Ibid.
88. Ibid., 983 (Scalia J., dissenting).
89. *Obergefell v. Hodges*, 135 S. Ct. 2584 (2015).

90. Ibid., 2601.
91. Ibid., 2598.
92. Ibid.
93. Ibid., 2602.
94. Ibid., 2629 (Scalia, J. dissenting).
95. Ibid., 2612 (Roberts, J. dissenting).
96. *Reynolds v. United States*, 98 U.S. 145 (1879).
97. *Obergefell*, 135 S. Ct. 2584, 2643 (Alito, J. dissenting).
98. Ibid., 2622 (Roberts, J. dissenting).
99. 198 U.S. 45 (1905).
100. 300 U.S. 379 (1937).
101. Ibid., 2626 (Roberts, J. dissenting).

CHAPTER 8: CRIMINAL PUNISHMENT

1. C. S. Lewis, *God in the Dock* (Grand Rapids: Eerdmans, 1970), 292.
2. Mary Sigler, "Mercy, Clemency, and the Case of Karla Faye Tucker," *Ohio State Journal of Criminal Law* 4 (2007): 458.
3. Ibid, 459.
4. Walter C. Long, "Karla Faye Tucker: A Case for Restorative Justice," *American J. Crim. Law* 27 126 (1999): 126.
5. Sigler, "Mercy, Clemency," 461.
6. Ibid., 459–60.
7. Ibid., 456, 460, 462; "International Appeals to Spare Tucker Fail," *CNN*, February 3, 1998, accessed May 16, 2016, http://www.cnn.com/US/9802/03/tucker.world/.
8. "Tucker Loses Clemency Bid; Bush Reprieve Still Possible," *CNN*, February 2, 1998, accessed May 16, 2016, http://www.cnn.com/US/9802/02/tucker.clemency.deny/.
9. Sigler, "Mercy, Clemency, and the case of Karla Faye Tucker," 456.
10. Ibid., 461.
11. Albert Alschuler, "The Changing Purposes of Criminal Punishment: A Retrospective on the Past Century and Some Thoughts about the Next," *University of Chicago Law Review* 70 (Winter 2003): 6.
12. Ibid., 9.
13. Ibid., 11.
14. Mark Memmott, "Cleveland's Convicted Idiot Finishes Punishment; Says She's Learned Lesson," *NPR*, November 13, 2012, http://www.npr.org/sections/thetwo-way/2012/11/13/165027763/convicted-idiot-driver-who-passed-school-bus-holds-her-sign-of-shame.
15. Jonathan Turley, "Silly Sentences," *The Virginian-Pilot*, October 23, 2005, J1.
16. "Controversy Over Sentences for Rioters," *ABC Radio Australia*, January 18, 2012, http://www.radioaustralia.net.au/international/radio/onairhighlights/controversy-over-sentences-for-uk-rioters.
17. Ibid.
18. Ibid.
19. Andrew Tilghman, "Man Who Slapped Wife Sentenced to Yoga," *Houston Chronicle*, January 22, 2004, accessed May 24, 2016, http://www.chron.com/news/houston-texas/article/Man-who-slapped-wife-sentenced-to-yoga-1474268.php.
20. Matthew Brown, "Court Stops Montana Judge from Undoing Rape Sentence," *Yahoo News*, September 6, 2013, accessed May 24, 2016, https://www.yahoo.

com/news/court-stops-mont-judge-undoing-rape-sentence-202124479.
html?ref=gs.

21. "Oscar Pistorius Given Five Years for Reeva Steenkamp Death," *BBC News*,
    October 21, 2014, accessed May 16, 2016, http://www.bbc.com/news/
    world-africa-29700457.

22. Ibid.

23. Texas Penal Code Ann. § 1.02 (West 2016).

24. Ibid.

25. New York Penal Law § 1.05 (McKinney 2016).

26. Jeremy Bentham, *An Introduction to the Principles of Morals and Legislation*
    (Oxford: Clarendon, 1970), 158.

27. Ibid.

28. Edwin Patterson, *Jurisprudence: Men and Ideas of the Law* (Brooklyn:
    Foundation Press, 1953), 450–51.

29. Joshua Dressler, *Understanding Criminal Law*, 6th ed. (San Francisco:
    Matthew Bender & Company, 2012), 15.

30. Richard L. Nygaard, "The Myth of Punishment: Is American Penology Ready
    for the 21st Century," *Regent Law Review* 5 (1995): 10.

31. Russell Christopher, "Deterring Retributivism: The Injustice of 'Just'
    Punishment," *Northwestern University Law Review* 96 (2002): 856.

32. Richard A. Posner, *Economic Analysis of Law*, 3rd ed. (Boston: Little, Brown
    and Co, 1986), 207.

33. Karl Menninger, *The Crime of Punishment* (New York: Viking, 1966), 18.

34. Ibid., 26; Dr. Menninger seems to have modified his views on determinism
    and moral accountability somewhat in a later book, *Whatever Became of
    Sin* (New York: Hawthorn, 1973); see also Ralph Slovenko, "Menninger:
    Whatever Became of Sin?" *DePaul Law Review* 23 (1974): 1437.

35. Nygaard, "The Myth of Punishment," 9.

36. Dressler, *Understanding Criminal Law*, 22.

37. Ibid.

38. Nygaard, "The Myth of Punishment," 6n19.

39. Nygaard, "The Myth of Punishment," 6n20.

40. Immanuel Kant, *Metaphysical Elements of Justice: Part 1 of The Metaphysics of
    Morals*, trans. John Ladd, 2nd ed. (Indianapolis: Hackett, 1999), 138.

41. Ibid.

42. Edwin Patterson, *Jurisprudence* (Brooklyn: Foundation Press, 1953), 380.

43. Kant, *Metaphysical Elements of Justice*, 138.

44. Lewis, *God in the Dock*, 288.

45. Ibid.

46. Stephen P. Garvey, "Punishment as Atonement," *UCLA Law Review* 46 (1999):
    1821.

47. Lewis, *God in the Dock*, 292.

48. Alschuler, "Changing Purposes of Criminal Punishment," 19.

49. Ibid., 2.

50. Menninger, *The Crime of Punishment*, 17.

51. Nygaard, "The Myth of Punishment," 8.

52. Quoted in Leo Katz, Michael S. Moore, and Stephen J. Morse, *Foundations of
    Criminal Law* (New York: Foundation Press, 1999), 80.

53. Lewis, *God in the Dock*, 287.

54. Ibid., 288.

55. Katz, Moore, and Morse, *Foundations of Criminal Law*, 89.

56. Alschuler, "Changing Purposes of Criminal Punishment," 3.

57. Kant, *Metaphysical Elements of Justice*, 138.

58. Lewis, *God in the Dock*, 292.

59. Ibid., 293.

60. Walter C. Kaiser, Jr., "Exodus," in vol. 2 of *The Expositor's Bible Commentary* (Grand Rapids: Zondervan, 1990), 434.

61. John Calvin, *Institutes of the Christian Religion*, ed. John T. McNeill (Philadelphia: The Westminster Press, 1960), 507–8; J. I. Packer, *Knowing God* (Downers Grove, IL: InterVarsity Press, 1973), 189.

62. For more on restorative justice, see Charles Colson and Pat Nolan, "Prescription for Safer Communities," *Notre Dame J.L. Ethics & Pub. Pol'y* 18 (2004): 387, 388–92; Mary Ellen Reimund, "The Law and Restorative Justice: Friend or Foe? A Systemic Look at the Legal Issues in Restorative Justice," *Drake L. Rev.* 53 (2005): 667, 670–87.

63. Garvey, "Punishment as Atonement," 1844.

64. Charles Colson, *Born Again* (Grand Rapids: Chosen Books, 1976), 369.

65. Michael Dobbs, "Charles Colson, Nixon's 'dirty tricks' man, dies at 80," *Washington Post*, April 21, 2012, https://www.washingtonpost.com/politics/whitehouse/chuck-colson-nixons-dirty-tricks-man-dies-at-80/2012/04/21/gIQAaoOHYT_story.html?utm_term=.eb8c78a1f6c8.

66. Prison Fellowship, "Our Approach," https://www.prisonfellowship.org/about/#.

67. Ibid.

CHAPTER 9: ENVIRONMENTAL INFLUENCE DEFENSES

1. William Shakespeare, *The Tragedy of King Lear*, ed. Jay L. Halio (Cambridge: Cambridge University Press, 1992), 117.

2. Alix M. Freedman, "In Milwaukee, the Raven Finds Its Victims," *Wall Street Journal* (February 28, 1992): A7.

3. Ibid.

4. *State v. Morgan*, 536 N.W.2d 425, 440–41 (Wis. Ct. App. 1995).

5. Patricia Falk, "Novel Theories of Criminal Defense Based Upon the Toxicity of the Social Environment: Urban Psychosis, Television Intoxication and Black Rage," *North Carolina Law Review* 74 (1996): 798.

6. *Morissette v. U.S.*, 72 S. Ct. 240, 246, 251 (1952).

7. William Blackstone, *Commentaries on the Laws of England, Volume 4* (Chicago: University of Chicago Press, 1979), 20–21.

8. Blackstone, *Commentaries, Volume 4*, 21.

9. Joshua Dressler, *Understanding Criminal Law*, 6th ed. (Dayton, OH: LexisNexis, 2012), 87.

10. Ibid., 205.

11. Paul Duggan, "Mom Charged with Drowning Her 5 Children," *Washington Post*, January 21, 2001, http://www.sfgate.com/crime/article/Mom-charged-with-drowning-her-5-children-2907880.php.

12. Andrew Cohen, "How Andrea Yates Lives, and Lives with Herself, a Decade Later," *The Atlantic*, March 12, 2012, http://www.theatlantic.com/national/archive/2012/03/how-andrea-yates-lives-and-lives-with-herself-a-decade-later/254302/.

13. "Andrea Yates case: Yates found not guilty by reason of insanity," *CNN*, December 31, 2007, http://www.cnn.com/2007/US/law/12/11/court.archive.yates8/index.html?_s=PM:US.

14. Wendy Davis, "Killer Buzz: Caffeine Intoxication is Now Evidence for an Insanity Plea," *ABA Journal* (June 2011): 16.
15. Ibid.
16. Falk, "Novel Theories of Criminal Defense," 742–43.
17. Ibid., 741.
18. Ibid.
19. Henry F. Fradella, "From Insanity to Beyond Diminished Capacity: Mental Illness and Criminal Excuse in the Post-Clark Era," *University of Florida Journal of Law & Public Policy* 18 (2007): 57–58.
20. "Jury Accepts Battered-wife Defense, Acquits N.Y. Woman of Murder," *Los Angeles Times*, October 6, 2011, http://latimesblogs.latimes.com/nationnow/2011/10/woman-acquitted-of-murder-jurors-accept-battered-wife-syndrome.html.
21. Ibid.
22. *New Jersey v. Kelly*, 478 A.2d 364 (N.J. 1984).
23. Ibid., 369.
24. Daina Chiu, "The Cultural Defense: Beyond Exclusion, Assimilation, and Guilty Liberalism," *California Law Review* 82 (1994): 1053.
25. Ibid.; see also Celestine Bohlen, "Holtzman May Appeal Probation for Immigrant in Wife's Slaying," *The New York Times*, April 5, 1989, http://www.nytimes.com/1989/04/05/nyregion/holtzman-may-appeal-probation-for-immigrant-in-wife-s-slaying.html?mcubz=0.
26. Falk, "Novel Theories of Criminal Defense," 739.
27. Ibid., 739–40.
28. Henry F. Fradella, "From Insanity to Beyond Diminished Capacity," 68.
29. Falk, "Novel Theories of Criminal Defense," 749.
30. "Life of crime is in the genes, study claims," *The Telegraph*, January 26, 2012, http://www.telegraph.co.uk/news/science/science-news/9040997/Life-of-crime-is-in-the-genes-study-claims.html.
31. Melissa Hogenboom, "Two genes linked with violent crime," *BBC News*, October 28, 2004, http://www.bbc.com/news/science-environment-29760212.
32. "Genetic link to suicidal behavior confirmed," *Science Daily*, October 7, 2011, http://www.sciencedaily.com/releases/2011/10/111007113941.htm.
33. "Media heralds the discovery of 'infidelity gene,'" *NHS Choices*, February 16, 2015, http://www.nhs.uk/news/2015/02February/Pages/Media-heralds-the-discovery-of-the-infidelity-gene.aspx.
34. Landon Hall, "Gene abnormality could be factor behind bad driving," *Virginian Pilot*, November 4, 2009.
35. Kevin Davis, "Brain Trials: Neuroscience is Taking a Stand in the Courtroom," *ABA Journal* (November 2012): 39.
36. Ibid., 41.
37. "PTSD: A Growing Epidemic," *NIH Medline Plus*, Winter 2009, https://www.nlm.nih.gov/medlineplus/magazine/issues/winter09/articles/winter09pg10-14.html.
38. Thomas L. Hafemeister and Nicole A. Stockey, "Last Stand? The Criminal Responsibility of War Veterans Returning from Iraq and Afghanistan with Posttraumatic Stress Disorder," *Indiana Law Journal* 85 (2010): 89–90.
39. Hafemeister and Stockey, "Last Stand," 137.
40. Ibid.
41. Ibid.

42. Fradella, "From Insanity to Beyond Diminished Capacity," 54.
43. David L. Bazelon, "Foreword—The Morality of the Criminal Law: Rights of the Accused," *Journal of Criminal Law and Criminology* 72 (1981): 1153–54.
44. *U.S. v Alexander*, 471 F.2d. 923, 959 (D.C. Cir. 1972) (Bazelon, J. dissenting).
45. Ibid., 960.
46. Ibid., 957.
47. Richard L. Nygaard, "The Myth of Punishment: Is American Penology Ready for the 21st Century," *Regent Law Review* 5 (1995): 9.
48. Marilyn Berger, "David Bazelon Dies at 83; Jurist Had Wide Influence," *The New York Times*, February 21, 1993, http://www.nytimes.com/1993/02/21/us/david-bazelon-dies-at-83-jurist-had-wide-influence.html?pagewanted=all.
49. *Durham v. United States*, 214 F.2d 862, 874–75 (D.C. Cir 1954).
50. Ibid., 869–74.
51. Falk, "Novel Theories of Criminal Defense," 810.
52. Ibid., 811.
53. B. F. Skinner, *Beyond Freedom and Dignity* (Indianapolis: Hackett, 1971), 74–75.
54. Phillip E. Johnson, "Human Nature and Criminal Responsibility: The Biblical View Restored," in *Christian Perspectives on Legal Thought*, ed. Michael W. McConnell, Robert F. Cochran Jr. & Angela C. Carmella (New Haven: Yale University Press, 2001), 428.
55. Ibid., 427.
56. Ibid., 428.
57. Ibid., 429.
58. Ibid.
59. Ibid.
60. Ibid., 433.
61. Ibid., 434.
62. *The Queen v. Dudley & Stephens*, 14 Q.B. 273 (1884).
63. Ibid., 274.
64. Ibid., 277.
65. Ibid., 279.
66. Ibid., 287.
67. Ibid., 288.
68. Ibid., 287.
69. Ibid., 287.
70. Ibid.
71. Ibid., 288.
72. Ibid.
73. Ibid.
74. Dennis McCann, "Excuses Wearing Thin," *Milwaukee Journal* (March 6, 1992): B1.
75. Davis, "Brain Trials," 39.

CHAPTER 10: CHRISTIAN UTOPIANISM

1. C. S. Lewis, *God in the Dock* (Grand Rapids: Eerdmans, 1970), 292.
2. Loraine Eaton, "Virginia's Prohibition history," *Norfolk Virginian-Pilot*, November 30, 2008, http://pilotonline.com/news/local/virginia-s-prohibition-history/article_20b31552-ad56-5547-aacb-f3524f731ae1.html.
3. Ibid.

4.   "Billy Sunday," *Christianity Today*, accessed May 10, 2017, http://www.
     christianitytoday.com/history/people/evangelistsandapologists/billy-
     sunday.html.

5.   Ibid.

6.   Eaton, "Virginia's Prohibition history."

7.   Ibid.

8.   "Al Capone," *History*, accessed September 26, 2012, http://www.history.com/
     topics/al-capone.

9.   "Photographs from the Chicago Daily News, 1902–1933," *Library of Congress*,
     accessed September 26, 2012, www.loc.gov/teachers/classroommaterials/
     connections/photos-chicago/history4.html.

10. Mark Thornton, "Alcohol Prohibition Was a Failure," *Cato Institute*,
     July 17, 1991, http://www.cato.org/publications/policy-analysis/
     alcohol-prohibition-was-failure.

11. Henry G. Levine and Craig Reinarman, "From Prohibition to Regulation:
     Lessons from Alcohol Policy for Drug Policy," *The Milbank Quarterly* 69
     (1991): 463.

12. Thornton, "Alcohol Prohibition Was a Failure," 6.

13. Ibid., 2.

14. Levine and Reinarman, "From Prohibition to Regulation," 467, 472.

15. Lawrence Bergreen, *Capone: The Man and the Era* (New York: Simon &
     Schuster, 1994), 130–31.

16. Thornton, "Alcohol Prohibition Was a Failure," 4.

17. U.S. Const. amend. XVIII.

18. U.S. Const. amend. XXI.

19. William Blake, "Preface" to *Milton*, in *The Complete Poetry & Prose of William
     Blake*, ed. David V. Erdman (New York: Doubleday, 1988), 95–96.

20. Groups like The American Vision continue to promote Christian
     Reconstructionism today. See https://americanvision.org/.

21. Arlen Specter, "Defending the Wall: Maintaining Church/State Separation
     in America," *Harvard Journal of Law & Public Policy* 18 (1995): 575–76.

22. Arlen Specter, "Defending the Wall," 576.

23. Ibid.

24. Edward Burman, *The Inquisition: The Hammer of Heresy* (New York: Dorset,
     1984), 62–74.

25. F. F. Bruce, *The Spreading Flame* (Grand Rapids: Eerdmans, 1958), 293.

26. John Warwick Montgomery, *The Law Above the Law* (Minneapolis: Bethany,
     1975), 79.

27. Montgomery, *The Law Above the Law*, 81.

28. Sheryl Nance-Nash, "The High Price of America's Gambling Addiction," *AOL
     Finance*, July 22, 2011, www.dailyfinance.com/2011/07/22/the-high-price-
     of-americas-gambling-addiction; United States National Gambling Impact
     Study Commission, *Final Report* (Washington: GPO, 1999), 16.

29. David Skeel and William Stuntz, "Christianity and the (Modest) Rule of
     Law," *University of Pennsylvania Journal of Constitutional Law* 8 (2006): 833.

30. Skeel and Stuntz, "Christianity and the (Modest) Rule of Law," 834.

31. *National Gambling Impact Study Final Report* (June 18, 1999): 104.

32. Ibid., 2.

33. Ibid., 3.

34. The Data Team, "The world's biggest gamblers," *The Economist*, February 9,
     2017, http://www.economist.com/blogs/graphicdetail/2017/02/daily-chart-4.

35. Skeel and Stuntz, "Christianity and the (Modest) Rule of Law," 835.
36. Ibid., 826.
37. Ibid., 836.
38. Bethany McLean and Peter Elkind, "The guiltiest guys in the room," *CNN Money*, July 5, 2006, http://money.cnn.com/2006/05/29/news/enron_guiltyest/.
39. "Enron Fast Facts," *CNN Library*, updated April 27, 2017, http://www.cnn.com/2013/07/02/us/enron-fast-facts/.
40. Tom Ehrich, "Not heard from the pulpit," *USA Today*, March 12, 2006, https://usatoday30.usatoday.com/news/opinion/editorials/2006-03-12-sexual-morality_x.htm.
41. Skeel and Stuntz, "Christianity and the (Modest) Rule of Law," 834.
42. Joel Belz, "A Minimal Civil Code," *World* (April 23, 1994): 3.
43. Thomas Aquinas presented this view in his *Treatise on Law*, insisting that an effect of this is to make men good. Citing Aristotle, he argued that "lawgivers make men good by habituating them to good works." Even if humans would not normally act in a certain way, they will learn to do so through law. He noted that law could also act to reinforce good behavior; it "preserves and fosters [virtue] when it already exists." St. Thomas Aquinas, *Treatise on Law*, ed. Ralph McInerny (Washington: Regnery, 1998), 32.
44. National Gambling Impact Study, *Final Report*, 47.
45. Skeel and Stuntz, "Christianity and the (Modest) Rule of Law," 836.
46. Belz, "Going to God's Law School," 3.
47. Aquinas, *Treatise on Law*, 92.
48. Montgomery, *The Law Above the Law*, 82.
49. Michael McConnell, Robert F. Cochran Jr., and Angela C. Carmella, eds. *Christian Perspectives on Legal Thought* (New Haven: Yale University Press, 2001), 8. Judge Michael McConnell warns, "Utopian politics is dangerous and deceptive. More importantly, it is a kind of idolatry."
50. Montgomery, *The Law Above the Law*, 80.
51. Louis Hensler, "Misguided Christian Attempts to Serve God Using the Fear of Man," *Regent Law Review* 17 (2004): 35.
52. Belz, "A Minimal Civil Code," 3.
53. Aquinas, *Treatise on Law*, 92.
54. Skeel and Stuntz, "Christianity and the (Modest) Rule of Law," 835.
55. Montgomery, *The Law Above the Law*, 82.
56. Skeel and Stuntz, "Christianity and the (Modest) Rule of Law," 831.

INDEX OF COURT CASES

SUBJECT/AUTHOR INDEX

freedom of speech, 19, 134–35
Freedom Rights Project, 138
free will, 22, 26, 77, 200
Freedom Strategy, 59
French Revolution, 24, 167–69,
183, 184
Frontline, 107
fundamental rights, under the
Fourteenth Amendment.
See under Constitution,
United States

Galton, Francis, 82
gambling, 248–49, 251, 252–53, 260,
261
National Gambling Impact
Study Commission, 249,
253, 261
selective enforcement of
gambling laws, 252–53,
260
Garrett, Danny, 186–87
Garvey, Stephen, 208
Gementera, Shawn, 190
general will, in Rousseau's
philosophy, 167–69
gene therapy, 65–68, 71–73, 74, 75,
78, 81, 84, 86, 89–90, 94
germline gene therapy, 65–67,
72–73, 74, 78, 82, 84, 90, 94
somatic cell gene therapy, 71–73,
89
genetic diseases, 66, 70–72, 74, 81,
83, 84, 88, 89, 109
genetic influence on behavior, 222,
224, 231
genetic testing, 67, 69–71, 84,
87–89
amniocentesis, 69–70
chorionic villus sampling (CVS),
69–70

noninvasive prenatal testing
(NIPT), 69–71
Geneva Conventions, 114, 120
genocide, 3–6, 11, 14, 33, 44, 95–122,
126, 139, 149, 171
Genocide Convention
(Convention on
the Prevention and
Punishment of the Crime
of Genocide), 6, 98, 110–12,
120, 126, 139
genome, human, 67, 68, 73, 90
George, Robert P., 87
Germany
Confessing Church, 103
and European Court of Human
Rights, 138
genetic research, 68
Holocaust, 6, 13, 14, 83, 97, 98,
101–3, 105–6, 107, 108–9,
110, 111, 122
Nuremberg trials, 13, 14
German Christians, 102
germline gene therapy, 65–67,
72–73, 74, 78, 82, 84, 90, 94
Ghosts of Rwanda, 107
Gimbert, Allen, 243
Ginsburg, Ruth Bader, 84
Glendon, Mary Ann, 126
Global Slavery Index, 39–40
Gourevitch, Philip, 4, 106
Graves, Asia, 37–38, 39, 44
Gulf War, 224, 237

Habyarimana, Juvenal, 3, 109
Hafemeister, Thomas, 223
Hall, Shyima, 40–41
Hamilton, Alexander, 165–66
Hardin, Shena, 190
Harris, John, 72–73
Haugen, Gary, 52–53, 147–48, 149
Havel, Václav, 117

Henkin, Louis, 133, 137
Hensler, Louis, 257
Herbert, Paul, 57
heresy, state punishment of, 248
High Commissioner for Human
   Rights, United Nations,
   127
High Commissioner for Refugees,
   United Nations, 150
Highfield, Ron, 23, 25
Hinckley, John, Jr., 229, 230
Hitler, Adolf, 13, 102, 108, 129
Hoche, Alfred, 108
Holmes, Oliver Wendell, 16–19, 20,
   33, 83, 108, 201
Holocaust, 6, 13, 14, 83, 97, 98,
   101–3, 105–6, 107, 108–9,
   110, 111, 122
House of Representatives, United
   States, 165, 166
Huang, Junjiu, 65–67, 72, 73, 90, 94
hubris, 93, 142, 183
Human Fertilisation and
   Embryology Authority,
   United Kingdom, 67
Human Genome Project, 68
human rights, 11, 13, 23, 56, 73, 98,
   111, 119, 120, 123–51, 156, 157,
   171, 180
Human Rights Commission, 128,
   143
Human Rights Council, 127, 134–35,
   138, 139, 143–44
human trafficking, 11, 33, 37–64,
   91, 130, 150, 171, 262, 263
humanitarian theory of
   punishment, 201–3
Hutus, in Rwandan genocide, 3–6,
   100–101, 104, 107, 109–10
hybrids, human and animal, 82

iEmphathize, 61

image of God, 11, 13–14, 16, 20–26,
   28–30, 263
   and biotechnology, 77–80, 86, 88,
      90, 93
   and criminal punishment, 186,
      198, 199, 200–201, 203, 205,
      206
   and environmental influence
      defenses, 235, 240
   and genocide, 106, 107–10, 120,
      121
   and human rights, 131–40
   and human trafficking, 45, 47–49
   and the rule of law, 163–64, 185
incapacitation, 188, 189, 192
Independent International
   Commission on Kosovo,
   117
India
   human trafficking in, 39, 41, 42,
      44–45, 47–48, 150
   nonparticipation in the
      International Criminal
      Court, 44
Indonesia
   human trafficking in, 48
   nonparticipation in the
      International Criminal
      Court, 44
induced pluripotent stem cells, 76
infanticide, 80
Inquisition, the, 248
insanity, 213–14, 216–19, 221, 223,
   225–26, 227–31, 237, 241
   American Law Institute (ALI)
      Model Penal Code rule,
      229–30
   Durham rule, 226, 229
   M'Naghten rule, 228–30
intelligent design, 228
Inter-American Commission on
   Human Rights, 135

incapacitation, 188, 189, 192
rehabilitation, 189, 190, 191, 192,
    194, 195, 197, 202–3, 207,
    210
retribution, 188, 189, 191, 192–93,
    195–208, 210, 216, 230
shame, 190
Purity Squad, London Bridge
    Baptist Church, 243
Putin, Vladimir, 140

Qatar, human trafficking in, 39
Queen's Bench, Court of, 234–36

Radio Télévision des Mille
    Collines (RTLM), 4, 109
Rambold, Stacey, 191
rape
  as a domestic crime, 191, 213, 262
  as a means of genocide, 3–4,
    95–97, 98–101, 110, 115
  as part of human trafficking, 38,
    44, 46, 48
  in the absence of the rule of law,
    52, 147
  in Zimbabwe election-related
    violence, 156
  rape trauma syndrome, 221
Ravensbrück concentration camp,
    107
Reagan, Ronald, 229, 230
Reconstructionism, Christian, 246
redemptive history, 10, 203
Reed, Ralph, 246
Regent University School of Law,
    10, 13
rehabilitation, 189, 190, 191, 192,
    194, 195, 197, 202–3, 207,
    210
religious liberty, 123–24, 130,
    134–35, 150, 174

and defamation of religions,
    134–35
Responsibility to Protect, 117–20
restitution, 207–8
restorative justice, 206–8
retribution, 188, 189, 191, 192–93,
    195–208, 210, 216, 230
Riley, Brad, 61
Roberts, John, 181, 182, 183–84
Robertson, Pat, 187
Robespierre, Maximilien, 169
Roman Catholic Church, 22, 23, 99,
    102, 105, 167
Roman Empire, 247–48, 258
Rome, genocide in Carthage, 97
Roosevelt, Franklin Delano, 172
Roslin Institute, University of
    Edinburgh, 73
Cloning of Dolly the sheep, 74
Rousseau, Jean-Jacques, 24,
    167–68, 169, 170
rule of law, 11, 53, 127, 130, 147–50,
    151, 155–86
Rushdoony, R. J., 246
Russia
  and genocide in Sudan, 113
  and intervention in Kosovo, 115,
    116, 117
  and Salvation Army, 123–24
  Law on Freedom of Conscience
    and Religious
    Associations, 123–24
Rwanda, genocide, 3–6, 33, 100–1,
    102, 104, 105, 106–7, 109–10,
    111–12, 117, 121, 149

Salvation Army, 123–24
same-sex marriage, 24, 178–82
Sanger, Margaret, 82
Sarbanes-Oxley Act, 250, 251
Scalia, Antonin, 162, 163, 178, 181
Schaefer, Brett, 143